WRITING THROUGH MODERN HISTORY

Level 2
"Cursive Models"

A Charlotte Mason Writing Program
"Gentle and Complete"

Modern History
1800's-1985

From Frederick Douglass to African Famine Relief

Historical Narratives, Primary Source Documents, Poetry, and Cultural Tales

BOOKS PUBLISHED BY BROOKDALE HOUSE:

The Writing Through Ancient History books
Writing Through Ancient History Level 1 Cursive Models
Writing Through Ancient History Level 1 Manuscript Models
Writing Through Ancient History Level 2 Cursive Models
Writing Through Ancient History Level 2 Manuscript Models

The Writing Through Medieval History books
Writing Through Medieval History Level 1 Cursive Models
Writing Through Medieval History Level 1 Manuscript Models
Writing Through Medieval History Level 2 Cursive Models
Writing Through Medieval History Level 2 Manuscript Models

The Writing Through Early Modern History Books
Writing Through Early Modern History Level 1 Cursive Models
Writing Through Early Modern History Level 1 Manuscript Models
Writing Through Early Modern History Level 2 Cursive Models
Writing Through Early Modern History Level 2 Manuscript Models

The Writing Through Modern History Books
Writing Through Modern History Level 1 Cursive Models
Writing Through Modern History Level 1 Manuscript Models
Writing Through Modern History Level 2 Cursive Models
Writing Through Modern History Level 2 Manuscript Models

The Fun Spanish Level 1

Sheldon's Primary Language Lessons
(Introductory grammar workbook for elementary students)

The Westminster Shorter Catechism Copybook
(Available in the following font styles: traditional, modern, italic, and vertical, both print and cursive)

The Geography Drawing Series
Drawing Around the World: Europe
Drawing Around the World: USA

Easy Narrative Writing

ISBN: 978-1-64281-010-3

Table of Contents

Introduction   v
Definitions—Narration, Copywork, Studied Dictation   vii
Scheduling   x

Chapter I

The Uplift of a Slave Boy's Ideal, about Frederick Douglass	(1818-1895)*	I-3
The Rescue of Jerry, about Fugitive Slave Act	(1793-1850)	I-8
The Lady with the Lamp, Crimea and Florence Nightingale	(1853-1856)	I-13
A True Story about a Girl, about Louisa Alcott	(1832-1888)	I-18
Dog Was "A Leetle Bit Ahead", tale by Abraham Lincoln	(1861-1865)	I-23
Elizabeth Van Lew (excerpt), about Union Spy	(1861-1865)	I-27
Peter Petersen, about Minnesota Indian War	(1862)	I-32
The Soldier's Reprieve, about Abraham Lincoln	(1861-1865)	I-38
Robert E. Lee, about Civil War	(1807-1870)	I-44
Stonewall Jackson, about Civil War	(1824-1863)	I-49
The Surrender of General Lee, about Civil War	(1865)	I-54
The War Is Over, death of Abraham Lincoln	(1865)	I-59
Thomas A. Edison the Great Inventor	(1847-1931)	I-64
Clara Barton and the Red Cross	(1821-1912)	I-69
Hobson and the Merrimac, about Spanish American War	(1898)	I-74
Conquering the Yellow Fever	(1900)	I-78
The Wright Brothers and Their Secret Experiments (excerpt)	(1903)	I-83
Saved by a Child's Wit (excerpt), about Great War	(1914-1918)	I-88
The Sinking of the Lusitania	(1915)	I-94
General J'offre, about childhood of French General--WWI	(1852-1931)	I-99
The Exploits of Sergeant York, American Hero WWI	(1918)	I-104
Caught in the Dust, about dust storms	(1930's)	I-109
The Navajo Code Talkers	(1942-1945)	I-114
Rosa Parks	(1955)	I-120
The Cuban Missile Crisis	(1962)	I-125
The Watergate Scandal	(1972)	I-131
You Feed Them, African Famine Relief	(1985)	I-136

Chapter II

Autobiography of Abraham Lincoln	(1859)	II-3
Gettysburg Address, by Abraham Lincoln	(1863)	II-6
Another Camp Meeting (excerpt), about Sojourner Truth	(1797-1883)	II-9
Emancipation Proclamation	(1863)	II-14
The Trial of Susan B. Anthony (excerpt), Women's suffrage	(1872)	II-18
Life and Adventures of Calamity Jane, by herself	(1852-1903)	II-25
The Atlanta Compromise (excerpt), by Booker T. Washington	(1895)	II-30
San Juan Hill, by General John J. Pershing	(1898)	II-34

*Note: Dates denote the year of the story or the life span of the central figure or event.

Sinking of the Titanic (excerpt)	(1912)	II-38
The Sinking of the Lusitania (excerpt)	(1915)	II-43
The Women of China (excerpt), foot binding	(1918)	II-48
To Every Englishman in India, by M. K. Gandhi	(1920)	II-53
Infamy Speech, by Franklin D. Roosevelt	(1941)	II-57
The Atomic Bombings of Hiroshima and Nagasaki, Eyewitness Account, (excerpt)	(1945)	II-61
Inaugural Address of President John F. Kennedy	(1961)	II-66
President Nixon's Resignation Speech (excerpt)	(1974)	II-71

Chapter III

All Things Obey God, from The Infant's Delight	(after 1850)	III-3
America the Beautiful, by Katharine Lee Bates	(1859)	III-6
The Battle Hymn of the Republic, by Julia Ward Howe	(1861)	III-9
Bed in Summer, by Robert Louis Stevenson	(1885)	III-12
The Charge of the Light Brigade, by Alfred Lord Tennyson	(1854)	III-15
Father William, by Lewis Caroll	(1886)	III-19
IF, by Rudyard Kipling	(1910)	III-22
John Littlejohn, by Charles Mackay	(1848)	III-25
The Lost Thought, by Emily Dickinson	(1896)	III-29
The New Duckling, by Ella Wheeler Wilcox	(1850-1919)***	III-32
O Captain, My Captain!, by Walt Whitman	(1865)	III-36
The Pessimist, by Ben F. King	(1898)	III-39

Chapter IV[+]

The Bonfire in the Sea, an Australian Tale		IV-3
The Capture of Father Time, by L. Frank Baum	(1901)	IV-8
The Half-Chick, a Spanish Tale by Andrew Lang		IV-16
The Lion and the Gnat, an African Tale		IV-21
Persevere and Prosper, an Arabian Tale		IV-27
The Star Wife, an American Indian Tale		IV-31
The Story of Caliph Stork, an Arabian Tale		IV-38
The Young Head of the Family, a Chinese Tale		IV-45

Appendix

Oral narration questions	2
Grammar Guide	3
Models from Chapter I Historical Narratives	6
Models from Chapter II Text Excerpt from Primary Source Documents	15
Models from Chapter III Poetry from Modern History	21
Models from Chapter IV Folktales from Various Cultures	27

**Note: The date of publication was not available, but the publishing company was in existence after 1850.
   (Poetry selections are in alphabetical order.)
***Note: The publication was not available for the author's work, the life span of the author is indicated.
 +Note: Not all of the publication dates for Chapter IV are included. These are very old tales with many variations published at various times.

Introduction

Writing Through Modern History Layout

Writing Through Modern History is a writing program that teaches grammar, spelling, penmanship, and history—all at once. This volume covers modern history, beginning in the early 1800's to 1985—the fourth year of a 4-year cycle.

Writing Through Modern History teaches writing the Charlotte Mason way for upper grammar stage students, third through fifth grade. It is divided into four chapters: short stories, text excerpts from primary source documents, poetry, and cultural tales. For Chapter I, short stories that give insight into people, places, and events during modern times have been selected. Chapter II contains excerpts from primary source documents including, but not limited to, personal letters and government documents from the establishment and development of America. Chapter III contains poetry from authors living during modern times. Chapter IV contains folk tales.

In all four chapters the reading selection is followed by a practice model, which is used for copywork and dictation. There are more than 60 selections included in *Writing Through Modern History*.

To coordinate *Writing Through Modern History* with your history topics, refer to the Table of Contents, which also serves as a timeline. Use the timeline provided to determine which selection would be the best fit for that week's history lesson. Historical narratives will primarily come from Chapters I and IV. Feel free to move around the book.

In the Appendix you will find two models for each reading selection. The first model is the same as the copywork model which followed the reading selection. The second model, which is in italics, is also from the reading selection. It has been added for those that like to use a separate model for dictation.

Because *Writing Through Modern History* was written for grades 3–5, some selections will be too long for some students. Simply reduce any of the models by drawing a line through the unneeded portion. Sometimes you will have to break the model in the middle of a sentence. In that case, stop at a semicolon (;) or coordinating conjunction (", and" ", or" ", but" ", nor" ", for" ", so" ", yet") to make the selection shorter. Semi-colons and coordinating conjunctions are used to separate main clauses—those with a subject and a predicate. If you must break the model into a shorter sentence, modify the new selection by adding a period at the end and ensure that you have a grammatically correct model. Explain to your student the use of semi-colons and coordinating conjunctions and why the change is being made. This is an excellent opportunity to reinforce and explain the grammar rules involved.

Note: Some of the works included were taken from the public domain; many have been edited for Writing Through Modern History. *Some of the narratives in Chapter I were written specifically for this volume.*

Note: Although titles of books and ships would normally be italicized in texts, they are underlined to teach children that these names are underlined in handwritten works.

Most of the principles in *Writing Through Modern History* are based on the work of Ms. Charlotte Mason. She advocated that children of the grammar or elementary stage practice narration, copywork, and dictation as their primary method of learning to write. But because Ms. Mason's methods have been interpreted differently over the years, I have included alternative suggestions on how to implement *Writing Through Modern History*. So to begin using *Writing Through Modern History* as your child's writing program, please read all of the introduction, pages v–ix, before your student begins.

Additional Information

Reading Levels

Chapters II and III contain excerpts from historical documents and history relevant poetry that may be well above the reading level of some grammar and even logic stage students. I recommend that these complex selections be read to your student. If you would like to stretch your student, ask him to read all or part of the selection back to you. These reading selections offer great opportunity to cover new vocabulary as well as new ideas.

Appendix "Models Only"

The Appendix lists all of the models by chapter. The first model is in normal typeface while the second model is italicized. Only the first model follows the reading selections. The second models were added to give the students a different model for dictation. For the sake of organization, the Appendix contains a copy of the models to assist the instructor with copywork and studied dictation.

Getting Started

On the following page, I have covered each area of the program: Narration, Copywork, and Dictation. I have also provided a guide suggesting how to incorporate grammar into the program. Please read these in their entirety.

Correcting Work

Correcting writing, whether written summations, copywork, or dictation, is always difficult. Ms. Mason advised teachers and parents to correct the student's writings occasionally. This makes perfect sense when realizing that Ms. Mason's methods did not require the need for extensive corrections. She consistently emphasized that work be done correctly the first time. She believed that a student should not be allowed to visually dwell on incorrect work. When a child made a mistake during dictation, Ms. Mason had stamps or pieces of paper available to cover the mistakes so that the mistakes were not reinforced visually.

When a child made a mistake during narrations, she withheld correcting him. I believe that she used the time after the oral narration was finished to discuss the material that had been narrated. When corrections are needed, it is good to practice the principle of praise before correcting children. Find out what is right with what they've done. Be impressed. Focus on their effort. Build them up. Ephesians 5:29 of the King James Bible says—

Let no corrupt communication
proceed out of your mouth, but
that which is good to the use of edifying,
that it may minister grace
unto the hearers.

A Note on Cultural Terms

Throughout this text, you will find the word *Indian* used in reference to Native Americans. The reason for this is two-fold. First, many of the stories used in this text were written at a time when the term *Indian* was commonly used to refer to those peoples that are now known as the First Americans. Second, the modern term—*Native American*—has not been and is not fully accepted by most people that are known as *Native Americans*. Because there is no one term that has been fully agreed upon and because the word *Indian* is not deemed derogatory but outdated, the original word *Indian* is used throughout this text. By leaving this term in place, instructors are giving an opportunity to discuss, with their students, how this term has been used and viewed throughout history, and how this term is being used, and is currently viewed, in today's modern times.

Also, you will throughout this text, see the term *Negro*. Because it is not deemed inappropriate, it has been left in context. Its use will give instructors the opportunity to discuss how and why this word was used throughout early modern history. Although the term *Negro* is no longer used in modern speech, Dr. Martin Luther King did use the term in his "I Have a Dream" speech.

Definitions

<u>Personal Narrations</u> –the act of retelling what you have learned

Ms. Mason believed narrations should be done immediately after the story was read to the student or by the student. Narrations are very simple, yet very effective in teaching writing. The act of narrating helps children to internalize the content of the reading material they have been exposed to and allows them to make it their own. In order to narrate, students must listen carefully, dissect the information, and then express that same information in their own words. It is a powerful tool, but very simple to put into practice.

<u>Oral narrations</u> Read all or part of the story only once before requiring the student to narrate! It will require him to pay attention. Simply ask your student to tell you what he has just heard or read.

If your student has trouble with this process, show him how to narrate by demonstrating the process for him. **Read a selection yourself and then narrate it to him. Ask him to imitate you.** If he continues to draw a blank, use the list of questions below to prompt him. (See the removable list of narration questions in the Appendix, page 2, for daily use. The Appendix also contains questions for poetry and primary source documents.)

Besides all of the previously mentioned benefits, oral narrations teach students to digest information, dissect it, and reorganize it into their own words while thinking on their feet. This practice helps students to develop the art of public speaking. This formal process will force them to express their ideas without a written plan. It strengthens the mind. And over time, their speech will become fluent and natural. (I sometimes have my children stand as they narrate. It makes the process more formal.)

If your student has difficulty with narrations, ask some or all of the following questions:

1. Who was the main character?
2. What was the character like?
3. Where was the character?
4. What time was it in the story?
5. Who else was in the story?
6. Does the main character have an enemy?
   (The enemy may be another character, himself, or nature.)
7. Did the main character have a problem? If not, what did the character want?
8. What does the main character do? What does he say? If there are others, what do they do?
9. Why does the character do what he does?
10. What happens to the character as he tries to solve his problem?
11. Is there a moral to the story? If so, what was it?
12. What happens at the end of the story? Or how does the main character finally solve his problem?

<u>Written Summations</u> Around the age of 10, students were required by Ms. Mason to write down their narrations for themselves. Many students can do this earlier. Written summations will allow your student to develop this skill. If your student is able, have him write as much as he can, as perfectly as he can, even around the age of 8.

At the end of each oral narration, ask your child to summarize the reading selection by identifying the beginning, the middle, and the end. He should be able to do this in about three to six sentences—fewer is best.

Younger students will sometimes begin each sentence with "First,…" or "At the beginning,…" This is okay. But once the student masters the summation, ask him to summarize without these types of words. Tell him to begin with the subject or the time.

> Ex: When Louisa May Alcott was a young girl, she was very happy because she spent her time playing with her sisters and writing in her diary.

The benefits of written summations are manifold. They will help your student to think linearly from the beginning of the reading selection to the end. They also provide the right amount of content for the reluctant writer. Additionally, the act of summarizing teaches students to identify the main thread or central idea of a passage. (Even though your child begins to write his written summations, have him continue his oral narrations without limit. These will help him to internalize and learn the historical content of the stories in *Writing Through Modern History* as well as develop his public speaking skills.)

Copywork and Grammar—copying a passage exactly as written

As your child copies the model before him, stay near so that you are able to correct any problems immediately.

Before your child begins, discuss the model with him. Point out the grammatical elements that he is learning. Have your child identify the part of speech in the model and circle it with a colored pencil. See page 3 of the Appendix for a grammar guide. (Spend approximately one month on each new part of speech.) When using the grammar guide, continue to review by including all previously learned work in the current lesson. For the second month, he is to identify both nouns and verbs. The third—nouns, verbs, and pronouns.

Ms. Mason recommended the formal study of grammar at about 4th or 5th grade. If you opt to add a formal program for your upper grammar stage student, that would be worthwhile. If you do so, you may omit the grammar study in this program.

Grammar
If you would prefer that your student study grammar with his copywork, see the grammar guide in the Appendix page 3. It focuses on the 8 parts of speech as well as fundamental punctuation. The process involves the student identifying the parts of speech and color-coding the copywork selections according to the guide. The process is cumulative in that students should roll the new grammar concept in with the old. By of the end of the year, students should be identifying all eight parts of speech in their copywork.

Studied Dictation—the act of writing from an oral reading

Once again, Ms. Mason's ideas are simple, yet effective. The goal in dictation is to teach your child to write correctly and from memory the sentences or clauses he has just heard. Ms. Mason let the child study the dictation for a few minutes. She wrote down any unknown or difficult words for him on a board. She then erased the board and read each passage only once. From this one reading, the child wrote; however, if the child made a mistake, she covered the mistake instantly so that the student was not allowed to visualize and internalize it.

For the child who has never done dictation, start by reading as many times as necessary so that your child memorizes the sentences. Work down to one reading per 2 or 3 sentences or main clauses. This is an advanced skill and may require time to achieve. Be patient, but consistent. (If needed, allow your student to repeat the model back to you before he writes. Some students may need this reinforcement; others may not.)

After you write the model on the whiteboard, discuss it, in depth, with your student. An example of the process follows.

MODEL

"Mary, did you spill the ink on the carpet?" asked Tom.
"No, Tom," answered Mary. "Did you, Will?"
"I did not, Mary, but I know who did," said Will.
"Who was it, Will?"
Will did not answer in words. He pointed a finger at Fido, and guilty
little Fido crept under the sofa.

QUESTIONS TO ASK:

1. What are the names of the people in this story? How does each name begin?
   The names of people always begin with capital letters.
2. Study this model, telling what words begin with capitals and why; which words are indented and why; what marks of punctuation are used and why.

FIRST PARAGRAPH

3. Why is Mary indented in this paragraph.
4. Why is Mary capitalized? Why are the names capitalized?
5. Why is there a comma to separate "Mary" from the rest of the sentence?
6. Why are there quotation marks around certain words?
7. Why does the quoted sentence end with a question mark?
8. Why do some sentences end with a period?

SECOND PARAGRAPH

9. Where does the second paragraph begin?
10. The paragraph begins with someone speaking. How do we know this?
11. Why is the word no capitalized?
12. Why is there a comma after no?
13. Why is there a comma after Tom? After you?
14. Why is there a period after Mary and a question after Will.

DO THIS WITH EACH PARAGRAPH

If there are any questions that your student cannot answer, tell him the answers. Discuss the grammar with him, and work with him until he can narrate why the model is punctuated the way it is.

Do the same with spelling. Identify the words that your student doesn't know and discuss why that word is spelled the way it is.

To see an example of studied dictation, visit the youtube video at the link below:
https://www.youtube.com/watch?v=xoTACGomwsw

or search "Studied Dictation Demonstration" on youtube.
There I demonstrate this dictation process.

Scheduling Information

Listed below is a recommendation for the use of *Writing Through Modern History*; however, this is **only a recommendation** and should be adjusted for your student's individual needs. **Further explanations and alternate methods** are included on the next page. Please feel free to adjust these methods to make writing as painless as possible for your student. Every child is different.

One Suggested Schedule:

Day 1   **<u>Reading, Oral Narrations, and Written Summations</u>**
From the Table of Contents, choose a story from Chapters I or IV.
Either you or your student should read the story selection once.
First, have the student orally narrate the story back to you.
(If he has difficulty, use the narration questions listed in the Appendix.)
Second, ask the student to summarize the story in about three sentences to six sentences. If he is able, have him write one or more sentences from his summation. Write for him, if needed. **(For more on narrations, see page vii.)**

Day 2   **<u>Copywork and Grammar</u>** Complete Model Practice 1 from Day 1's reading selection. Discuss/explain the grammar and punctuation in the model. Do a color-coded grammar study.
(For more on copywork and grammar, see page viii.)

Day 3   **<u>Studied Dictation</u>** Complete Model Practice 2, using the additional model located in the Appendix, also from Day 1's reading selection. Follow the guidelines for studied dictation on page viii. Neatly write the italic model provided in the Appendix for your student on a separate paper or white board. Allow the student to study the model before writing. Erase the model and dictate.

Day 4   **<u>Oral narrations and Copywork</u>**
From the Table of Contents, choose a selection from Chapters II or III.
Read all **or part** of the primary source document to your student. He may read the poem himself. If so, teach him to read with expression.
Discuss the complicated ideas in the document. Have your student narrate what he has learned. Complete Model Practice 1 using the copywork model.

Day 5   **<u>Studied Dictation</u>** Complete Model Practice 2, also from Day 4's reading selection. Follow the guidelines for studied dictation on page viii. Neatly write the Italic model provided in the Appendix for your student on a separate piece of paper or a white board. Allow the student to study the model before writing. Erase the model and dictate.

If the models are too long

If the models are too long for your student, reduce them. Third graders, or even older reluctant writers, should not be forced to do more than they are able. See the bold paragraph on page v for guidelines on reducing the models.

If your child isn't ready for dictation

Replace the dictation with copywork of the same model, or write the dictation model from the Appendix into the model practice 2 area. Have your student copy your written model in the model practice 3 area.

Optional Schedules

Charlotte Mason's Methods

Ms. Mason used narration, copywork, and dictation simultaneously throughout a young child's education. Narrations were done immediately after he had listened to or read the selection. Copywork was done from well-written sentences. And while many don't believe copywork to be valuable once a student learns to write from dictation, Ms. Mason believed that copywork was extremely valuable for many years alongside dictation. Dictation was a separate part of the process, mostly for the purpose of teaching spelling.

Ms. Mason allowed students to look at the dictation passages and study them before the student began writing. This process was helpful because it allowed the student to visualize how the passage should look. It taught him to study with intention. It taught him to focus on the words. After the passage was read once, the student wrote the passage from memory. This method improved a child's spelling and his grasp of correct punctuation as well.

But not everyone who follows Ms. Mason's methods follows each area of narration, copywork, and dictation in the same way. Below are some ways to incorporate some or all of these ideas into your child's learning adventure.

Different Copywork Passages Daily

Simply use *Writing Through Modern History* as written, covering two stories per week. **Day 1**, pick a selection from Chapters I or IV. Read and have the student do an oral narration and a written summation. **Day 2**, do copywork and a color-coded grammar study of the model. **Day 3**, the teacher should write all or part of the italicized model from the Appendix onto the Model Practice 2 area, in ink. The student should copy the model and then do a color-coded grammar study of the model in the Model Practice 2 area. **Day 4**, pick a selection from Chapters II or III, a primary source selection or poetry selection. Do oral narration, copywork, and a color-coded grammar study of the model. **Day 5**, the teacher should write the italicized model from the Appendix onto the Model Practice 2 area, in ink. The student should copy the model and do a color-coded grammar study of the model in the Model Practice 2 area. This will provide your student with four different copywork selections each week from two different sources.

Copywork as Dictation

Day 1, pick a selection from Chapters I or IV. Read and have the student do an oral narration and a written summation. **Day 2**, do copywork and a color-coded grammar study of the model. **Day 3**, do studied dictation of the same model. Have your student write in the Model Practice 2 area. **Day 4**, pick a selection from Chapters II or III, a primary source selection or poetry selection. Do an oral narration, copywork, and a color-coded grammar study of the model. **Day 5**, do a studied dictation of yesterday's copywork. Have your student write in the Model Practice 2 area.

Copywork and Dictation

Follow the suggested schedule on page x.

Reminders and Helps

- Use *Writing Through Modern History* in the best way possible to serve your student's needs. Adapt any area as necessary.
- Help students with spelling as necessary. Set your student up for success.
- In the case of dialogue, remind your student that each time a different character is speaking, a new paragraph is started via indentions. When he first encounters this, show him an example before requiring it of him.
- If the size of the selection is too large, **simply reduce it and require less.**
- Set your student up for success. He shouldn't be expected to know what he has not yet been taught.
- To sum up Charlotte Mason's methods:
-

Quality over quantity.
Accuracy over speed.
Ideas over drill.
Perfection over mediocrity.

Added Note on Paragraphing
For full-length written narrations (not summations, but the whole story)

You may want your student to occasionally write his narrations in place of the summation. Ms. Mason had children begin writing their narrations around the age of 10. This is equivalent to fourth or fifth grade, and it is a good time for most students. To make the transition to written narrations, have your student orally narrate first, then ask him to write down his narration. Eventually he won't need the oral narration.

In the actual writing of the narration, the difficult elements for most students will be punctuation, grammar, spelling, and paragraph breaks. Through the copywork and dictation, students actively learn correct punctuation, grammar, and spelling. And although they make mistakes, with practice in these areas, they will improve.

Paragraph breaks, however, are not often taught—in any curriculum. Many students intuitively learn when to begin a new paragraph because they read well-written literature. But this isn't always enough.

Paragraphing is easy to learn. Each time the who, what, when, where, why, or how of the story changes, a new paragraph is begun. Look at the following story—

The Penny-Wise Monkey
re-told by Ellen C. Babbitt
from <u>More Jataka Tales</u>

    Once upon a time the king of a large and rich country gathered together his army to take a faraway little country. The king and his soldiers marched all morning long and then went into camp in the forest.
(who=king and soldiers, what=march and went, when=once upon a time, where=camp in forest, why=to take a country)

    When they fed the horses, they gave them some peas to eat. One of the Monkeys living in the forest saw the peas and jumped down to get some of them. He filled his mouth and hands with them, and up into the tree he went again, and sat down to eat the peas.

(New paragraph, a change in the what, what=gave the horses peas, change in the when, when=feeding the horses, the monkey is introduced)

As he sat there eating the peas, one pea fell from his hand to the ground. At once, the greedy Monkey dropped all the peas he had in his hands and ran down to hunt for the lost pea. But he could not find that one pea. He climbed up into his tree again and sat still looking very glum. "To get more, I threw away what I had," he said to himself.

(New paragraph, a change in the who, the story is now focused on the monkey and not the king, who=monkey)

The king had watched the Monkey, and he said to himself, "I will not be like this foolish Monkey, who lost much to gain a little. I will go back to my own country and enjoy what I now have."

(New paragraph, a change in the who, who=the king, the story is now focused on the king again)

So he and his men marched back home.

(New paragraph, a change in the what, what=marched back home)

Also, when writing dialogue in a conversation, a new paragraph is started each time a different character is speaking.

Bonus Materials

To learn of new publications and free educational resources, sign up for our newsletter at

www.brookdalehouse.com

or

scan:

CHAPTER
I

Historical Narratives
Covering
Modern History

The Uplift of a Slave Boy's Ideal

by Orison Swett Marden

Born a slave, with the feelings and possibilities of a man, but with no rights above the beast of the field, Fred Douglass gave the world one of the most notable examples of man's power over circumstances.

He had no knowledge of his father, whom he had never seen. He had only a dim recollection of his mother, from whom he had been separated at birth. The poor slave mother used to walk twelve miles when her day's work was done, in order to get an occasional glimpse of her child. Then she had to walk back to the plantation on which she labored, so as to be in time to begin to work at dawn next morning.

Under the brutal discipline of the "Aunt Katy" who had charge of the slaves who were still too young to labor in the fields, he early began to realize the hardships of his lot and to rebel against the state of bondage into which he had been born.

He was often hungry and was clothed in hottest summer and coldest winter alike in a coarse tow linen shirt, scarcely reaching to the knees. He had neither bed to lie on nor blanket to cover him. His only protection—no matter how cold the night—was an old corn bag, into which he thrust himself, leaving his feet exposed at one end and his head at the other.

When about seven years old, he was transferred to new owners in Baltimore where his kind-hearted mistress, who did not know that in doing so she was breaking the law, taught him the alphabet. He thus got possession of the key that was to unlock his bonds, and, young as he was, he knew it. It did not matter that his master, when he learned what had been done, forbade his wife to give the boy further instructions. He had already tasted of the fruit of the tree of knowledge. The prohibition was useless. Neither threats nor stripes nor chains could hold the awakened soul in bondage.

With infinite pains and patience, and by stealth, he enlarged upon his knowledge of the alphabet. An old copy of Webster's <u>The American Spelling Book,</u> cast aside by his young master, became his greatest treasure. With the aid of a few good-natured white boys who sometimes played with him in the streets, he quickly mastered its contents. Then he cast about for further means to satisfy his mental craving. How difficult it was for the poor, despised slave to do this, we learn from his own pathetic words. "I have gathered," he says, "scattered pages of the Bible from the filthy street gutters, and washed and dried them, that, in moments of leisure, I might get a word or two of wisdom from them."

Think of that, boys and girls of the twentieth century, with your day schools and evening schools, libraries, colleges, and universities,—picking reading material from the gutter and mastering it by stealth! Yet this boy grew up to be the friend and co-worker of Garrison and Phillips, the eloquent spokesman of his race, the honored guest of distinguished peers and commoners of England; one of the noblest examples of a self-made man that the world has ever seen.

Under equal hardships he learned to write. The boy's wits, sharpened instead of blunted by repression, saw opportunities where more favored children could see none. He gave himself his first writing lesson in his master's shipyard by copying, from the various pieces of timber, the letters with which they had been marked by the carpenters to show the different parts of the ship for which they were intended. He copied from posters on fences, from old copybooks, from anything and everything he could get hold of. He practiced his new art on pavements and rails, and he entered into contests in letter making with white boys in order to add to his knowledge. "With playmates for my teachers," he says, "fences and pavements for my copybooks, and chalk for my pen and ink, I learned to write."

While being "broken in" to field labor under the lash of the overseer, chained and imprisoned for the crime of attempting to escape from slavery, the spirit of the youth never quailed. He believed in himself, in his God-given powers, and he was determined to use them in freeing himself and his race.

How well he succeeded in the stupendous task to which he set himself while yet groping in the black night of bondage. With no human power outside of his own indomitable will to help him. His life work attests in language more enduring than "storied urn" or written history. A roll call of the world's great moral heroes would be incomplete without the name of the slave-born Douglass who came on the stage of life to play the leading role of the Moses of his race in one of the saddest and, at the same time, most glorious eras of American history.

Written Summation

While being broken in to field labor under the lashes of the overseer, chained and imprisoned for the crime of attempting to escape from slavery, the spirit of the youth never quailed. He believed in himself and in the right to freedom for all men.

Model Practice 1 (adapted from the original)

_____

_____

_____

_____

_____

_____

_____

_____

_____

_____

_____

_____

_____

Model Practice 2

Model Practice 3

The Rescue of Jerry

by Lawton B. Evans

Not all the slaveholders in the South were kind masters, nor were all the slaves treated properly; sometimes they ran away to places in the North. Then the law allowed them to be captured and returned to their masters.

Jerry McHenry was an athletic mulatto who had lived for a number of years in Syracuse, New York, working quietly and expertly as a cooper. No one inquired where he came from, how he had reached the town, or who he was. The people were content to let Jerry alone and not ask too many questions. If he were an escaped slave, it was the duty of the officers of the law to return him to his master. And no one wanted to do that.

One day, an agent came to Syracuse and obtained a warrant for the arrest of Jerry, declaring he was a former slave owned by a Mr. Reynolds of Missouri. And that, under the Fugitive Slave Law, he must be arrested and sent back to his master.

Going to his place of business, the agent, accompanied by an officer, said, "Jerry, you are an escaped slave and belong to Mr. Reynolds. You must come with us and stand trial."

Jerry was struck dumb with astonishment and dismay. He thought his hiding-place was still a secret. He said little, but, with despair in his heart, he laid aside his tools and went with the agent to appear before the Judge.

The testimony was one-sided. The agent thus stated the case: "This man, Jerry McHenry, is by birth a slave. He belongs to Mr. Reynolds of Missouri. He escaped from his master and has been hiding in the North. The law requires him to be returned to his owner."

Jerry said nothing in his defense and was not asked any questions. He sat looking on and not very closely guarded—though his hands were manacled with handcuffs. The Judge and the agent were arranging some papers and were talking about the case. A young man standing near the prisoner leaned over and whispered, "Now, Jerry, here is a good chance for you to slip out of the courtroom."

In a moment, Jerry had risen from his seat, slipped through the bystanders, run down the steps, and was in the street below. The crowd cheered him and made way for him. There was no vehicle for him to escape in, but Jerry was a swift runner and disappeared up the street.

The police officers raised a great cry and started in hot pursuit. Jerry had turned a corner and was fleeing as fast as his manacled condition would let him. He had run about a mile and was quite out of breath before his pursuers came near to him.

"Stop and surrender, or it will be the worse for you!" they cried.

"Never!" answered the fugitive and made one last despairing effort before they closed in on him. Jerry fought like a tiger against overwhelming odds. He was surrounded, by the police and their followers, and struck from before and behind. He was thrown down and bruised, his clothes being sadly torn.

In this condition, he was put in a wagon, four policemen guarding him. He was brought back to the city and confined in the back room of the station under a heavy guard. The crowd of citizens outside watched the proceedings with ill-concealed anger.

They proposed to rush in and rescue the poor man. But one of their number advised them in this fashion:

"Wait a little while, and it will be quite dark. Proper arrangements can then be made for the poor fellow to be disposed of, after we rescue him. Stay nearby until all is made ready."

In the meantime, Jerry was in a perfect rage of passion. He beat his ironbound hands on the table before him and cried out in his fury, "Take these irons off my hands and give me a chance! I will fight my way through all the guard and escape; if I do not, you can send me where you will!"

One of his friends came in to quiet him and told him in a low voice that a crowd was getting ready to rescue him when it was dark. He then sat down, with his head on the table, and said nothing else.

About thirty picked men met outside and planned how to effect the escape of the prisoner. They did not sympathize with the Fugitive Slave Law and were anxious to give Jerry a chance to get away. All arrangements were carefully made. At a given signal, the doors and windows were smashed in, and the rescuers rushed into the room. The officers were seized and held. There was little opposition, for the crowd was so determined that any show of force would have been useless.

Several men seized Jerry in their arms and bore him outside to a waiting buggy to which a swift horse was hitched and where a willing driver sat ready.

"Now, go for your life," was the order, and the horse started at a rapid pace. The driver managed to escape all followers, and, after about an hour's journey, he delivered Jerry into the hands of a kind woman who gave him shelter for the night. His pursuers were off the track, and Jerry was safe for a while.

After a day or two, a covered wagon with a pair of fleet horses was seen standing in front of the house where Jerry had found lodging. An old and infirm man was noticed coming out of the house and getting into the vehicle which started off at a rapid rate.

Several persons saw the unusual sight, and told the police that they were suspicious of the old man, and thought he might be Jerry. The police at once started in chase. The pursuit lasted for a short while, but they were not very eager to capture their former prisoner and did not go very far. After ten miles, they gave up and returned to town.

The supposed old man was, in reality, Jerry who was making his way into Canada. There no person could be held as a slave, and, once there, all fugitives were safe. In fact, there were many provisions made for helping escaped slaves get over the border into Canada.

After several days, Jerry and his rescuers came to one of the Great Lakes where a friendly Captain took him on board a boat. At dark, the boat sailed across the Lake, and Jerry was landed in Canada where he soon established himself again in business as a cooper.

Written Summation

In a moment, Jerry had risen from his seat, slipped through the bystanders, run down the steps, and was in the street below. The crowd cheered him and made way for him. There was no vehicle for him to escape in, but Jerry was a swift runner and disappeared up the street.

Model Practice 1 (adapted from the original)

Model Practice 2

_____

_____

_____

_____

_____

_____

_____

_____

_____

Model Practice 3

_____

_____

_____

_____

_____

_____

_____

_____

_____

The Lady with the Lamp

by F. J. Cross

The Story of Florence Nightingale

"Lo! in that house of misery
A lady with a lamp I see
Pass through the glimmering gloom,
And flit from room to room."
　　　　　—Longfellow

"She would speak to one and another, and nod and smile to many more. But she could not do it to all, you know, for we lay there by hundreds; but we could kiss her shadow as it fell and lay our heads on our pillows again, content."

So wrote one of the soldiers from the hospital at Scutari of Florence Nightingale, the soldier's nurse and the soldier's friend.

Let us see how it happened that Florence Nightingale was able to do so much for the British soldiers who fought in the Crimea, and why she has left her mark on the history of our times.

Miss Nightingale was born in the city of Florence in the year 1820, and it is from that beautiful Italian town that she derives her Christian name.

Her father was a good and wealthy man who took great interest in the poor, and her mother was ever seeking to do them some kindness. Thus Florence saw no little of cottage folk. She took them dainties when they were ailing and delighted to nurse them when ill.

She loved all dumb animals, and they seemed to know by instinct that she was their friend. One day she came across her father's old shepherd, looking as miserable as could be. On inquiring the cause, she found that a mischievous boy had thrown a stone at the shepherd's favorite dog. It seemed the boy had broken the dog's leg, and, now, he was afraid that the poor animal would have to be killed.

Going together to the shepherd's home they found the dog very excited and angry, but on Florence speaking to it in her gentle voice, it came and lay down at her feet and allowed her to examine the damaged limb.

Happily, she discovered it was only bruised; and she attended to it so skillfully that the dog was soon running about in the field again. A few days later she met the shepherd; he was simply beaming, for the dog had recovered and was with him.

When Florence spoke to the man, the dog wagged its tail as much as to say, "I'm mighty glad to see 'you' again"; whereupon the shepherd remarked: "Do look at the dog, Miss, he be so pleased to hear your voice."

The fact that even her dolls were properly bandaged when their limbs became broken or the sawdust began to run out of their bodies will show that even then she was a thoughtful, kindly little person. When she grew up she wished very much to learn how to nurse the sick.

But in those days it was not considered at all a ladylike thing to do; and, after trying one or two nursing institutions at home, she went to Germany and afterwards to Paris in order to make a study of the subject and to get practical experience in cities abroad.

Miss Nightingale thus learned nursing very thoroughly and, when she came back to England, turned her knowledge to account by taking charge of an institution in London. By good management, tact, and skill the institution became a great success; but she was too forgetful of self. And after a time the hard work told upon her health, and she was obliged to take a rest from her labors.

The time came when the Russian war broke out, and Great Britain and France sent their armies into the Crimea. Our men fought like heroes. But it was found out ere many months had passed that those brave fellows, who were laying down their lives for the sake of their country, were being so badly nursed when they were sick and wounded that more were being slain by neglect than by the guns of the enemy.

Then there arose a great cry in Britain; every one demanded that something should be done to remedy this state of things. But nobody knew quite what to do or how to do it except one woman; that woman was Florence Nightingale.

Mr. Sidney Herbert, the War Minister, was one of the very few people who knew anything about her great powers of organization. Happily, he knew how thoroughly fit she was for the task of properly directing the nursing of the sick soldiers.

So, on the 15th of October 1854, he asked her to go to the Crimea to take charge of the nursing arrangements. In less than a week she started, with about forty nurses, for Scutari—the town where the great hospital was situated.

All Britain was stirred with admiration at her heroism, for it was well known how difficult was the task she was undertaking. But the quiet gentlewoman herself feared neither death, disease, nor hard work. The only thing she did not like was the fuss the people made about her.

Scutari, whither she went, is situated on the eastern side of the Bosphorus, opposite Constantinople. Thither the sick and wounded soldiers were being brought by hundreds. It took four or five days to get them from the field of battle to the hospital, their wounds during that time being generally unattended to. When they arrived at Scutari, it was difficult to land them. There was a steep hill up which they had to be carried to the hospital; so that by the time they arrived, they were generally in a sad condition. But their trials were not over then. The hospital was dirty and dismal. There was no proper provision for the supply of suitable food, everything was in dire disorder, and the poor fellows died of fever in enormous numbers.

But "the lady with the lamp" soon brought about a revolution, and the soldiers knew, to their joy, what it was to have proper nursing. No wonder the men kissed her shadow! Wherever the worst cases were to be found, there was Florence Nightingale. Day and night she watched and waited, worked and prayed. Her very presence was medicine and food and light to the soldiers.

Gradually disorder disappeared, and deaths became fewer day by day. Good nursing, care and cleanliness, nourishing food, and—perhaps beyond and above all—love and tenderness wrought wonders. The oath in the soldier's mouth turned to a prayer at her appearance.

Though the beds extended over a space equal to four miles, yet each man knew that all that human strength could do to forward his recovery was being done.

Before her task was finished, Miss Nightingale had taken the fever herself, but her life was mercifully spared.

Since those days, Florence Nightingale has done many kind and noble deeds. She has always lived as much out of the public sight as possible, though her work has rendered her dear to all hearts.

Though she has had much ill health herself, she has been able to accomplish a splendid life's work and to advance the study of nursing in all parts of the globe.

Written Summation

Her father was a good and wealthy man who took great interest in the poor, and her mother was ever seeking to do them some kindness. Thus Florence saw no little of cottage folk. She took them dainties when they were ailing and delighted to nurse them when ill.

Model Practice 1 (edited from the original)

_____

_____

_____

_____

_____

_____

_____

_____

_____

_____

_____

_____

_____

_____

Model Practice 2

_____

_____

_____

_____

_____

_____

_____

_____

Model Practice 3

_____

_____

_____

_____

_____

_____

_____

_____

A True Story about a Girl

by Sara Cone Bryant

Once there were four little girls who lived in a big, bare house in the country. They were very poor, but they had the happiest times you ever heard of because they were very rich in everything except money. They had a wonderful, wise father, who knew stories to tell and who taught them their lessons in such a beautiful way that it was better than play. They had a lovely, merry, kind mother, who was never too tired to help them work or watch them play. Moreover, they had all the great green country to play in. There were dark, shadowy woods, fields of flowers, and a river. And there was a big barn.

One of the little girls was named Louisa. She was very pretty, and ever so strong. She could run for miles through the woods and not get tired. She had a splendid brain in her little head; it liked study, and it thought interesting thoughts all day long.

Louisa liked to sit in a corner by herself, sometimes, and write thoughts in her diary; all the little girls kept diaries. She liked to make up stories out of her own head, and sometimes she made verses.

When the four little sisters had finished their lessons and had helped their mother wash up and sew, they used to go to the big barn to play. The best play of all was theatricals. Louisa liked theatricals better than anything.

They made the barn into a theatre, and the grown-up people came to see the plays they acted. They used to climb up on the hayloft for a stage, and the grown people sat in chairs on the floor. It was great fun. One of the plays they acted was "Jack and the Beanstalk". They had a ladder from the floor to the loft, and on the ladder they tied a vine all the way up to the loft to look like the wonderful beanstalk. One of the little girls was dressed up to look like Jack; she acted that part. When it came to the place in the story where the giant tried to follow Jack, the little girl cut down the beanstalk, and the giant came tumbling down from the loft. The giant was made out of pillows with a great, fierce head of paper and funny clothes.

Another story that they acted was Cinderella. They made a wonderful big pumpkin out of the wheelbarrow, trimmed with yellow paper. Cinderella rolled away in it when the fairy godmother waved her wand.

One other beautiful story they used to play was the story of Pilgrim's Progress. (If you have never heard it, you must be sure to read it as soon as you can read well enough to understand the old-fashioned words.) The little girls used to put shells in their hats for a sign they were on a pilgrimage, as the old pilgrims used to do. Then they made journeys over the hill behind the house, through the woods, and down the lanes. When the pilgrimage was over they had apples and nuts to eat in the happy land of home.

Louisa loved all these plays, and she made some of her own and wrote them down so that the children could act them.

But better than fun or writing, Louisa loved her mother; and by and by as the little girl began to grow into a big girl, she felt very sad to see her dear mother work so hard. She helped all she could with the housework, but nothing could really help the tired mother except money. She needed money, for food and clothes, and someone grown up to help in the house. But there never was enough money for these things, and Louisa's mother grew more and more weary and sometimes ill. I cannot tell you how much Louisa suffered over this.

At last, as Louisa thought about it, she came to care more about helping her mother and her father and her sisters than about anything else in all the world. And she began to work very hard to earn money. She sewed for people; and when she was a little older, she taught some little girls their lessons; and then she wrote stories for the papers. Every bit of money she earned, except what she had to use, she gave to her dear family. It helped very much, but it was so little that Louisa never felt as if she were doing anything.

Every year she grew more unselfish, and every year she worked harder. She liked writing stories best of all her work; but she did not get much money for them; and some people told her she was wasting her time.

At last, one day, a publisher asked Louisa, who was now a woman, to write a book for girls. Louisa was not very well; and she was very tired; but she always said, "I'll try," when she had a chance to work, so she said, "I'll try," to the publisher. When she thought about the book, she remembered the good times she used to have with her sisters in the big, bare house in the country. So she wrote a story and put all that in it. She put her dear mother, her wise father, and all the little sisters in it. And besides the jolly times and the plays, she put the sad, hard times in—the work and worry and going without things.

When the book was written, she called it <u>Little Women</u> and sent it to the publisher.

And, children, the little book made Louisa famous. It was so sweet and funny and sad and real—like our own lives—that everybody wanted to read it. Everybody bought it and much money came from it. After so many years, little Louisa's wish came true. She bought a nice house for her family; she sent one of her sisters to Europe, to study; she gave her father books; but best of all, she was able to see to it that the beloved mother, so tired and so ill, could have rest and happiness. Never again did the dear mother have to do any hard work, and she had pretty things about her all the rest of her life.

Louisa Alcott, for that was Louisa's name, wrote many beautiful books after this, and she became one of the most famous women of America. However, I think, the most beautiful thing about her is what I have been telling you: that she loved her mother so well that she gave her whole life to make her happy.

Written Summation

Another story that they acted was Cinderella.
They made a wonderful big pumpkin out of the
wheelbarrow, trimmed with yellow paper.
Cinderella rolled away in it when the fairy
godmother waved her wand.

Model Practice 1 (adapted from the original)

Model Practice 2

_____

_____

_____

_____

_____

_____

_____

_____

_____

Model Practice 3

_____

_____

_____

_____

_____

_____

_____

_____

_____

Dog Was "A Leetle Bit Ahead"

by Colonel Alexander K. McClure

Lincoln could not sympathize with those Union generals who were prone to indulge in high-sounding promises, but whose performances did not by any means come up to their predictions as to what they would do if they ever met the enemy face to face. He said one day, just after one of these braggarts had been soundly thrashed by the Confederates:

"These fellows remind me of the fellow who owned a dog which, so he said, just hungered and thirsted to combat and eat up wolves. It was a difficult matter, so the owner declared, to keep that dog from devoting the entire twenty-four hours of each day to the destruction of his enemies. He just 'hankered' to get at them.

"One day a party of this dog-owner's friends thought to have some sport. These friends heartily disliked wolves and were anxious to see the dog eat up a few thousand. So they organized a hunting party and invited the dog-owner and the dog to go with them. They desired to be personally present when the wolf killing was in progress.

"It was noticed that the dog-owner was not over-enthusiastic in the matter; he pleaded a 'business engagement,' but, as he was the most notorious and torpid of the town loafers and wouldn't have recognized a 'business engagement' had he met it face to face, his excuse was treated with contempt. Therefore he had to go.

"The dog, however, was glad enough to go, and so the party started out. Wolves were in plenty, and soon a pack was discovered. But when the wolfhound saw the ferocious animals, he lost heart and, putting his tail between his legs, endeavored to slink away. At last—after many trials—he was enticed into the small growth of underbrush where the wolves had secreted themselves, and yelps of terror betrayed the fact that the battle was on.

"Away flew the wolves, the dog among them, the hunting party following on horseback. The wolves seemed frightened, and the dog was restored to public favor. It really looked as if he had the savage creatures on the run, as he was fighting heroically when last sighted.

"Wolves and dog soon disappeared, and it was not until the party arrived at a distant farmhouse that news of the combatants was gleaned.

"'Have you seen anything of a wolf-dog and a pack of wolves around here?' was the question anxiously put to the male occupant of the house, who stood idly leaning upon the gate.

"'Yep,' was the short answer.

"'How were they going?'

"'Purty fast.'

"'What was their position when you saw them?'

"'Well,' replied the farmer in a most exasperatingly deliberate way, 'the dog was a leetle bit ahead.'

"Now, gentlemen," concluded the President, "that's the position in which you'll find most of these bragging generals when they get into a fight with the enemy. That's why I don't like military orators."

Written Summation

The dog, however, was glad enough to go, and so the party started out. Wolves were in plenty, and soon a pack was discovered. But when the wolf-hound saw the ferocious animals, he lost heart and, putting his tail between his legs, endeavored to slink away.

Model Practice 1

Model Practice 2

Model Practice 3

Elizabeth Van Lew (excerpt)

by Kate Dickinson Sweetser

Down the aisles of the hastily converted hospitals and into dim prison cells came almost daily a little woman with a big smile, always with her hands full of flowers or delicacies, and with a basket swinging from her arm. As she walked she hummed tuneless airs, and her expression was such a dazed and meaningless one that the prison guards and other soldiers paid little heed to the coming and going of "Crazy Bet" as she was called. "Mis' Van Lew-poor creature, she's lost her balance since the war broke out. She'll do no harm to the poor boys, and maybe a bit of comfortin'. A permit? Oh yes, signed by General Winder himself. Let her be!" Such was the verdict passed from sentry-guard to sentry in regard to "Crazy Bet," who wandered on at will humming her ditties and ministering to whom she would.

One day a cautious guard noticed a strange dish she carried into the prison. It was an old French platter with a double bottom in which water was supposed to be placed to keep the food on the platter hot. The dish roused the guard's suspicions, and to a nearby soldier he muttered something about it. Apparently unheeding him, "Crazy Bet" passed on beyond the grim, gray walls, carrying her platter; but she had heard his words. Two days later, she came to the prison door again with the strange dish in her hand, wrapped in a shawl. The sentry on guard stopped her.

"I will have to examine that," he said.

"Take it!" she said, hastily unwrapping it and dropping it into his hands. It contained no secret message that day as it had before—only water scalding hot, and the guard dropped it with a howl of pain and turned away to nurse his burned hands. "Crazy Bet" went on into the prison, smiling a broad and meaningless smile.

Well did the Spy play her role as months went by; more loudly she hummed, more vacantly she smiled, and more diligently she worked to obtain information regarding the number and placing of Confederate troops-information she sent on at once to Federal headquarters. Day by day she worked, daring loss of life and spending her entire fortune, for the sake of the cause that was dearer to her than a good name or riches-the preservation of the Union and the abolishing of slavery.

From the windows of the Libby and from Belle Isle, the prisoners could see passing troops and supply-trains and give shrewd guesses at their strength and destination, making their conjectures from the roads by which they saw the Confederates leave the town. Also they often heard scraps of conversations between surgeons or prison guards, which they hoarded like so much gold to pass on to "Crazy Bet," and so repay her kindness and her lavish generosity, which was as sincere as her underlying motive was genuine. Meals at the Van Lew mansion grew less and less bountiful, even meager. Not one article did either Elizabeth Van Lew or her loyal mother buy for themselves, but they spent their ample fortune without stint on the sick and imprisoned in their city. There was never an hour of her time that the Federal Spy gave to her own concerns. If there was nothing else to be done, she was writing a home letter for some heartsick prisoner from the North, and secretly carrying it past the censors to be sure that it should reach the anxious family eagerly awaiting news of a loved one.

"Crazy Bet" loaned many books to the prisoners. They returned them with a word or sentence or a page number faintly underlined here and there. In the privacy of her own room, the Spy would piece them together and read some important bit of news which she instantly sent to Federal headquarters by special messenger as she had ceased using the mails in the early stages of the war. Or a friendly little note would be handed to her with its hidden meaning impossible to decipher except by one who knew the code.

Important messages were carried back and forth in her baskets of fruit and flowers in a way that would have been dangerous had not "Crazy Bet" established such a reputation for harmless kindness. She had even won over Lieutenant Todd, brother of Mrs. Lincoln, who was in charge of the Libby, by the personal offerings she brought him of delectable buttermilk and gingerbread. Clever Bet!

So well did she play her part now, and with such assurance, that she would sometimes stop a stranger on the street and begin a heated argument in favor of the Union. The person who did not know her simply looked on the outspoken little woman with a mixture of admiration and contempt. At that time her lifelong persecution, by those who had before been her loyal friends, began. Where before she had been met with friendly bows and smiles, there were now averted glances or open insults. She encountered dislike, even hatred, on every side, but at that time it mattered little to her, for her heart and mind were occupied with bigger problems.

The old Van Lew house, in its capacity of Secret Service station, was a hive of industry, which was carried on with such smooth and silent secrecy that no one knew what went on in its great rooms. And watching over all those who came and went on legitimate business—or as agents of the Federal Government on secret missions—was a woman, alert of body and keen of mind, standing at her post by day and by night. After all members of her household were safely locked in their rooms for the night, the Spy would creep down, barefooted, to the big library with its ornamented iron fireplace. On either side of this fireplace were two columns, on each of which was a small, carved figure of a lion. Possibly by accident, probably by design, one of these figures was loosened so that it could be raised like a box-lid. And in the darkness of the night, the swift, silent figure of the Spy would steal into the big room, lift the carved lion, deftly slip a message in cipher into the cavity beneath the figure and cautiously creep away, with never a creaking board to reveal her coming or going.

With equal caution and swift dexterity, early the next morning an old Negro servant would steal into the room, duster and broom in hand, to do his cleaning. Into every corner of the room he would peer, to be sure there were no watching eyes. Then he would slip over to the fireplace, lift the lion, draw out the cipher message, and place it sometimes in his mouth, sometimes in his shoe. As soon as his morning chores were done he would be seen plodding down the dusty road leading to the farm, where someone was eagerly waiting for the tidings he carried. Well had the Spy trained her messengers!

Elizabeth Van Lew was indeed a Spy working against the city of her birth and the friends of her love and loyalty—a traitor in one sense of the word. But above all, she was tireless in working for her highest ideals, and so is she worthy of respect and honor wherever the Stars and Stripes float free over united America.

Written Summation

One day a cautious guard noticed a strange dish carried by Crazy Bet into the prison. It was an old French platter with a double bottom in which water was supposed to be placed to keep the food on the platter hot. The dish roused the guard's suspicions, and to a nearby soldier he muttered something about it.

Model Practice 1 (adapted from the original)

_____

_____

_____

_____

_____

_____

_____

_____

_____

_____

_____

_____

_____

Model Practice 2

Model Practice 3

Peter Petersen
A Story of the Minnesota Indian War
by Edward Eggleston

Peter Petersen was a very little boy living in Minnesota. He lived on the very edge of the Indian country when the Indian War of 1862 broke out.

Settlers were killed in their cabins before they knew that a war had begun. As the news spread, the people left their houses and hurried into the large towns. Some of them saw their houses burning before they got out of sight. The roads were crowded with ox wagons full of women and children.

Peter Petersen's father was a Norwegian settler. When the news of the Indian attack came, Peter's father hitched up his oxen and put his wife and daughters and little Peter into the wagon. They drove the oxen hard and got to Mankato in safety.

The town was crowded with frightened people. Many were living in woodsheds and barns. In their hurry, these country people had not brought food enough with them. Before long they began to suffer hunger. Peter Petersen's father thought of the potato field he had at home. If he could only go back to his house long enough to dig his potatoes, his family would have enough to eat.

When he made up his mind to go, Peter wanted to go along with him. As there were now soldiers within a mile of his farm, Peter's father thought the Indians would not be so bold as to come there. So he and Peter went back to the little house.

The next morning Peter's father went out to dig potatoes. Peter, who was but five years old, was asleep in his bed. He was awakened by the yells of Indians. He ran to the door just in time to see his father shot with an arrow.

Little Peter ran like a frightened rabbit to the nearest bushes. The Indians chased him and caught him. They were amused to see him run, and they thought he would be a funny little plaything to have. So they just set him up on the back of a cow and drove the cow ahead of them. They laughed to see Peter trying to keep his seat on the cow's back.

The little boy lived among the Indians for weeks. They did not give him anything to eat. When he came into their tents to get food, they would knock him down. But he would pick up something to eat at last and then run away. When he could not get any food, he would go out among the cows the Indians had taken from the white people. Little as he was, he would manage to milk one of the cows. He had no other cup to catch the milk in but his mouth. Whenever any of the Indians threatened to kill him, he would run away and dodge about between the legs of the cows or among the horses, so as to get out of their way. Sometimes he was so much afraid that he slept out in the grass, in the dew or rain.

After some weeks, Peter and the other captives were retaken by the white soldiers sent to fight the Indians. But the poor little boy could speak no language but Norwegian. He could not tell whose child he was nor where he came from. His mother and sisters had left the dangerous country near the Indians. They had gone to Winona, a hundred and fifty miles away. One of his sisters heard somebody read in the paper that such a little boy had been taken from the Indians. The kind-hearted doctor in whose house she lived tried to find the boy, but nobody could tell what had become of little Peter. His family at last gave up all hope of seeing him again.

When Peter was taken by the soldiers, he had worn out all his clothes in traveling through the prairie grass. He had nothing on him but part of a shirt. The soldiers took an old suit of uniform and made him some clothes. He was soon dressed from top to toe in army blue.

He was as much of a plaything for the soldiers as he had been for the Indians. They laughed at his pranks as they might have done if he had been a monkey. He passed from one squad of soldiers to another. They fed him on hard tack and shared their blankets with him. He was the pet and plaything of them all. But after a while the Indians were driven away from the settlements, and the soldiers were ordered to the South, for it was in the time of the Civil War.

The regiment that Peter happened to be with got on a steamboat, and Peter went aboard with them. The soldiers knew that if Peter should be taken to the South, he would be farther than ever away from his friends. So the soldiers made up their minds to put him ashore at Winona. It was the last place at which he would find Norwegian people. To put such a little fellow ashore in a large and busy place like this was a hard thing to do. Peter was hardly more than a baby, and he could not speak English. He stood about as much chance of starving to death here as he had in the Indian camp.

When the boat landed at Winona, the soldiers gave some money to one of the hotel porters and told him to give the child something to eat and send him out into the country where there were Norwegian people. But as soon as Peter had eaten the dinner they gave him at the hotel, he slipped away and went back to the river. He expected to find his friends, the soldiers, waiting for him; but the boat had gone. Peter was now in a strange city, without friends. Not without friends, either, for his sisters were in this same city. But he did not think any more of getting to his mother or his sisters. He was only thinking of the soldiers who had been so kind to him.

When the next boat came down the river, Peter Petersen, in his little blue uniform, marched aboard. He thought he might overtake the soldiers, but the boatmen put him ashore again. He stood gazing after the boat, not knowing what to do or where to go.

There stood on the bank that day a Norwegian. He was a guest at the Norwegian hotel in the town. He heard Peter say something in his own language, and he thought the boy must be a son of the man who kept the hotel. So he said to him in Norwegian, "Let's go home."

It had been a long time since Peter had heard his own language spoken. Nobody had said anything to him about home since he was taken away from his father's cabin by the Indians. The words sounded sweet to him. He followed the strange man. He did not know where he was going, except that it was to some place called home. When he got to the hotel, he went in and sat down. He did not know what else to do.

Presently the landlady came in. Seeing a strange little boy in army blue, she said, "Whose child are you?"

Peter did not know whose child he was. Since the soldiers left him, he did not seem to be anybody's child. As he did not answer, the landlady spoke to him rather sharply.

"What do you want here, little boy?" she said.

"A drink of water," said Peter.

A little boy nearly always wants a drink of water.

"Go through into the kitchen there and get a drink," said the landlady.

Peter opened the door into the kitchen and went through. In a moment two arms were about him. Peter knew what home meant then. His sister, Matilda, had recognized her lost brother Peter in the little soldier boy. The next day he was put into a wagon and sent out to Rushford, where his mother was living. The wanderings of the little captive were over.

Written Summation

The town was crowded with frightened people. Many were living in woodsheds and barns. In their hurry, these country people had not brought food enough with them. Before long they began to suffer hunger. Peter Petersen's father thought of the potato field he had at home. If he could only go back to his house long enough to dig his potatoes, his family would have enough to eat.

Model Practice 1 (adapted from the original)

_____

_____

_____

_____

_____

_____

_____

_____

_____

_____

_____

_____

_____

_____

Model Practice 2

_____

_____

_____

_____

_____

_____

_____

_____

_____

_____

Model Practice 3

_____

_____

_____

_____

_____

_____

_____

_____

_____

_____

The Soldier's Reprieve

from <u>The New York Observer</u>

"I thought, Mr. Allen, when I gave my Bennie to his country, that not a father in all this broad land made so precious a gift-no, not one. The dear boy only slept a minute, just one little minute at his post; I know that was all, for Bennie never dozed over a duty. How prompt and reliable he was! I know he only fell asleep one little second-he was so young and not strong, that boy of mine. Why, he was as tall as I, and only eighteen! And now they shoot him because he was found asleep when doing sentinel duty. 'Twenty-four hours,' the telegram said, only twenty-fours hours. Where is Bennie now?"

"We will hope with his heavenly Father," said Mr. Allen soothingly.

"Yes, yes; let us hope; God is very merciful! 'I should be ashamed, Father,' Bennie said, 'when I am a man to think I never used this great right arm'—and he held it out proudly before me— 'for my country when it needed it. Palsy it, rather than keep it at the plow.' 'Go, then, my boy, and God keep you!' I said. God has kept him, I think, Mr. Allen!" And the farmer repeated these last words slowly, as if in spite of his reason his heart doubted them.

"Like the apple of the eye, Mr. Owen; doubt it not."

Blossom sat near them listening with blanched cheek. She had not shed a tear. Her anxiety had been so concealed that no one had noticed it. She had occupied herself mechanically in the household cares. Now, she answered a gentle tap at the door, opening it to receive from a neighbor's hand a letter. "It is from him," was all she said.

It was like a message from the dead! Mr. Owen took the letter, but could not break the envelope on account of his trembling fingers and held it toward Mr. Allen with the helplessness of a child. The minister opened it and read as follows:

"Dear Father: When this reaches you I shall be in eternity. At first it seemed awful to me, but I have thought so much about it that now it has no terror. They say they will not bind me nor blind me but that I may meet death like a man. I thought, Father, that it might have been on the battlefield, for my country, and that when I fell it would be fighting gloriously; but to be shot down like a dog for nearly betraying it—to die for neglect of duty! O, Father! I wonder the very thought does not kill me! But I shall not disgrace you; I am going to write you all about it, and when I am gone, you may tell my comrades. I cannot, now.

"You know I promised Jemmie Carr's mother I would look after her boy; and when he fell sick, I did all I could for him. He was not strong when he was ordered back into the ranks, and the day before that night, I carried all his luggage besides my own on our march. Towards night we went in on double quick, and though the luggage began to feel very heavy, everybody else was tired, too; and as for Jemmie, if I had not lent him an arm now and then he would have dropped by the way. I was all tired out when we came into camp, and then it was Jemmie's turn to be sentry. I would take his place; but I was too tired, Father. I could not have kept awake if a gun had been pointed at my head; but I did not know it until—well, until it was too late."

"God be thanked" interrupted Mr. Owen, reverently, "I knew Bennie was not the boy to sleep carelessly at his post."

"They tell me today that I have a short reprieve, 'time to write to you,' the good Colonel says. Forgive him, Father, he only does his duty; he would gladly save me if he could; and do not lay my death against Jemmie. The poor boy is heart-broken and does nothing but beg and entreat them to let him die in my place.

"I can't bear to think of mother and Blossom. Comfort them, Father! Tell them I die, as a brave boy should; and that when the war is over, they will not be ashamed of me, as they must be now. God help me! It is very hard to bear! Good-bye, Father. God seems near and dear to me; not at all as if he wished me to perish forever, but as if he felt sorry for his poor sinful, broken-hearted child and would take me to be with him and my Savior in a better life."

A deep sigh burst from Mr. Owen's heart. "Amen," he said solemnly, "amen."

"Tonight, in the early twilight, I shall see the cows all coming home from the pasture and precious little Blossom standing on the back stoop, waiting for me! But I shall never, never come! God bless you all! Forgive your poor Bennie!"

Late that night the door of the "back stoop" opened softly, and a little figure glided out and down the footpath that led to the road by the mill. She seemed rather flying than walking, turning her head neither to the right nor left, looking only now and then to heaven, and folding her hands as if in prayer. Two hours later the same young girl stood at the mill depot, watching the coming of the night train; and the conductor, as he reached down to lift her into the car, wondered at the tear-stained face that was upturned toward the dim lantern he held in his hand. A few questions and ready answers told him all; and no father could have cared more tenderly for his only child than he for our little Blossom. She was on her way to Washington to ask President Lincoln for her brother's life. She had stolen away, leaving only a note to tell them where and why she had gone.

She had brought Bennie's letter with her; no good, kind heart like the President's could refuse to be melted by it. The next morning they reached New York, and the conductor hurried her on to Washington. Every minute, now, might be the means of saving her brother's life. And so, in an incredibly short time, Blossom reached the Capitol and hastened to the White House.

The president had just seated himself to his morning task of overlooking and signing important papers; when without one word of announcement the door softly opened, and Blossom, with downcast eyes and folded hands, stood before him.

"Well, my child," he said in his pleasant, cheerful tone, "what do you want so bright and early this morning?"

"Bennie's life, sir," faltered Blossom.

"Who is Bennie?"

"My brother, sir. They are going to shoot him for sleeping at his post."

"O, yes," and Mr. Lincoln ran his eye over the papers before him. "I remember. It was a fatal sleep. You see, my child, it was a time of special danger. Thousands of lives might have been lost by his culpable negligence."

"So my father said," replied Blossom, gravely. "But poor Bennie was so tired, sir, and Jemmie so weak. He did the work of two, sir, and it was Jemmie's night, not his; but Jemmie was too tired, and Bennie never thought about himself that he was tired too."

"What is this you say, child? Come here, I do not understand," and the kind man caught eagerly as ever at what seemed to be a justification of the offense.

Blossom went to him; he put his hand tenderly on her shoulder and turned up the pale face toward his. How tall he seemed! And he was the President of the United States, too! A dim thought of this kind passed for a minute through Blossom's mind, but she told her simple, straightforward story and handed Mr. Lincoln Bennie's letter to read.

He read it carefully; then taking up his pen, wrote a few hasty lines, and rang his bell.

Blossom heard this order: "Send this dispatch at once!"

The President then turned to the girl and said: "Go home, my child, and tell that father of yours, who could approve his country's sentence even when it took the life of a child like that, that Abraham Lincoln thinks the life far too precious to be lost. Go back or—wait until tomorrow. Bennie will need a change after he has so bravely faced death; he shall go with you."

"God bless you, sir!" said Blossom, and who shall doubt that God heard and registered the request?

Two days after this interview, the young soldier came to the White House with his little sister. He was called into the President's private room and a strap fastened upon his shoulder. Mr. Lincoln then said: "The soldier that could carry a sick comrade's baggage and die for the act so uncomplainingly deserves well of his country." Then Bennie and Blossom took their way to their Green Mountain home. A crowd gathered at the mill depot to welcome them back; and as Farmer Owen's hand grasped that of the boy, tears flowed down his cheeks, and he was heard to say fervently: "The Lord be praised!"

Written Summation

I thought, Father, that I might meet death on the battlefield, for my country, and that when I fell it would be fighting gloriously. But to be shot down like a dog for nearly betraying it! To die for neglect of duty! O, Father! I wonder the very thought does not kill me!

Model Practice 1 (adapted from the original)

_____

_____

_____

_____

_____

_____

_____

_____

_____

_____

_____

_____

_____

_____

Model Practice 2

_____

_____

_____

_____

_____

_____

_____

_____

_____

Model Practice 3

_____

_____

_____

_____

_____

_____

_____

_____

_____

Robert E. Lee

by Lawton B. Evans

Robert E. Lee was the son of General Henry Lee, a hero of the Revolution known as "Light Horse Harry." He was born in Virginia. He was no more than a mere boy when his father died, leaving him to the training of a devoted mother. When Robert was not at school, he spent his time with her, helping her to keep house, taking her out to ride in the old family coach, and reading aloud the books she liked to hear.

Some days, however, he spent in hunting of which he was very fond. Then he would ride all day with his hounds or tramp for hours through the woods looking for game. In this way, he developed the splendid strength that never failed him in his after life.

When he was eighteen years old, he went to West Point to be trained as a soldier. He was there for four years and never received a demerit. He was a model cadet. His clothes were always clean and well cared for. His gun, belt, and sword were as bright as they could be polished. His lessons were studiously prepared. So good a record did he make that he graduated second in his class.

Like many great men, Lee was always gentle, generous, and good. He was simple in his habits, never using tobacco nor any intoxicating liquors. Upon one occasion, a lady gave him a bottle of whisky to use, if he "ever needed it." Lee took it with him through the Mexican War, and then sent it back to his friend, saying, "I have gotten along very well without it and am returning it to you, for I have never found that I really needed it."

Lee served as a Captain of Engineers during the War with Mexico. It was his duty to make roads and bridges, to plant big guns, to draw maps, and to direct the marches of the fighting men. He was with General Scott in all the big battles and was of such assistance that that General said: "Lee is the greatest soldier I have ever known."

In after years, General Scott said, "If I knew that a battle was to be fought for my country, and the president were to say to me, 'Scott, who shall be my commander?' I would say 'Robert E. Lee! Nobody but Robert E. Lee.'"

In Mexico, while the battle of Cerro Gordo was raging, Captain Lee heard the cries of a little girl and, following the sound, found a Mexican drummer-boy badly wounded and lying on the ground with a big Mexican soldier, who had been shot, fallen on top of him. Lee stopped; he had the Mexican thrown off the boy's body and the little fellow taken to a place of safety.

His small sister stood by, her eyes full of tears, her hands crossed over her breast. Her feet and arms were bare, and her hair hung down in a long plait to her waist. She looked up into the kind face of Captain Lee and said, in her own language, "I am very grateful, kind sir. May God bless you for saving my brother."

Once, on a long march, a part of Scott's army had lost its way. General Scott sent seven engineers to guide the men into the right road. They had to cross a huge bed of lava and rocks. Six of the engineers came back and said they could not get across. Captain Lee, however, on foot and alone, pressed on through darkness and danger and brought the men out in safety. General Scott said, "It was the greatest feat done by any one man during the war."

When the Civil War came on, Lee resigned from the United States Army to fight for Virginia and the South. He was offered the chief command of the Union forces, if he would remain in the service of the United States. He said to Mr. Blair, who came to offer him this command:

"If I owned the four millions of slaves in the South, I would give them all up to save the Union; but how can I draw my sword upon Virginia, my native State?"

After the war had been going on for nearly a year, Lee became the commanding General of all the Confederate army. His soldiers were devotedly attached to him and had supreme confidence in his ability. They referred to him affectionately as "Marse Robert."

On one occasion, General Lee placed himself at the head of a body of Texas troops and, waving his sword, ordered them to follow him into battle. The situation was critical, and Lee wanted to save the day.

But the soldiers would not move. They cried out, "Lee to the rear! Lee to the rear." One of his Generals rode up and, taking his horse by the bridle, said, "General Lee, there are Georgians and Texans here willing to charge, but unwilling to see you in danger. If you will go back, we will go forward."

To this Lee replied, "You are brave men and do not need me"; and, turning his horse's head, he rode back of the charging lines.

An old soldier relates that one-day he was in the trenches when a big gun was ready to be fired. Lee came in and walked about, asking after the men and speaking words of cheer. Approaching the big gun, he asked an officer to fire it that he might see the result.

The officer hesitated and respectfully answered, "If I fire this gun, the enemy will return the fire at once in great force. Some of us will be killed, but that does not matter so long as you are not here. If you will retire out of danger, I shall fire it as long as you order, but I beg you not to have it fired while you are standing here."

Lee was greatly touched by this devotion and did not insist upon the big gun going into action while he was present.

General Lee ever felt kindly toward Union soldiers. He never called them the enemy but always spoke of them as those people. Once, he remarked about the Northern troops, "Now, I wish all those people would go back to their homes and leave us to do the same."

A lady who had lost her husband in the war spoke in sharp terms of the North, one day, to General Lee. He said gently, "Madam, do not train up your children as foes of the government of the United States. We are one country now. Bring them up to be Americans."

Throughout his life, he had but one purpose, and that was to do his duty. He often said, "Duty is the sublimest word in the English language," and, in accordance with this belief, he regulated his great life upon what seemed to him to be the only course he ought to pursue at the time.

Written Summation

The officer hesitated and respectfully answered, "If I fire this gun, the enemy will return the fire at once in great force. Some of us will be killed, but that does not matter so long as you are not here. If you will retire out of danger, I shall fire it as long as you order, but I beg you not to have it fired while you are standing here."

Model Practice 1 (adapted from the original)

Model Practice 2

Model Practice 3

Stonewall Jackson

by Lawton B. Evans

His real name was Thomas Jonathan Jackson, and he was born in what is now West Virginia of poor parents who had to work hard for a living. His father died when he was three years old, leaving his mother to support three little children. They all lived in one room where the mother taught a little school and did sewing for her friends and neighbors.

Thomas grew up rosy-cheeked and blue-eyed with waving brown hair, very determined to have his way and full of confidence in himself. Fortunately, his was a good way, and from the start he was a very dependable boy.

He was fond of arithmetic and easily learned all the hard rules and could work any of the problems given him. His other studies were not so easy, but he never stopped anything he had once started until he had mastered it, or it had mastered him. One of the maxims of his life was, "You may be whatever you resolve to be."

He gained a reputation for telling the exact truth. At one time, he walked a mile in the rain to correct a statement he had made.

"Why do you go to so much trouble for such a mere trifle as that?" someone asked him on his return.

He answered, "Simply because I found out that what I said was not true, and I never carry anything to bed with me that will rob me of sleep."

He was a leader in sports, particularly in climbing and jumping. He was generally selected as Captain of one side, and this was the side that nearly always won, for he was a master of strategy in games.

At eighteen, he resolved to be a soldier. Dressed in a plain homespun suit and carrying his clothes in a saddlebag, he rode into Washington and asked to be made a cadet at West Point, the military academy of the nation. He received the appointment.

His appearance caused much sport among the students there, for he was awkward and ill at ease, but always good-natured. It was not long before his ability to master his studies, however, made him sought after by others; and he soon won admiration and respect.

From early life, he was very religious. He taught in the Sunday school and even gathered the slaves of his town together every Sunday afternoon and made them familiar with the truths of the Bible. Later on, when he had become a great soldier, it was his habit to go off to a quiet place and pray before a battle.

Jackson's servant used to say, "I can tell when there is going to be a big fight, for Marse Tom always prays a long time before one."

When the Civil War began, Jackson threw his lot in with Virginia and enlisted in the Confederate army. He was commissioned a General. The first great battle of this war was known as Bull Run, or the Battle of Manassas. The Confederate troops were driven back, but were rallied on a half-plateau by General Jackson.

Here they stood immovable, for Jackson refused to retreat a step. An officer rushed up and said, "General, they are beating us back, and we are without ammunition."

"Then, sir," replied Jackson, "we will give them the bayonet."

A few minutes later, seeing the troops around Jackson, standing their ground so firmly, General Bee, a Confederate officer, cried out to his own men:

"Look at Jackson's brigade! It stands like a stone wall."

After this incident, the great soldier was known in history as "Stonewall" Jackson.

Like many other soldiers, Jackson never used coffee, tobacco, or whisky. Nor could he bear to hear any one utter profane language. He never refrained from expressing his disapproval of swearing.

Often, in winter, he would go without an over-coat, saying, "I do not wish to give in to the cold." Once, when told by his surgeon that he needed a little brandy, he replied, "I like it too well; that is the reason I never take it. I am more afraid of it than of Federal bullets."

Jackson always shared the hardships of his men. On one occasion, when his brigade was worn out with marching, he said, "Let the poor fellows sleep. I will guard the camp myself." Accordingly, he acted as sentinel during the night while his tired men took their rest.

Jackson became the ablest Lieutenant of General Lee, who relied upon him implicitly. He was often sent upon the most important and most dangerous missions, but his skill was so great that he always returned victorious. So rapid were the movements of his troops that they became known as "Jackson's foot cavalry."

At the battle of Chancellorsville, Lee sent Jackson around to the rear of Hooker's army. Jackson fell so suddenly upon the flank of the Federals that they were thrown into confusion. The result of the attack was to defeat Hooker's plan and to check his advance.

The victory was dearly bought. Jackson had ridden out in the gathering darkness to reconnoiter the positions of the enemy and was returning to camp. He ran into a body of his own troops, who, mistaking his party for Federal cavalry, fired upon them. Jackson fell from his horse mortally wounded.

He was borne on a stretcher to a farmhouse nearby, where he died after a few days. His final thoughts were of the battle, and he muttered orders to his men as his life ebbed away.

His last words were: "Let us cross over the river and rest under the shade of the trees."

His death was a great loss to the Confederate cause. Lee wept when he heard the sad news and said, "I have indeed lost my right arm."

Written Summation

Thomas grew up rosy-cheeked and blue-eyed with waving brown hair, very determined to have his way and full of confidence in himself. Fortunately, his was a good way, and from the start he was a very dependable boy.

Model Practice 1

Model Practice 2

Model Practice 3

The Surrender of General Lee
by Lawton B. Evans

At a house in the little town of Appomattox, Virginia on April 9, 1865, a memorable event took place. General Robert E. Lee here met General Ulysses S. Grant and surrendered the Confederate army under his command.

For four years, the terrible war between the North and South had been going on, until the Southern army was reduced to a bare handful of ill-fed and badly clothed men. The South had been drained of her men and supplies, and Lee saw it was useless to continue the unequal struggle any longer.

The two great Generals met by agreement in this village to arrange terms for the cessation of hostilities.

The contrast between the two men was striking. Grant was forty-three years of age, five feet, eight inches tall with brown hair and full brown beard. He wore a single-breasted blouse, of dark blue flannel, an ordinary pair of top boots, with his trousers inside; he was without spurs, and he had no sword. A pair of shoulder straps was all to show his rank. Around him sat or stood a dozen of his staff officers.

Lee, on the other hand, was six feet tall, and faultlessly attired. His hair and beard were silver gray and quite thick for one of his age. He was sixteen years older than Grant. He wore a new Confederate uniform, and by his side, was a sword of exquisite workmanship, the hilt studded with jewels. It was the sword presented to him by the State of Virginia. His boots were new and clean, and he wore a pair of handsome spurs. He was attended by a single officer, his military secretary.

Lee was the first to arrive, and when Grant entered he arose and bowed profoundly. Grant and his officers returned the greeting. Grant then sat at a marble top table, in the center of the room, while Lee sat at a small oval table, near a window.

General Grant began the conversation by saying, "I met you once before, General Lee, while we were serving in Mexico. I have always remembered your appearance, and I think I should have recognized you anywhere."

"Yes," replied Lee, "I know I met you in Mexico, and I have often thought of it. Those were wonderful experiences for us, when we were young soldiers."

After a few more remarks about Mexico, Lee said, "I suppose, General Grant, that the object of our meeting is understood. I asked to see you to find out upon what terms you would receive the surrender of my army."

Grant replied, "The terms are that all officers and men surrendered are to be paroled and are not to take up arms again; and all guns, ammunition, and supplies are to be handed over as captured property."

Lee suggested that the terms be written out for his acceptance. This was done, Grant adding that the side arms, horses, and baggage of the officers were not to be included in the terms of surrender. There was no demand made for the surrender of Lee's sword, nor was there any offer of it on Lee's part. In fact, nothing was said about it.

When the document was written, Lee took out his glasses and slowly put them on. Reading the terms of surrender, he remarked,

"I would like to mention that the cavalry and artillery own their horses. I would like to know whether those men will be permitted to retain their own stock."

Grant immediately replied, "I take it that most of the men in the ranks are small farmers. And, as the country has been so raided by the armies, it is doubtful if they will be able to put in a crop to carry them through next winter without the aid of the horses they now have. I will instruct the officers to let the men who claim to own horses or mules take the animals home with them to work their little farms."

Lee appreciated this concession and said, "This will have the very best possible effect upon the men. It will do much toward conciliating our people." He then wrote out his acceptance of the terms of the surrender.

When this was done, General Grant introduced the members of his staff to General Lee. Some of them Lee had known before, and the conversation became general and cordial. Lee at length said, "General Grant, I have a thousand or more of your men as prisoners, a number of them officers. I shall be glad to send them into your lines as soon as possible, for I have no provisions for them. I have indeed nothing for my own men. They have been living for the last few days on parched corn, and we are badly in need of both rations and forage."

General Grant immediately offered to receive the prisoners back into his own lines and said, "I will take steps to have your army supplied with rations at once." Turning to an officer, he gave him the command for the issuing of the rations to the hungry Confederate army.

The two Generals then shook hands, and, bowing gravely to the others, Lee prepared to depart. Reaching the porch, he signaled for the orderly to bring up his horse. When it was ready, he mounted and rode away to break the sad news to the brave fellows he had so long commanded.

The news of the surrender reached the Union lines, and firing of salutes began at several places. Grant sent orders to stop this, saying,

"The war is over, and it is ill-becoming to rejoice in the downfall of a gallant foe."

When Lee appeared among his soldiers, they saw by his sad countenance that he brought them news of surrender. They stood in silence as he rode before them, every hat raised; and down the bronzed cheek of thousands of hardened veterans, there ran bitter tears.

As Lee rode slowly along the lines, the old soldiers pressed about him; trying to take his hand, to touch his person, or even to lay their hands upon his splendid gray horse, thus, showing for him their deep affection. Then General Lee, with bare head and tears flowing, bade adieu to his soldiers. In a few words, he told the brave men, who had been so true, to return to their homes and begin to rebuild their wastelands.

Written Summation

Lee was the first to arrive, and when Grant entered he arose and bowed profoundly. Grant and his officers returned the greeting. Grant then sat at a marble-top table, in the center of the room, while Lee sat at a small oval table, near a window.

Model Practice 1

Model Practice 2

Model Practice 3

The War Is Over

by Mara L. Pratt

Picture to yourself if you can, the joy of the people in the North when the news of these surrenders spread over the land! The telegraphs flashed it over the wires from city to city and from town to town, until the news reached the lonely homes away out on the prairies and away up on the mountains.

Our "Union boys," the "boys in blue" tossed up their hats for joy. Faces in the homes—even in those whose soldier boys would never come back to them—shone with thankfulness that this cruel war was over.

But nobody was happier than Lincoln himself. Washington was all one blaze of light; fireworks were shooting, bonfires were blazing, and bands were playing.

President Lincoln stepped out upon the balcony of the White House and asked one of the bands to play the tune of "Dixie." This had been the favorite tune of the Confederates all through the war, just as "John Brown's Body" had been the favorite with our soldiers.

"I have always thought Dixie one of the best songs I ever knew. Our enemies over the way tried to make it their own; but I think we captured it with the rest; and I now ask the band to give us a good turn on it."

This was Abraham Lincoln's last public speech.

Next evening, the 14th of April, the president went to the theatre to see an English play called "Our American Cousin." For four years the heavy duties of his great office, the sorrow which he had felt at the horrors of the war, had made an evening of amusement almost impossible for him.

But the war was over; he could lay off some of his cares. There was now to be a little time for laughter and enjoyment, a holiday for the nation and its president. So Mr. Lincoln went to the theatre, sitting in a box just above the stage. About half-past ten o'clock in the evening, as the play drew near its close, a man named John Wilkes Booth, wrapped closely in a cloak, entered the box. He came up behind the president and shot him in the back of the head. The ball entered the brain, Lincoln's head drooped forward, his eyes closed, and he never spoke afterwards. It is hoped that he felt no more pain, though he lingered until next morning, and then quietly passed away.

After the shot, the murderer with the cry, "Thus may it be always with tyrants," leaped over the box railing down upon the stage. Rushing hastily through the frightened actors, hardly conscious of what had been done, he escaped through a back entrance, mounted a horse made ready for him at the theatre door, and rode rapidly away.

This news of horror, so quickly following that of joy, spread over the country, filling it with gloom. This good, simple man, Abraham Lincoln, —this gentleman of the people—had won to himself all loyal hearts. His face, so full of pathos, winning in spite of its rugged plainness; his manly, truthful nature; his noble humanity had gained him the regard even of those who at first sneered at the "vulgar rail-splitter." Across the ocean in England where he had been held up to ridicule, his name was now mentioned with reverence.

The assassin, as he leaped from the box upon the stage, had caught his foot in the American flag, which draped the front of the President's box. He fell forward and broke his leg in the fall. A party was at once sent in pursuit of him. On April 21, 1865, he was found in a barn near Fredericksburg. Defiant to the last, he stood at bay, like a hunted wild animal with loaded weapon, prepared to take the life of any one who attempted to take him alive.

The barn was set on fire, and, as he attempted to escape, he was shot at by one of those in pursuit and so captured. He died soon after from the effects of the wound, and his body was buried secretly.

Andrew Johnson the vice-president, now, became president, and the people set to work to bring the country back into its old condition of peace and prosperity. Since then the country has grown very rapidly, and we are today the freest, the happiest, the richest, the best nation—I hope you all think—on the face of the earth.

Peace shall unite us again and forever,
Though thousands lie cold in the graves of these wars;
Those who survive them shall never prove, never,
False to the flag of the Stripes and the Stars!

Written Summation

The assassin, as he leaped from the box upon the stage, had caught his foot in the American flag, which draped the front of the President's box. He fell forward and broke his leg in the fall. A party was at once sent in pursuit of him. On April 21, 1865, he was found in a barn near Fredericksburg.

Model Practice 1

Model Practice 2

Model Practice 3

Thomas A. Edison the Great Inventor

by Lawton B. Evans

The story of our great inventors would not be complete without telling about Edison, the greatest of them all. When he was a boy, he sold papers for a while on a train. On one occasion, while he was standing at a station, he saw a little child playing on the track. Just at that moment, a train came thundering along. Edison jumped on the track, in front of the moving engine, and rescued the child. The father was the telegraph operator at the station. To show his gratitude, he offered to teach telegraphy to the young newsboy.

In a few years, Edison became a swift and competent operator. He was offered employment in a Boston office. When he appeared dressed in shabby clothes, for he was very poor, the other operators in the room made fun of him. But Edison did not care and took his place at his desk. In a short time an operator from New York, noted for his swiftness, called up the Boston office.

"Let the new man take the message," said the chief. He desired to try out Edison, of whose ability he knew nothing.

Edison sat down and for four hours and a half wrote the message as it came over the wire. Not once did he ask the operator to go more slowly, but kept up with him easily. Faster and faster ticked the instrument, while Edison's fingers flew over the pages, taking down every word as it came. The other operators gathered around in amazement to see this exhibition of speed, but Edison paid them no attention.

At the end of a long period, the operator sending the message inquired over the wire, "Who are you taking this message?" Edison replied, "I am Thomas A. Edison, the new operator."

"You are the first man in the country," was the reply, "who could ever take me at my fastest, and the only one who could sit at the other end of my wire for more than two hours and a half. I am proud to know you."

All the time that Edison was an operator, his mind was busy on inventions and improvements. When he was seventeen, he invented the duplex telegraph by which several messages could be sent on the same wire at the same time, even in opposite directions without causing any confusion. This was a great saving of time.

Shortly afterwards, he went to New York where he soon became known as an electrical expert. The first invention that brought him any considerable money was the ticker for stockbrokers' offices. This ticker was an electrical machine for recording quotations in the stock market. He was paid forty thousand dollars for this invention.

He next persuaded some men in New York to furnish the money for him to experiment in making a lamp for the electric light. They agreed to pay all his expenses, and, if it were a success, a share of the profits would be theirs. Edison moved to Menlo Park, New Jersey and opened a little shop and laboratory.

After awhile, he announced that he had made an electric lamp that would burn and soon had eighty electric lights in Menlo Park. This was very promising, and everybody was greatly interested in the results. Suddenly, the lamps went out, and Edison was much discouraged, but he was not the man to give up.

For five days and nights he remained at his laboratory, sleeping only a few hours at a time. The world declared the electric lamps a failure. One prominent man said they could not be made.

"I will make a statue of that man, light it with electric lights, and put a sign on it saying 'Here is the man that said the Edison lamp will not burn,'" was the inventor's reply.

After much hard labor, Edison discovered that the reason why his lamp would not burn was because the air had not been sufficiently exhausted from the glass bulbs. So he set about remedying the defect, after which the lamps burned brightly and lasted a long time. Now, all the world uses electric light.

Edison invented the first electric railway, and because of him the electric cars are used on the streets of nearly every city, large and small. He invented the phonograph for recording and reproducing sound. He also invented the kinetoscope, which was the beginning of the moving pictures.

Many other inventions have been made by him. So many, indeed, that he has accumulated a large fortune and is known as "The Wizard of Menlo Park," though his laboratories are now at Orange, New Jersey.

It is quite certain that no other inventor has produced so many things that have added to the comfort and pleasure of the world as Thomas A. Edison.

Written Summation

Edison sat down and for four hours and a half wrote the message as it came over the wire. Not once did he ask the operator to go more slowly, but kept up with him easily. Faster and faster ticked the instrument, while Edison's fingers flew over the pages. The other operators gathered around in amazement to see this exhibition of speed, but Edison paid them no attention.

Model Practice 1 (adapted from the original)

Model Practice 2

Model Practice 3

Clara Barton and the Red Cross
by Lawton B. Evans

At the outbreak of the Civil War, a young woman who was a clerk in the Patent Office at Washington gave up her position and volunteered to nurse soldiers without pay. She knew that the sick, wounded, and dying men would need the comfort that only a woman's hand can give. Her name was Clara Barton. She did not go to hospitals where it was safe for her to be, but she went on the battlefields where the awful carnage of death was around her.

Inspired by her example, other women undertook the same work, some going to the hospitals, others following the armies, but all nursing the sick, comforting the dying, and keeping their last messages for the loved ones at home.

After the war, Clara Barton went to Europe. In 1859, one hot day in summer, there was fought the great Battle of Solferino at the end of which more than thirty-five thousand men lay dead and wounded on the field of battle. There was no aid for them. For hours and even days they lay where they had fallen. A Swiss, by the name of Henri Dunant, visited the battlefield and was so overcome by its horrors that he wrote circular letters and delivered lectures, calling upon all nations to form some sort of a society to relieve the distress of the wounded.

"If nations will go to war, then there should be some means to help those who suffer by it. I call upon all nations to send representatives to Geneva, Switzerland in order to establish a society for this purpose," said he.

The conference met and formed an organization, which had for its purpose the care of the sick and wounded on the battlefield and in hospitals. The society adopted a badge, or flag, which was a red cross on a white ground. This was done in compliment to the Swiss Republic, whose flag was a white cross on a red ground. The organization soon became known as The Red Cross Society. Many nations signed an agreement to respect the principals of this Society.

When Clara Barton, who was in Switzerland recovering her health, heard of this society, she was filled with joy and hope. It was the kind of work she most loved, and she resolved to give her whole life to the Red Cross.

At the beginning of the Franco-Prussian War, in 1870, Clara Barton saw her opportunity for service. After the siege of Strasbourg, there were twenty thousand people without homes and employment, and starvation threatened them all. Clara Barton secured materials for thirty thousand garments and gave them out to the poor women of the city to be made up. She paid the women good wages for the work. Everywhere she went, the soldiers and people lent a helping hand.

After the war, the city of Paris was in the hands of lawless men of the lowest character. The Army of the Republic besieged the city, and the most dreadful scenes of conflict occurred. There was fighting on the streets, and many innocent persons were killed. In the midst of these horrors, Clara Barton entered the city on foot and began her work of helping the sick and wounded.

One day, a great crowd surged through the streets of Paris, crying for bread. The soldiers were powerless before such a mob. Clara Barton raised her head as if to speak to them. The crowd stopped, and she spoke in calm and hopeful words. In the end, they cried out, "It is an angel that speaks to us," and quietly went back to their homes.

When the war was over, there were removed from Paris ten thousand wounded men, who otherwise would have suffered and perhaps died through lack of care. All this was done by the Red Cross Society, working under the direction of Clara Barton.

She now returned to America, to found a similar society in this country. It was not until 1882 that the United States signed the treaty of Geneva and joined the family of nations in this great work. The American plan, however, went further in its purpose than relief in times of war. It included relief for the distressed at any time and to meet any calamity such as earthquake, flood, fire, and pestilence. Clara Barton was the first President of the American Red Cross.

A great fire swept through the forests of Michigan. For many days it raged in unchecked fury. Homes, farms, woods were swept away, and thousands of people were left homeless and penniless. The Red Cross Society was there promptly with its offers of relief. The call for aid went forth, and supplies poured in from every direction until eighty thousand dollars in money, food, and clothing were available for the suffering people of Michigan.

Then came floods along the Ohio and Mississippi rivers, fearful cyclones in the West, an earthquake in South Carolina, and a long and terrible drought in Texas. To them all the Red Cross went, with Clara Barton as its inspiration.

In 1889, the city of Johnstown, Pennsylvania was swept away by a flood caused by the breaking of a dam. Nearly five thousand lives were lost, and twelve million dollars worth of property was destroyed. It was a most dreadful calamity. Hardly had the news reached the country before Clara Barton and the Red Cross were in Johnstown, organizing relief for the severely stricken people. For five months she stayed amid those scenes of desolation and woe.

"The first to come and the last to go," said one of the newspapers, "she has indeed been an elder sister to us—nursing, tending, caring for the stricken ones through a season of distress such as no other people may ever know."

When the war with Spain occurred, Clara Barton was seventy years old, but she went to Cuba and did heroic work there. At the time of the Galveston flood, she was eighty years old, but she went to that stricken community and for many days labored to relieve the sufferings of the people.

The American Red Cross has grown into a very large and useful society and has many thousands of members. It has contributed a great deal of money to a suffering world. For the victims in the Japanese famine, it contributed nearly a quarter of a million dollars. For those rendered homeless by the eruption of Mt. Vesuvius in 1905, it gave twelve thousand dollars. For the sufferers in the great California earthquake in 1906, it gave more than three million dollars. Wherever humanity has a need, wherever it raises a cry for help, the Red Cross holds out its hand in relief and comfort.

In the recent World War, the American Red Cross sent its workers into the home camps and overseas to be with the soldiers in time of need. Whatever the men desired in the way of comfort and help, which the Government could not supply, the Red Cross was ready and willing to give. Its doctors, nurses, and directors numbered many thousands. What they did for the wounded and the dying will be the subject of many an inspiring story for years to come.

Written Summation

After the siege of Strasbourg, there were twenty thousand people without homes and employment, and starvation threatened them all. Clara Barton secured materials for thirty thousand garments and gave them out to the poor women of the city to be made up. She paid the women good wages for the work. Everywhere she went, the soldiers and people lent a helping hand.

Model Practice 1

Model Practice 2

Model Practice 3

Hobson and the Merrimac

by Lawton B. Evans

The war with Spain was undertaken for the purpose of delivering Cuba from the oppressive rule of Spain. It was therefore natural that the main object of the United States Government should be to drive the Spaniards from that island. When the war began, there was some uncertainty as to the size and strength of the Spanish navy. We knew that Spain had fine battleships, but we did not know how they were equipped and manned or what training their gunners possessed. It was feared that the Spanish fleet might appear off the Atlantic Coast and bombard New York or Boston. As it turned out, we can now afford to laugh at such foolish fears.

The Spanish navy was under command of Admiral Cervera. Our own fleet hunted for weeks before it was discovered that the Spaniards had taken refuge in the harbor of Santiago. Immediately, the American fleet blockaded the harbor so that the Spanish boats could not get out. The Spanish admiral knew the weakness of his vessels. He had five ships, but his crews were not trained, and his gunners had but little practice; they were by no means the equal of the American marksmen.

Days and weeks passed in idleness. Cervera refused to come out, and the American Commanders guarded the mouth of the harbor day and night. It was feared that the Spanish ships would slip out under cover of darkness and be free to inflict damage along the United States coast before they could be destroyed. But they did not attempt to offer battle to the American fleet.

To prevent their escape, a daring exploit was planned by Lieutenant Richard P. Hobson. He proposed to sink the collier, Merrimac, in the channel of the harbor so as, effectually, to prevent any ships from passing in or out. Lieutenant Hobson, with seven companions, started out on the collier, in the dead of night, and slowly steamed away.

When the Spaniards discovered the approach of the collier, they opened fire upon her from the shore, batteries on both sides. It seemed that the shells must certainly pierce her through and through. Escape for the men aboard appeared impossible.

But they were cool-headed and kept on until they reached the desired position. Just before they were ready to sink the collier and take to their boats, the rudder of the Merrimac was shot away. Hence, she sank diagonally instead of across the channel. The position of the wreck did not entirely block the entrance; it left a passage open for the unfortunate dash for liberty, which was made later by the Spanish fleet.

When the Merrimac was sunk in the channel, Hobson and his men took to a raft, and there they clung till morning. It was impossible to escape the searching fire of the enemy, afloat as they were in the open harbor. But, when day came and the Spaniards saw their helpless plight, they sent a boat out and took them prisoners. Admiral Cervera, himself, helped lift Hobson out of the water and was so filled with admiration for his daring that he sent a flag of truce to the American fleet with the news that all the men were safe in his hands.

The prisoners were treated with great respect and, later, were exchanged for a number of Spanish prisoners held by our forces.

Written Summation

When the Spaniards discovered the approach of the collier, they opened fire upon her from the shore, batteries on both sides. It seemed that the shells must certainly pierce her through and through. Escape for the men aboard appeared impossible.

Model Practice 1

Model Practice 2

Model Practice 3

Conquering the Yellow Fever

by Lawton B. Evans

There was an enemy that for hundreds of years no one learned to conquer. Its presence spread terror wherever it appeared. It lurked in Southern cities, but, often, it stalked broadcast over the whole country, scattering death wherever it came. That enemy was the yellow fever.

Its ravages had been endured with hopeless despair, with no chance to escape but in flight; and, often, flight was denied to those who lived in the stricken districts. Quarantine was rigidly enforced. So terrified were those who lived in the uninfected regions that refugees from yellow fever cities were turned back by loaded shotguns.

Household goods were destroyed, bedding and clothing and even houses were burned, to prevent the spread of the disease. Yet it was only held in check, and the people continued to live in terror of it. Just the announcement that yellow fever had appeared in a town was enough to make the bravest heart turn sick with the awful consequence of the horror it might mean.

Yellow fever had always been present in Cuba. Ships from that island brought it into Southern cities, and the contagion, once started, went on its ravages for months at a time. When Cuba was occupied by the United States, the problem of the yellow fever was in the hands of our Government.

Our soldiers were going into Cuba, and it was said that those who went would sooner or later have the fever. Many lives were thus imperiled. It was for our Government to find out what measures could be taken to save the men.

A Board of Medical Commissioners was appointed to go to Cuba and investigate the yellow fever. Of this Board, Major Walter Reed, an army surgeon, was appointed chairman. Major Reed had never had the fever, but he was too brave an officer and too devoted a surgeon to do otherwise than welcome this opportunity for service.

He had to deal with a treacherous enemy, that stalked up and down in the dark, attacking its unsuspecting victims. No one knew how it came or by what means it spread. It was found wherever filth and darkness prevailed and was supposed to be a filth disease.

"The first thing we will do will be to clean up Havana and not leave any place for fever germs to lurk," said Major Reed.

For a year and a half the most rigid sanitary measures were enforced. Deaths from other causes were reduced, but yellow fever went on its way unchecked. Plainly it was not a filth disease. Dr. Carlos Finlay, a physician in Cuba, offered the suggestion that the fever might be carried by the bite of a mosquito. The other members of the Commission scoffed at the idea.

"Everything else has failed in explaining why the disease spreads. I see no reason why we should scoff at this idea," remarked Dr. Reed. "It is certainly worth investigating."

There was but one way to find out, and that was for those who had not had the fever to be bitten by a mosquito that had come from the body of a yellow fever patient. The members of the Commission tried the experiment on themselves. Dr. Carroll was bitten by an infected mosquito, took the fever, and came near dying. Dr. Lazear allowed himself to be bitten by a mosquito, took the disease in its worst form, and died a martyr to the cause of science.

"It seems that we must try this experiment on a large scale and build special houses for the purpose," said Dr. Reed to the Commission. "I am beginning to think the mosquito has much to do with it."

An experiment camp was therefore built, named "Camp Lazear" in honor of the dead doctor who had sacrificed his life in the cause of investigation. Two houses were erected. One was filled with infected clothing, soiled articles, bedding, and everything that could possibly spread the disease from one person to another. All mosquitoes were carefully excluded from this building. Nothing was left to carry the disease, but the clothing and bedding.

The other building was clean, airy, and free from infected articles of any kind. But inside the screens were placed a number of mosquitoes that were known to be infected. Then came the call for volunteers. Dr. Reed addressed the soldiers:

"Men, I shall not detail anyone to enter these wards. I am asking for volunteers. Dr. Lazear has just died from the results of an experiment. It may mean death to some of you, but it may mean the saving of hundreds of thousands of others."

One by one the soldier boys volunteered, until Dr. Reed had enough for his purpose. He explained to them their danger and their duties. He then offered to each one a sum of money. "We take no money for this," they replied. "It is a condition of our going that we receive no pay."

"Gentlemen, I salute you in the name of humanity and your own great Government," said Dr. Reed.

For twenty days and nights, the men lived in their different quarters. In the clothes-infected house the men slept in the yellow fever beds, handled the clothing of patients, and breathed the air that had passed over infected articles. Not one of them took the fever.

In the other house, clean, sweet, airy, but full of mosquitoes, ten out of thirteen came down with the fever, but the cases were light and not one of them died.

The experiment proved conclusively that yellow fever was carried by the bite of a female mosquito which had previously bitten a yellow fever patient. It was not carried by the clothing, and it did not infect the house. Its spread could be controlled by killing the mosquito or by screening the sick-room.

Dr. Reed died shortly after he had announced the results of his investigations. In a letter to his wife, he wrote,

"The prayer that has been mine for twenty years, that I might be permitted in some way and at some time to do something to alleviate human suffering, has been granted."

Written Summation

There was an enemy that for hundreds of years no one learned to conquer. Its presence spread terror wherever it appeared. It lurked in Southern cities, but, often, it stalked broadcast over the whole country, scattering death wherever it came. That enemy was the yellow fever.

Model Practice 1 (adapted from the original)

Model Practice 2

_____

_____

_____

_____

_____

_____

_____

_____

_____

Model Practice 3

_____

_____

_____

_____

_____

_____

_____

_____

_____

The Wright Brothers and Their Secret Experiments (excerpt)
by William J. Claxton

In the beginning of the twentieth century many of the leading European newspapers contained brief reports of aerial experiments which were being carried out at Dayton, in the State of Ohio. So wonderful were the results of these experiments and so mysterious were the movements of the two brothers—Orville and Wilbur Wright—who conducted them that many Europeans would not believe the reports.

No inventors have gone about their work more carefully, methodically, and secretly than did these two Americans, who, hidden from prying eyes, "far from the maddening crowd", obtained results which brought them undying fame in the world of aviation.

For years they worked at their self-imposed task of constructing a flying machine which would really soar among the clouds. They had read brief accounts of the experiments carried out by Otto Lilienthal, and in many ways the ground had been well paved for them. It was their great ambition to become real "human birds"; "birds" that would not only glide along down the hillside, but would fly free and unfettered, choosing their aerial paths of travel and their places of destination.

Though there are few reliable accounts of their work in those remote American haunts during the first six years of the present century, the main facts of their life history are now well known. And we are able to trace their experiments, step by step, from the time when they constructed their first simple airplane down to the appearance of the marvelous biplane which has made them world-famed.

For some time the Wrights experimented with a glider, with which they accomplished even more wonderful results than those obtained by Lilienthal. These two young American engineers—bicycle makers by trade—were never in a hurry. Step by step they made progress: first with kites, then with small gliders, and ultimately with a large one. The latter was launched into the air by men running forward with it until sufficient momentum had been gained for the craft to go forward on its own account.

The first airplane made by the two brothers was a very simple one, as was the method adopted to balance the craft. There were two main planes made of long spreads of canvas arranged one above another, and on the lower plane, the pilot lay. A little plane in front of the man was known as the ELEVATOR, and it could be moved up and down by the pilot. When the elevator was tilted up, the aeroplane ascended; when lowered, the machine descended.

But it was in the balancing control of their machine that the Wrights showed such great ingenuity. Running from the edges of the lower plane were some wires which met at a point where the pilot could control them. The edges of the plane were flexible; that is, they could be bent slightly either up or down, and this movement of the flexible plane is known as WING WARPING.

You know that when a cyclist is going round a curve his machine leans inwards. Perhaps some of you have seen motor races, such as those held at Brooklands; if so, you must have noticed that the track is banked very steeply at the corners, and when the motorist is going round these corners at, say, 80 miles an hour, his motor makes a considerable angle with the level ground, and looks as if it must topple over. The aeroplane acts in a similar manner, and, unless some means are taken to prevent it, it will turn over.

Let us now see how the pilot worked the "Wright" glider. Suppose the machine tilted down on one side, while in the air, the pilot would pull down, or warp, the edges of the planes on that side of the machine which was the lower. By an ingenious contrivance, when one side was warped down the other was warped up, with the effect that the machine would be brought back into a horizontal position.

It must not be imagined that as soon as the Wrights had constructed a glider fitted with this clever system of controlling mechanism they could fly when and where they liked. They had to practice for two or three years before they were satisfied with the results of their experiments: neglecting no detail, profiting by their failures, and moving logically from step to step. They never attempted an experiment rashly; there was always a reason for what they did. In fact, their success was due to systematic progress achieved by wonderful perseverance.

Written Summation

The first airplane made by the two brothers was a very simple one. There were two main planes made of long spreads of canvas arranged one above another, and on the lower plane, the pilot lay. A little plane, which could be moved by the pilot, was known as the elevator. When the elevator was tilted up, the airplane ascended; when lowered, the machine descended.

Model Practice 1 (adapted from the original)

Model Practice 2

Model Practice 3

Saved by a Child's Wit (excerpt)
by Ruth Royce from <u>The Children of France</u>

"This time I will tell you about a quick-witted little French girl," said Captain Favor. "She was a stout-hearted little woman, full of spirit and as fearless as she was keen, as you shall see.

"It is not only the French lads who are quick-witted and brave. The girls are fully as much so, and all are filled with the same wonderful spirit of patriotism and love of country, as you already have learned from the stories I have told you.

"This little woman's name was Jeanne; she had just turned eleven years when the incidents I am about to relate occurred. For some time the news had been coming to the village in which she lived of the wicked deeds of a company of German lancers. These lancers were roving from village to village, stealing whatever they could lay their hands on and mistreating the women and children. It was a terrible thing to do, but nothing new for the Prussians. As in other towns of which I have told you, all the able-bodied men of this village had gone to the war.

"To guard against surprise the inhabitants of Jeanne's home town had placed watchers on the outskirts of the village that the people might be notified in advance of the approach of the enemy's detachments.

"One afternoon the warning came; and, while expected, it was a shock to the people, and their hearts were filled with fear. They closed and locked their doors, pulled down the shades, and took refuge in their cellars. Not a person was to be seen in the streets; the village appeared to be deserted.

"'The Prussians are coming!' was the startling cry that had sent the inhabitants flying to the cellars, after which a great silence reigned in the little place.

"Soon after that a troop of Prussian lancers rode quietly into the village, alert for surprises, for they had confidently expected to see French soldiers ere this. Not a French soldier was in sight, so the invaders concluded there was nothing to fear. However, they decided to question some of the villagers.

"The house that Jeanne lived in was the first one the lancers came to. Jeanne, like others, had taken to the cellar with her parents, where they remained for a long time, tremblingly awaiting the arrival of their enemies. Not a sound thus far having been heard, the family wondered if the Prussians had come and gone. They fervently hoped this were true.

"'I will go and find out,' volunteered the little girl.

"'It is not safe,' objected the mother. 'If they are still here and should discover you, all would not be well with you, My Daughter. You might be killed. I cannot permit it.'

"'Have no fears, Mother; I will listen for every sound in the street and will go no further than the door. They shall neither see nor hear me.'

"The mother reluctantly gave Jeanne her consent, and Jeanne crept upstairs, stepped quietly to the door and unbolted it, intending to open the door a few inches and peer out.

"At that instant the door was rudely forced open from the outside. A German officer and several men pushed their way in. The officer caught Jeanne in a listening attitude.

"'Halt!' he commanded, the lances of his men thrust out so close to the little girl that it seemed as if they already had pierced her. 'Listening, are you?'

"'Yes, monsieur,' she answered truthfully.

"'Why?'

"'That I might know if you had gone so I might once more go out to the street.'

"The officer laughed.

"'You have nothing to fear if you tell us the truth. We would have certain information from you, child.'

"'Yes, monsieur.'

"'If you do not truthfully answer all my questions, you and all the rest will be shot.'

"'I do not fear you, sir. I will answer you well.'

"'Good. Then tell me, are there any French soldiers here?'

"'There are none here, sir.'

"'Neither here nor elsewhere in the village?'

"'There are none here, as I have said. I know not whether there are any in the village or not, for I have not seen any since a detachment passed through here two days ago.'

"'Is this the truth?'

"She looked at the officer with an expression of amazement that he should doubt her word.

"'Come, I will show you; I will prove to you that what I say is the truth.'

"'It is well,' answered the Prussian officer, now reassured. 'We will pass on. It is good that you have not lied to us, child,' he said. 'It were better if all the French were so truthful, but, alas, they are not. Forward!'

"The Prussians departed, Jeanne watching them from the door. 'No, there are no French soldiers here,' she chuckled. 'Perhaps there may be just outside the village. And if so, alas for the Prussians!'

"A short distance beyond the village stood a large farmhouse in a vast yard, the latter being surrounded by a high stone wall. Within were trees and shade, so the place looking very attractive to the tired Prussians. Their commander ordered a halt and, opening the gate that led to the grounds, he ordered his men in for a rest. They tied their horses to trees and threw themselves down on the grass in great content.

"The place seemed deserted, but that some one was about was evidenced when the gate through which they had entered was quietly closed and locked by no less a person than the little Jeanne herself. She had followed the Prussians at a distance, hoping to be able to give a signal to her friends if they might still be in the farmhouse, but, finding a better opportunity for serving them, had locked the lancers within the enclosure. Having done this, she ran as fast as her nimble feet would carry her for her own home.

"The tired lancers lay down to sleep while their commander strolled up to the house and beat on the door with the hilt of his saber. To his amazement, the door was suddenly jerked open, and a French dragoon dragged him in by the collar. The commander was a prisoner.

"A detachment of French soldiers were secreted in the house where they had been waiting for some days for this very opportunity, knowing that the Prussians were headed that way. Yet, though the German commander had been deceived, little Jeanne had not told him an untruth. She knew the French soldiers had been at the farmhouse three days before, for she had taken food to them, but she did not know of her own knowledge that they still were there. If she did not tell the officer the whole truth it was because he had not asked her, and for the sake of her beloved France she would not volunteer information that would aid the Germans.

"'Betrayed!' raged the Prussian when he saw how neatly he had been tricked. He groaned when a volley rang out from the house and several of his lancers fell.

"His men made a frantic rush for their horses; then, when they discovered that the gate was locked and that they were caught, they threw up their hands and surrendered to the foe that they had not yet seen.

"The French made every one of the lancers a prisoner. Several had been wounded, but none was killed.

"Credit was given to little Jeanne for placing the lancers in the hands of the French soldiers, for had she not done this the French would have attacked the Prussians in the open and might have lost many men in the fight that would have followed.

"For her part in this fine capture, little Jeanne, in time, received a letter from the President of the French Republic, thanking her in the name of France for her quick wit and for her heroism."

Written Summation

"Have no fears, Mother; I will listen for every sound in the street and will go no further than the door. They shall neither see nor hear me.

"The mother reluctantly gave Jeanne her consent, and Jeanne crept upstairs, stepped quietly to the door and unbolted it, intending to open the door a few inches and peer out.

Model Practice 1

_____

_____

_____

_____

_____

_____

_____

_____

_____

_____

_____

_____

_____

_____

Model Practice 2

_____

_____

_____

_____

_____

_____

_____

_____

_____

Model Practice 3

_____

_____

_____

_____

_____

_____

_____

_____

_____

The Sinking of the Lusitania

by Lawton B. Evans

During the World War, it was the declared policy of Germany to torpedo any vessel flying an enemy flag in the waters adjacent to the British Isles, regardless of its character or who was on board.

One bright morning, the first day of May 1915, the huge British liner, <u>Lusitania</u>, lay at her dock ready to sail from New York to Liverpool. Her decks were crowded with passengers. They had read in the morning papers that "vessels flying the flag of Great Britain or any of her Allies are liable to destruction—and that travelers sailing in the war zone on ships of Great Britain or her Allies, do so at their own risk."

In spite of this warning, the ship was crowded with a large and happy throng, who were not deterred by any threat of destruction. She steamed down the harbor amid the waving of hands from the shore, and the sound of music on her deck. There were many confident souls on board, but along with them were many who were wondering if destruction really lay in wait for the great vessel.

The voyage was pleasureful. The decks were crowded with promenaders, and the smoking-room and cabins were centers of amusement and conversation. There was little thought of danger, and but few discussed the possibility of the ship being torpedoed. It was an event that no one wished to consider for a moment.

The morning of May 7 came with a heavy fog over the sea. The blowing of the siren awakened the passengers, and some of them commented on the fact, saying it might attract the submarines. Later on the fog lifted, leaving the sky without a cloud and the sea as smooth as glass. The shores of Ireland were in sight. Everybody was glad that the voyage was nearly over, and that, in a few hours, the ship and its passengers would be safe.

The morning passed, and the ship steamed steadily on. Luncheon hour came, and the passengers thronged below for their midday meal. Nearer and nearer came the friendly shores, and less and less grew the danger that threatened the vessel. The British flag was flying, as if in defiance to the threat of Germany.

Having finished luncheon, some of the passengers came on deck, some went to their rooms to rest, while others turned to the smoking rooms. The ship settled down to the usual afternoon routine.

At a few minutes after two o'clock, some of the passengers saw what looked like a whale or porpoise, rising about three-quarters of a mile to starboard. They knew that it was a submarine, but no one dared name it. All eyes now fastened in silence and dread on the menace that lay so quietly and sullenly in the distance.

Then a long white line, making a train of bubbles across the water, started from the black object. It came straight for the ship. No one spoke until it was about sixty yards away. Then someone cried out, "It is a torpedo!"

There was no chance for the great ship to get out of the way. Its movement was too ponderous for the swiftly coming torpedo. It was plain that it could not miss its mark. It was aimed ahead of the vessel and timed to strike under the bridge. As the missile of death came nearer, it dived, and the passengers held their breath. Would it hit or would it miss?

Suddenly, there was a terrific explosion, and the fore part of the ship was torn into great holes. Pieces of the wreckage came through the upper deck and fell among the frightened passengers. Germany had carried out her threat and had dealt death to the great Trans-Atlantic liner!

There was no second torpedo; there was no need of one. The boiler exploded immediately, and the ship listed heavily to starboard. The passengers rushed to the high side of the deck—the port side. There was such a lift to starboard that the lifeboats on the port side swung so far in that they could not be launched.

The vessel began to settle, and the lifeboats on the starboard side were launched. The first boat dropped clear of the ship and floated away with no one in it. One man jumped from the deck, swam toward the boat, and got in alone.

Everyone was frightened, but there was no panic. The cry was raised, "Women and children first!" These were placed in the lifeboats that were launched. The ship settled down on the starboard side, and also by the head. Those who could not get into the lifeboats trusted to the life preservers and made ready for the plunge into the cold water. The officers of the ship acted with bravery and coolness, trying to launch the lifeboats and get the women and children into safety. The wireless telegraph apparatus was put out of commission shortly after the explosion, but not before a distress message, calling for help, was sent out and answered.

So quickly did the ship sink that it was impossible to get life preservers from the lower deck cabins. Many had to leap into the sea without them. The shock of the cold water was so benumbing that those who jumped in were not able to swim, and many of them soon sank out of sight.

With one great plunge, the stricken vessel, that so often had crossed the Atlantic and that only an hour before was so full of life and power, sank head foremost into the sea. A great wave, rushing over her decks, cast the remaining passengers into the water.

Then followed a scene of indescribable tragedy. Two boats full of people were overturned. Another was swamped as the vessel went down, and still another was dragged down by catching in the davits. The sea was piled with wreckage to which people were clinging. Some were struggling to swim, others were depending on life preservers; all were battling with the waves in mad endeavor to save their lives.

Women were holding on to their husbands, while both went down. Children were floating helpless, trying to catch any object and crying piteously for their parents, before their little mouths were closed forever.

One by one they went down beneath the cruel waves. Thus, eleven hundred and fifty-two were drowned. Of these, one hundred and fourteen were known to be American citizens. Of the two thousand and more passengers, nine hundred and fifty-two were saved in the lifeboats and on the rafts picked up by friendly vessels that hastened to the scene of disaster.

Thus did the German submarine carry out the threat of the German Government and sink a noble ship with its precious freight of human lives.

Written Summation

Then a long white line, making a train of bubbles across the water, started from the black object. It came straight for the ship. No one spoke until it was about sixty yards away. Then someone cried out, "It is a torpedo!"

Model Practice 1

Model Practice 2

Model Practice 3

General J'offre

by Donald A. Mackenzie

General Joffre, the French Commander-in-Chief, is usually referred to among his countrymen as "Silent Joffre". He never utters an unnecessary word, but what he does say is worth listening to. In appearance he is not very soldierly, and certainly not at all like Kitchener. He is of short stature and some-what stout, and he has a habit of thrusting his hands into his pockets. In civilian attire, one might mistake him for a shrewd and prosperous city businessman who has spent much of his time at a desk. His jaw is broad and resolute, his nose prominent with wide nostrils, and his gray-blue eyes are as kindly as they are penetrative. He has heavy, pondering lips, over which droops a large white moustache, and deep lines seam his broad forehead. You can see at a glance that he is a man accustomed to think deeply and long. When he smiles his face beams with unaffected good humor.

There is nothing about him to suggest the popular idea that all Frenchmen are gay and light-hearted. The grave, silent Joffre is a modest man of simple habits and manners. But he is "as hard as nails", as the saying goes, and always "wide awake."

The great general is a man of humble origin. It is said that one of his ancestors, a century ago, was a travelling peddler in the Eastern Pyrenees, who used to go from village to village driving a van with all kinds of household wares. Because he was in the habit of shouting "Joffre", which signifies "I offer", he became known as "Joffre", and his descendants adopted the nickname as a surname. If this story is true, the Joffre family must have had no cause to be ashamed of their connection with the honest broker of village fame.

In boyhood General Joffre was regarded as being of rather daring and reckless character. Bathing was his favorite recreation, and he won among his fellows a great reputation as a diver and swimmer. But his feats alarmed his parents, and especially his mother, who feared he would some day meet with a grave mishap. It was his custom to have a plunge in a river near his home every morning before breakfast. He was ordered to discontinue it, because he could not be prevailed upon to keep out of danger. "Some morning you'll be drowned," his mother exclaimed nervously. "I have never heard of such a foolhardy boy as you are."

The lad fretted under the restriction and at length began to steal out of the house before anyone was up. So he was put to sleep in a room in a second story of the old-fashioned country house, and his mother locked him in every night. The river was strictly forbidden. "He can't be trusted," declared his mother; "he seems to enjoy risking his life."

But young Joffre was difficult to restrain. He soon hit on a plan to have his morning dip unknown to anyone. Securing an old sheet, he tore it up and made a "rope ladder" of it. He went early to bed and woke with the lark. In the gray dawn he lowered his ladder from the window, clambered down it, and ran to the riverside. Then he had a cool plunge in a deep pool, diving headlong from a jutting rock, and swam about where the current was strongest as nimbly as a seal. Those who had occasional glimpses of him in the water were not surprised that his mother should feel nervous. After his bathe he did not wait to dry himself, but scampered home across the fields and climbed up his ladder to his bedroom before anyone in the house had wakened up.

These exploits went on for a time until one morning the frail ladder snapped, and the boy fell heavily into the garden and broke his leg. He lay there for nearly two hours before he was discovered. "Oh, my dear, foolish boy," exclaimed his mother, "I knew something terrible would happen to you one day! Will you never be warned?"

His mother's tears hurt him more than his injury. So he resolved to be obedient to her wishes in future. To please her he began to study seriously, and when he was going about on crutches he got into the habit of reading a good deal.

"After all," his mother remarked to a friend one day, "this accident he has had may be a blessing in disguise."

At the same time she felt that her son had better have experience of strict discipline. He had been so wayward and determined and cunning that she feared he would return to his bathing exploits again. So the boy was sent to a college sooner than was intended, before he had ceased to limp as he walked. He made good progress and was looked upon as a lad of great promise. In time he decided to study for the army and, like Kitchener, showed a preference for the Engineers. The ambitious spirit he had displayed in rivaling the feats of other boys in river bathing was then given a more serious turn. He determined to acquit himself with distinction in his military studies, and he certainly did so. Young Joffre was pointed out as an example to his comrades.

Before he was nineteen, the war of 1870 broke out between Germany and France. He took part in the defense of Paris and learned much by bitter experience regarding the military needs of his country. After the French capital fell and peace was declared, he did useful work in connection with the reconstruction of the city defenses and was promoted to the rank of captain at the age of twenty-two. He was already marked out as a young soldier of great promise. It is of special interest to know that as an Engineer officer he had to do with the rebuilding of the famous fortifications of Verdun.

Subsequently he saw much active service in the French colonies. He took part in expeditions in Cochin-China, where he overlooked the erection of forts, and in West Africa. He also performed important duties in Madagascar and Algeria.

His promotion was rapid and well deserved. Ultimately, after his return home, he became the youngest general in the French army. His interests were entirely bound up in profession. He studied the art of warfare continually, preparing himself for the struggle with Germany, which he felt fully convinced was bound to come in his own lifetime. In politics he took no part. When he appeared on a public platform he spoke simply as a soldier and never feared to be frank regarding the seriousness of the coming conflict. In the army he was known as a reformer. He cared nothing for display. He worked hard for efficiency. His belief was that French soldiers were too apt to trust to their daring and fearless methods of attack. He wanted to have them trained to maintain a tenacious and enduring defensive, so that they might wear down the enemy and strike hard when they got them at a disadvantage. At maneuvers he displayed great ability as a strategist who did the unexpected and outwitted his opponents. Nobody ever knew what Joffre's next move would be. He always showed himself strongest where his opponents thought he was weakest. Everyone admired the clever manner in which he handled large forces of men. The army and the public learned to place entire confidence in the silent, determined, and watchful General Joffre. His character has been well summed up by one of our own public men who paid him a visit at the seat of war. "General Joffre", he said, "is not only a great soldier; he is also a great man."

Written Summation

The lad fretted under the restriction and at length began to steal out of the house before anyone was up. So he was put to sleep in a room in a second story of the old-fashioned country house, and his mother locked him in every night. The river was strictly forbidden. "He can't be trusted," declared his mother; "he seems to enjoy risking his life."

Model Practice 1

_____

_____

_____

_____

_____

_____

_____

_____

_____

_____

_____

_____

_____

Model Practice 2

_____

_____

_____

_____

_____

_____

_____

_____

_____

Model Practice 3

_____

_____

_____

_____

_____

_____

_____

_____

_____

The Exploits of Sergeant York

by Lawton B. Evans

Alvin York came from the mountains of Tennessee. He was the second elder in the Church of Christ and Christian Union. His Church is opposed to any form of fighting, and, when York was drafted into the World War, the members wanted him to ask for exemption on the ground that fighting was against his conscience.

But York's patriotism was as great as his religion. He asked one of those who had been urging him, "Suppose some man should come into your house, maltreat your wife, and murder your children, what would you do?"

"I think I would kill him," was the reply. After that they let him alone. He went to Camp Gordon, at Atlanta, Georgia, and began to train for a soldier.

But York was still troubled about war and the killing of men. His religious convictions worried him a great deal, in spite of the fact that his country was at war. He often discussed the matter with his Captain, and they read the Bible together, sometimes far into the night.

At last, after one long talk and the reading of many passages of Scripture bearing on the subject, York was convinced by Captain Danforth that the killing of one's enemies was in accordance with the teachings of the Bible.

"All right," exclaimed the big mountaineer, "I am satisfied." From that time, especially after his company went to France, he threw himself with all his heart into the war.

Up in his mountain home, York had learned to be very expert with rifle and pistol. His aim was certain; his fire was rapid; and when he pulled the trigger it meant sure death. He had won many prizes shooting at turkeys and targets. Once, he stopped a fight, showing his skill to a man who was quarreling with him, by deliberately shooting the head off a lizard running on a tree. In a contest with an officer, York, who had become a Sergeant, hit a penny match-box at forty paces every time.

He had worked on a farm and as a blacksmith and had developed a powerful body. He was six feet high, weighed over two hundred pounds, and had a lot of red hair.

On October 8, 1918, the chance came for Sergeant York to show the material of which he was made. His battalion was in the Argonne section in France. The men left their position on Hill 223, in order to attack the Decauville railroad, nearly two miles to the westward. The battalion had to pass through a valley, on both sides of which were hills from which the German machine-guns poured a deadly fire into their ranks. In front was another hill filled with machine-guns. Thus the battalion was caught in a fire from three directions.

York's platoon was on the extreme left. The line seemed to melt away before the enemy's bullets. The squad to which York belonged was ordered to put the machine-guns out of action.

The men leaped to their task and advanced toward the hill. There were sixteen in all. Sergeant York and the others rushed up the steep slope, under cover of bushes, slipping behind trees and hiding in the ditches. The enemy's fire was fierce and dangerous. Fortunately, the men escaped observation and pursued their way back of the lines.

They came upon an old trench, formerly used by the French, and into it they dropped for protection. It led over the hill, and behind the nest of machine-guns. Single file and cautiously, they crept along, now in the trench and now under the bushes, keeping a sharp lookout for Germans. At last, they came to a little stream on the other side of the hill and ran into a party of twenty or thirty Germans, holding a conference and getting ready to eat.

The Americans yelled and opened fire, as if a whole regiment had arrived. The astonished Germans, not expecting an attack and being unprepared, held up their hands, shouting "Kamerad," in token of their surrender.

"Who are you? Are you English troops?" shouted the German Major.

"No. We are a force of Americans," was the reply, which seemed to bring no great surprise to the Major.

Before arrangements could be made to secure their prisoners, the machine-guns opened fire, not thirty yards away. The Americans had been discovered. The valley became a bedlam of shrieking sounds as the rain of bullets whistled by. The German prisoners dropped to the ground and hugged the earth for protection from the fire of their own guns. The Americans followed their example, but not before a number of their party were killed.

By this time, the sixteen men had been reduced to eight—Sergeant York and seven others. It took the whole seven to guard the prisoners who were lying down and afraid to move for fear of the awful machine-gun fire passing overhead. York alone remained to fight the enemy. He was lying in a narrow path, leading toward the guns, the prisoners directly before him, the gunfire barely missing him where he lay. The enemy could not lower their fire without killing their own men. But York was as cool as though he was at a shooting match in the mountains. He began potting the Germans in their foxholes, from behind the trees, and under shelter of the logs. With every shot, he brought down an enemy. His fire was deadly.

"If I had moved, I would have been killed. The prisoners saved me, for the Germans had to fire high to keep from hitting their own men," said York afterwards.

Finally, a Lieutenant and seven men rose from a machine-gun and charged down the hill toward the place where York lay. He shot all eight of them before they ran halfway. As soon as the Germans saw the Lieutenant and his men drop, the battle quieted down, for they were amazed at the way their men were being killed and did not know what force was attacking them. They had no idea York was doing it all.

The Major of the prisoners called out, "Don't shoot any more, and I'll make them surrender." With that, York lowered his pistol, and the Major raised his hands.

The Germans came down the hill in droves. Their arrival made a list of ninety prisoners. York and the others placed them in columns and marched off toward the American lines.

"How many men have you in your command?" asked the Major.

"I have plenty to hold you prisoners," answered York. "Drop your guns and equipment and move on!" The Germans obeyed promptly.

On the way back, they ran into other machine-gun nests. Using their prisoners as screens, the Americans made the Major demand the surrender of them as fast as they were discovered, under penalty of having his men shot by their own machine-guns. It soon became a procession.

In this way, York and his few companions added to their list as they went along, until, when they arrived at their destination and turned over their prisoners, they had one hundred and thirty-two! The Major was the gloomiest man in Europe when he found out that he had surrendered to a handful of Americans. York himself had killed twenty men with his own pistol, and thirty-five machine-guns had been put out of action!

Written Summation

"Who are you? Are you English troops?" shouted the German Major.

"No. We are a force of Americans," was the reply, which seemed to bring no great surprise to the Major.

Model Practice 1 (adapted from the orignal)

Model Practice 2

_____

_____

_____

_____

_____

_____

_____

_____

Model Practice 3

_____

_____

_____

_____

_____

_____

_____

_____

Caught in the Dust
by R. J. M. Marks, (a fictional story about a 14-year-old girl and her brother)

It was a school day like any other school day. Everything seemed normal, that is until our walk home that afternoon. The sky, which had been clear and beautiful all day, suddenly turned dark and evil. At the time, I was busy talking to myself, practicing Charles Wesley's hymn "Jesus, Lover of my Soul" for school. I wasn't paying attention to the change in the weather, and I would not have noticed the dust cloud coming, if it hadn't been for Jimmy.

I was reciting the hymn in my head—

> Jesus, lover of my soul,
> Let me to Thy bosom fly,
> While the waters nearer roll,
> While the tempest still is high;
> Hide me, O my Savior, hide,
> Till the storm of life is past;
> Safe into the haven glide,
> O receive my soul at last.

"Emma, wait for me," screamed Jimmy, rudely interrupting my practice.

"Stop, dawdling, Jim," I said without turning around. "I have to help mother with cooking and cleaning and washing and gardening and whatever else she wants me to do. And then, after all of that, I have homework."

"But, Em, I have a rock in my shoe."

"Most kids don't even have shoes. Now, hurry up, please!"

I turned around to see if Jimmy really needed my help, and that's when I saw it—a big black wave of sand—looming over the horizon and heading right for us. It was rushing toward us, ready to fall upon us and swallow us whole. I ran back to Jimmy, grabbed his hand, and tried to drag him on.

"Hey, what are you doing? Let me go." he complained as I pulled his arm a little too hard.

"It's a dust storm! And it's coming right at us!"

Without another word Jimmy stumbled forward, the rock completely forgotten. He recovered quickly and began sprinting as fast as his 9-year-old legs could go. Both of us had heard stories of people dying in dust storms, half-buried and suffocating to death by sand.

Jimmy was running faster than I've ever seen him run before, but he couldn't keep pace with me. So I held tighter and pulled harder. Our legs leaped across the ground. In other circumstances this might have been fun, but not now. We were running for our lives.

"Let me to Thy bosom fly," the words echoed in my mind. They were no longer lines of a hymn, memorization work, or simply words to ponder; they had become my prayer. The ground disappeared from under us, as we flew toward home. But even flying creatures can't survive a dust storm. The dust rolls on top of them, smashes them to the ground, and suffocates them to death.

"While the dust clouds nearer roll." The words streamed into my head, and the dust into my mouth. I didn't need to turn around to see if it was coming. It was here. The sky grew darker and darker; it was gritty with dirt. We were finally close enough to see the shape of the house, but it seemed so far away.

Jimmy was hanging back more and more;

I tightened my grip. My legs were burning and my arm hurt from half-pulling, half-dragging Jim down the road. I needed air; but the harder I breathed, the more dust I swallowed. It was everywhere, swirling around us. The air grew thick as the dark clouds surrounded us, causing the house to slowly disappear from view.

"While the tempest still is high." I knew what the songwriter meant. The tempest roared on top of us like a wave at sea. It was pushing us from behind, barreling over us-trying to throw us to the ground, swallowing us in its path.

"Hide me, O my Savior, hide." Where do we go? The barn—it was a thought from outside of me. I'm sure I heard it. I dragged Jimmy across the yard where the barn should be. We ran with our eyes somewhere between squinting and closed, trying to keep out the dust while hoping to catch sight of the barn.

"Till the storm of life is past." With the wind at our backs and dust swirling around us, we ran into the barn wall. We couldn't find the door. I kept pulling Jimmy, his hand in mind. I dragged him with me to the south side of the barn, downwind of the dust, where we clung to each other tightly.

"Safe into the haven glide." The clouds blanketed us in dust and darkness. I tasted the dirt; I felt it between my teeth and in my ears. I was breathing dirt, and it was painful. Dust wasn't meant to be breathed in. I tried to cover Jimmy's mouth by burying his face into my shoulder and braced myself for death. Dirt piled up over my feet, climbing to my ankles and higher. We were being buried alive.

"O receive my soul at last." I felt my father's arms wrap around me and remove me from the dirt piled up around my legs. I thought I must be in heaven until the fog lifted from my mind and the pain moved in.

That's when the uncontrollable coughing started. I couldn't stop coughing and spitting. "Blood and dirt," I heard one of my older brothers say. I wish I could stop it; but the dirt had to come out. Little Jimmy was coughing too, but not like me. At least we were both alive.

Father laid me in my bed where I rested on and off for a couple of weeks. After a while, I started to move around again. The blood and dirt were gone, but my cough was still there. The doctor came to see me and told me that I was fine. Later, I heard him telling my parents they needed to bring me to the hospital, but Daddy said no. I heard Daddy say there was no way was he putting his little girl around dying people. So I stayed home.

Slowly, I got better. I started sitting up and even walking around some, and the coughing was less and less. I was going to live. Life was getting back to normal.

Normal, however, still included dirt. So mother and father decided that they weren't taking any chances on the safety of their children. They decided to move our family to California right along with everyone else. All of us were a little sad about it at first, but we quickly became excited at the idea of being free of the dust storms. I never thought we'd move, but Daddy's sure we can make a new start farther out west, far away from the dust where rain falls, grass grows, and the air is clean.

Written Summation

The words streamed into my head, and the dust into my mouth. I didn't need to turn around to see if it was coming. It was here. The sky grew darker and darker; it was gritty with dirt. We were finally close enough to see the shape of the house, but it seemed so far away.

Model Practice 1

Model Practice 2

Model Practice 3

The Navajo Code Talkers
by R. J. M. Marks

It was February 1942, and the Japanese had recently bombed Pearl Harbor, a United States naval base on the island of Hawaii. Philip Johnston, a World War I veteran and engineer for the city of Los Angeles, sat at his desk reading about the participation of the United States in the Second World War. Johnston knew it was not possible to re-enlist at the age of 49, but he had no greater desire than to be involved in the fight to protect America and her people. He sympathized with the plight of the American soldier. Historically, the U.S. had faced their enemies with strength and confidence. However, after the bombing of Pearl Harbor, it seemed the enemy had the upper hand.

Following military activities and military training through local newspaper articles, was a normal part of Johnston's routine. And on this day, one particular article covering training maneuvers in Louisiana piqued his interest. The article claimed that Canadians attempted to utilize Native Americans during World War I to relay secret messages while fighting the Germans. And even though they had experienced only limited success, an American military division was attempting the same. Reading this article gave Johnston an idea. He reasoned that the Navajo language could be used as the basis for a military code; and because of his military experience and his fluency in Navajo, he understood how to do it.

From the age of four years old, Johnston had lived with the Navajo Indians. His father, Reverend William Johnston, had moved his family from Kansas City, Kansas to the Navajo Reservation, hoping to bring Christianity to the Navajo people. Young Philip had played with the Navajo children, had learned the Navajo ways, and had become fluent in the Navajo language. He had lived on the reservation for 22 years. During that time, nine-year-old Philip had acted as an interpreter between President Roosevelt and the Navajo leaders—the Navajo people had requested that more land be assigned to their reservation. After moving from the reservation, Johnston had still remained in contact with the Navajo people.

Johnston presented his idea for a military code to Colonel James E. Jones. "Colonel," he asked, "what would you think of a device that would assure you of complete secrecy when you send or receive messages on the battlefield?"

Based on his experience with military codes, the Colonel responded that no code could be completely secure. Johnston proceeded to explain his idea of using an Indian language "to build a code" using Indian words such as "iron rain for a barrage" and "fast shooter to designate a machine gun." Interest slowly crept into the Colonel's eyes as understanding set in.

Johnston demonstrated with a series of clicks, guttural sounds, and nasal tones.

Colonel Jones bolted upright in his chair. Suddenly, he knew that Johnston's idea was a good one. To further illustrate his point, Johnston asked Colonel Jones to repeat a word after him. The colonel twisted and contorted his lips, trying to pronounce that one word; he failed miserably, but Johnston had succeeded. They scheduled a demonstration meeting for two weeks later.

Johnston located four educated tribesmen and returned with them to Camp Elliot. Before the demonstration, the Navajos were given a list of typical military messages and one hour to develop Navajo words for military expressions such as dive-bombing and anti-tank guns. Colonel Jones then escorted them to the headquarters of Major General Vogel where the demonstrators were paired off and separated.

A member of the staff handed a "typical" message to one of the men who transmitted the message in Navajo; the recipient wrote the Navajo message in English. Upon conclusion of the test, Major General Vogel gave his opinion: "These are excellent translations, as good as might be possible from any language. There's no doubt in my mind that Navajo words could be used for code purposes."

With this success, a pilot project of 30 recruits was authorized; 29 entered the program. After enlisting, the group faced boot camp (military recruit training). Because the Navajo men were smaller than most men in the military, barely making the 122-pound weight requirement, many military personnel were uncertain of the Navajo men's ability to pass basic training. However, harsh conditions on the reservation had more than prepared them for the rigors of boot camp. From their Navajo lifestyles, they were accustomed to locating water in the desert, running or hiking for miles at-a-time for trading, and working cooperatively as a team. (Competition was not a part of the Navajo lifestyle.)

After passing with exemplary performance, the pilot group of 29 faced eight weeks of intensive training. During this time they developed the Navajo Code, which consisted of approximately 400 of the most frequently used military terms and the 26 letters of the English alphabet. Names and infrequent terms were to be spelled out by way of the alphabet code. For example, the Navajo word for cat, moasi, was code for the letter C, and the Navajo word for fly, tsa-e-donin-ee, was code for the letter F. During training, the code proved to be quick, unbreakable, and almost error-free.

Unlike English, the vowel sounds in Navajo have many variations. Changing the vowel sounds along with moving the location of the origin of the vowel sound—making the sound in the front or back of the mouth or speaking through the nose—can modify the meaning of the word. This makes Navajo extremely difficult to learn by anyone other than a child, and the Navajo code impossible to break.

Here is a table of words taken from the Navajo Code Dictionary

Military Term	Navajo Code	Code Translation
Dive Bomber	Gini	Chicken Hawk
Submarine	Besh-Lo	Iron Fish
December	Yas-Nil-Tes	Crusted Snow
Alternate	Na-Kee-Go-Ne-Nan-Dey-He	Second Position
Before	Bih-Tse-Dih	Before
Capacity	Be-Nel-Ah	Capacity
Dispatch	La-Chai-En-Seis-Be-Jay	Dog Is Patch
District	Be-Thin-Ya-Ni-Che	Deer Ice Strict
Establish	Has-Tay-Dzah	Establish
Limit	Ba-Has-Ah	Limit
Not	Ni-Dah-Than-Zie	No Turkey
Notice	Ne-Da-Tazi-Thin	No Turkey Ice
Now	Kut	Now

(Accents indicating stress and tone are not included in the dictionary. The Code Talkers passed on this information orally.)

Cryptographers (code specialists) were ordered to try to break the code. They couldn't. They claimed it sounded like drivel. Even other Navajos could not break the code. At once, the Code Talkers were dispatched from Guadalcanal to Okinawa. And they proved their service to be invaluable.

In one instance, during battle on Saipan, the Japanese retreated under the cover of night. Within hours the American battalion advanced forward, taking the former position of the Japanese. Soon after, artillery from American headquarters exploded near the new American location. An American radioman dispatched a message to inform headquarters of their new position. But the onslaught of weapons continued, coming ever closer, spraying them with dirt and mud.

Headquarters could not be sure that Americans had sent the message. The Japanese had become quite skilled at imitating Americans, from a Texas drawl to a New York accent. Finally someone from headquarters called back: "Do you have a Navajo?"

They did. The only Navajo present in the battalion relayed a single message in the Navajo Code. Within minutes, headquarters re-directed the attack from the Americans and onto the Japanese, saving the entire battalion.

From the time of the implementation of the code talkers program in September 1942 to the end of the war in August of 1945, when Emperor Hirohito surrendered, the Navajo code was used extensively by the Marines. Approximately 400 Navajos served their country as code talkers during World War II. The Navajo code proved at that time to be the fastest and most secure means of sending coded messages during battle. Because of the hard work, dedication, and service of the code talkers, many believe that World War II was shortened and countless lives were saved.

Written Summation

From the age of four years old, Johnston had lived with the Navajo Indians. His father, Rev. William Johnston, had moved his family from Kansas City, Kansas to the Navajo Reservation, hoping to bring Christianity to the Navajo people. Young Philip had played with the Navajo children, had learned the Navajo ways, and had become fluent in the Navajo language.

Model Practice 1 (adapted from the original)

Model Practice 2

_____

_____

_____

_____

_____

_____

_____

_____

Model Practice 3

_____

_____

_____

_____

_____

_____

_____

_____

Rosa Parks

by R. J. M. Marks

(Note: Dialogue is adapted from My Story by Rosa Parks.)

> Don't ride the bus to work, to town, to school, or any place Monday, December 5. Another Negro woman has been arrested and put in jail because she refused to give up her bus seat. Don't ride the buses to work, to town, to school, or anywhere on Monday. If you work, take a cab, or share a ride, or walk. Come to a mass meeting, Monday at 7:00 P.M, at the Holt Street Baptist Church for further instruction.

These words were printed on 7000 leaflets that were passed out one-by-one to African Americans in Montgomery, Alabama. Rosa Parks had just been arrested, and black people had had enough. They had had enough of the injustices, the slander, and the discrimination that they faced daily when riding the buses in Montgomery, Alabama.

Bus riders were separated by race. And since most of the riders were black, the middle and the back sections of the bus were available for their use. The "whites only" section was in the front of the bus. However, when the "whites only" section was filled, the "colored section" was pushed back; the seats were given to the white passengers; and the black riders had to move to seats further back or stand. Blacks were never allowed to ride in the white section. These seating arrangements were not just rules; they were the law. And when Rosa Parks did not give up her seat to a white passenger, she broke the law.

Four days earlier, Rosa Parks had made her way to the store across the street from the tailor's shop where she worked. She finished her errands and proceeded to the bus stop for a long ride home.

When she paid her fare that day, she walked to the "colored" seats. She placed her packages on her lap and began to rest her tired body from a hard day's work. She was glad to be going home.

The bus ride seemed uneventful at first. The driver made his stops, and the bus began to fill. Eventually, the "whites only" section filled up, but more white passengers boarded. Because of the law, the passengers in the front of the "colored" section had to move back and give up their seats.

James Blake, the bus driver, made his way to the "colored" sign located in the middle of the bus-in front of Mrs. Parks. He picked it up and moved it behind her and three other black passengers.

"Get up. Let me have these seats," he ordered.

No one moved.

"Y'all better make it light on yourselves and let me have those seats," he demanded.

This time, all four of them moved. Three of the black passengers moved to the back of the bus, but Rosa Parks moved closer to the window, tired of submitting to racism, steeling herself for the battle to come.

"Why aren't you standing up?" the angry driver demanded.

"I should not have to," answered Mrs. Rosa Parks, calmly, politely, and wearily.

"Are you going to stand up?"

"No, I am not."

"Stand up or I'm going to have you arrested!"

"You may do that," replied the 42-year-old woman (Parks, 116).

The bus driver called the police who promptly arrested Mrs. Parks. She was charged with breaking the segregation law. Edgar Nixon, a family friend and civil rights activists, bailed her out of jail. Immediately, plans were put in place for a one-day boycott. Fliers were handed out, and announcements were made in churches.

On the day of the trial, Mrs. Parks was found guilty. But this was not defeat. The boycott was a success. The buses were almost completely void of black passengers. They had left the buses and had joined together in protesting the infringement of their civil rights.

That evening, the Montgomery Improvement Association was formed, and Dr. Martin Luther King was elected the president. The boycott continued for over a year. Black people did not ride the buses. They took cabs. They carpooled. And they walked—sometimes 20 miles.

Finally in November of 1956, the United States Supreme Court declared that segregation laws were against the law and were a violation of the constitutional rights of the people. When the news reached Montgomery, Alabama, the boycott ended, although the struggle for equal rights continued on.

Rosa Parks and all of the citizens that boycotted the buses had had enough of racism and segregation. They faced injustice and they overcame. And although the struggle continued with more arrests, more fights, and even deaths, they had, in fact, already won. The victory came when they embraced civil rights for themselves and refused to accept anything less.

Parks, Rosa and Jim Haskins. My Story. New York: Puffin Books, 1992.

Written Summation

"Why aren't you standing up?" the angry driver demanded.

"I should not have to," answered Mrs. Rosa Parks, calmly, politely, and wearily.

"Are you going to stand up?"

"No, I am not."

"Stand up or I'm going to have you arrested!"

Model Practice 1

_____

_____

_____

_____

_____

_____

_____

_____

_____

_____

_____

_____

_____

_____

Model Practice 2

_____

_____

_____

_____

_____

_____

_____

_____

_____

Model Practice 3

_____

_____

_____

_____

_____

_____

_____

_____

_____

The Cuban Missile Crisis
by R. J. M. Marks

(Dialogue is adapted from an audio transcript of Executive Committee meeting at the White House dated October 16, 1962 11:50 AM http://www.mtholyoke.edu/acad/intrel/transcri.htm)

The year was 1962, and Nikita Khrushchev was the Premier of the Soviet Union. He was short, stout, bald, and loud. He was known for interrupting meetings by shaking his fist in the air, taking off his right boot and banging it on the table, and calling the speakers names if he disagreed with their presentation. He had fought his way up from a peasant's life through the ranks of the Red Army to First Secretary of the Communist party, and as a result, the Premier of the Soviet Union—being First Secretary automatically made him the Premier. As leader of one of the two great Super Powers, Khrushchev aimed to expand his brand of communism and eradicate capitalism.

Khrushchev partnered with Fidel Castro, the bearded militant dictator of Cuba, and garnered his support in establishing a communist influence in the Western Hemisphere. He convinced Castro to allow him to place Soviet Nuclear missiles in Cuba, only 90 miles from the United States and within striking distance. He calculated his chances and gambled that the new American President, John F. Kennedy, would be too weak and ineffective to challenge him. The young president had just admitted responsibility for the embarrassing fiasco of The Bay of Pigs Invasion.

After learning of the missiles, Kennedy and his Cabinet sat in the White House Cabinet Room. The meeting was filled with tension and apprehension as the cabinet members deliberated their options. A quiet urgency filled the room.

"Secretary Rusk," said the President as he turned and nodded to the Secretary of State.

"Mr. President," he answered gravely, "this is a serious development, and one that we did not believe the Soviets would carry out. I think we must eliminate those missile sites. The question is whether we do it by a quick strike or whether we allow the Soviets time to give in."

"Mr. President," added Robert McNamara, "if we conduct an air strike, we must attack before the missiles are fully operational. If the Soviets deploy these missiles, we can expect chaos in a radius of 600 to 1000 miles from Cuba."

General Taylor began, "Well, Sir, I'm thinking that we act in phases. In phase one, we pause as we determine the scope of the air strikes and possible invasion. Then, at the same time, we attack missiles and airfields and implement a naval blockade. As we are preparing for the air strike, we can determine whether or not to invade Cuba."

With intense concentration, the President listened as the Cabinet members discussed America's options. Leaning back in his executive leather chair, he let the information resonate deep within him. Slowly, he formed a plan.

"How effective can the air strikes be?" he asked and turned to General Taylor.

"They'll never be 100 percent effective, Mr. President. We hope to take out a vast majority in the first strike, but there would be a continuous air attack whenever we discover a missile site."

With determination and resolve, President Kennedy restated their options: "Well, what we're really talking about is a two- or three-phase operation. One is the air strike on these three known bases. The second is a broader air strike on airfields and anything else connected with the missiles. Third is doing both of these and at the same time, launching a naval blockade."

The debate continued. Attorney General Robert Kennedy, the President's brother, pointed out that while an outright invasion of Cuba was an option, a Soviet retaliation would probably follow. Others disagreed.

After much deliberation, the president decided to carry out a naval blockade while continuing the preparations for an air strike and for a possible Soviet attack. American military vessels around the world were placed at Defense Readiness Position 2. The United States was ready for war.

On October 22, 1962, President Kennedy informed the public of the nuclear missiles in Cuba, and of America's determination to confront this threat with these words:

> "We will not prematurely or unnecessarily risk the costs of worldwide nuclear war in which even the fruits of victory would be ashes in our mouth; but neither will we shrink from that risk at any time it must be faced."

In response, Nikita Khrushchev sent the following correspondence to President Kennedy:

> "The Soviet government considers the violation of the freedom of Navigation in international waters and air space to constitute an act of aggression propelling humankind into the abyss of a world nuclear missile war."

Fear hovered over the United States and the world. And Americans, living under the threat of a nuclear attack on American soil, took action to protect themselves.

Anticipating the worst, families filled their basements with bottled water, non-perishable foods, and medical supplies. Others stockpiled supplies in closets and under beds. Schools added bomb drills to their schedules. When the alarms sounded, students and faculty members scrambled under desks, expecting to use them as protection from fallen debris caused by a nuclear attack. Shocked and frightened, Americans clung to their loved ones, preparing for death, praying for a miracle.

After secret meetings and many delivered messages, Premier Khrushchev agreed to disassemble and remove the missiles from Cuba if the United States pledged to abstain from invading Cuba. The following day, he sent a second message demanding that the United States remove missiles that had been placed in Turkey. And even though the United States had already planned to remove them, President Kennedy refused to authorize their removal under the terms dictated by the Soviet Union for fear of setting a precedent of capitulation.

The entire world waited, fearful of World War III, nuclear fall out, or worse—worldwide nuclear destruction.

On October 28, President John F. Kennedy, at the suggestion of his brother, agreed to the terms of the first letter sent by President Khrushchev. The United States responded that they would not invade Cuba. And Khrushchev agreed to the compromise. He removed the missiles. (Later, on his own terms, Kennedy removed the American missiles from Turkey.)

America was safe, the crisis was over, and Kennedy became a hero. But it was the beginning of the end for Khrushchev's career. He had underestimated Kennedy's resolve and ultimately yielded to Kennedy's terms. However, if Khrushchev had not agreed to Kennedy's terms when he did, thousands of lives could have been lost and the Cuban Missile Crisis could have escalated into World War III. Although war was avoided, his fellow Communists Party members believed he mishandled the entire crisis from the installation of the missiles to their removal. Two years later, Khrushchev was removed from office.

Written Summation

"Mr. President," added Robert McNamara, "if we conduct an air strike, we must attack before the missiles are fully operational. If the Soviets deploy these missiles, we can expect chaos in a radius of 600 to 1000 miles from Cuba."

Model Practice 1

Model Practice 2

Model Practice 3

The Watergate Scandal

by R. J. M. Marks

When Benjamin Franklin was a young boy, he and his friends built a fishing wharf with stolen stones. His excuse was that the wharf could be used by everyone, therefore he was justified in taking the stones. When his actions were discovered and relayed to his father, his father was very disappointed and said, "...evil can produce only evil, that good ends must be wrought by good means." This lesson is one for all great men and women of power and influence to live by. But there is a time in history upon which we can look back and see the effects of not living up to this ideal. It happened in 1972 when Richard M. Nixon was President.

During this time, the Vietnam War was raging, and many people—old and young—wanted it over. President Nixon felt threatened because of the opposition to the war. He believed that those who did not support him were against him. To monitor and control the actions of these people, President Nixon created a list, his Enemies List.

On this list were reporters, members of his White House staff, actors, activists, Presidents of Universities, Supreme Court Justices, and regular American citizens. Nixon believed that everyone on this list was his enemy and posed a threat to the welfare of the United States.

Nixon and his closest men formed an organization known as the Committee to Re-Elect the President (CREEP). They schemed and plotted to protect the country and to keep Nixon in office.

They concocted legal problems for those on the Enemies List, hoping to keep them too busy to cause trouble for Nixon. The Internal Revenue Service illegally audited them, and the Federal Bureau of Investigations (FBI) investigated them. To monitor these enemies, Nixon and CREEP called the Plumbers. The Plumbers were a secret group that "leaked" stories about people on the Enemies List. These stories were meant to discredit Nixon's enemies in the eyes of the American people. In the dark of night, the Plumbers broke into buildings and spied on Nixon's enemies.

For one of their most well known assignments, the Plumbers were ordered to break into the office of the Democratic National Committee (DNC) which was located at the Watergate Hotel. President Nixon, a Republican, wanted documentation on any illegal activity committed by the Democratic Party to use against them.

The Plumbers disguised themselves in business suits, carried briefcases, and held a fake banquet in a small room near the elevator leading to the DNC office. There they ate dinner, watched films, and waited for the office to empty.

The DNC office stayed open very late that night, and eventually the on-duty guard ordered them to leave. Two of the Plumbers, the leader and the lock-picker, decided to hide in a nearby closet and sneak out after the guard left, then let everyone else back into the hotel. The two men entered the closet and closed the door. The door locked behind them, and they had to spend the entire night in the hotel closet, standing up. They decided to try again the next night.

This time, they waited for the lights to go out in the DNC office, and then they entered the hotel front door. They publicly took the elevator to the 8th floor. From there, they secretly took the stairs down to the 6th floor where the DNC office was located. They tried to enter the hallway leading to the DNC office, but the door was locked. They had failed again. They decided to try again the next night.

Finally, everything seemed to work as planned. The Plumbers entered the Watergate Hotel from the garage. They broke into the DNC office, planted wiretaps, and took photographs of any documents that might be helpful in tarnishing the reputation of the DNC. When finished, the group left, and each of the men went to their separate homes. Eventually, they learned that one of the wiretaps did not work properly. About three weeks later, they returned to the hotel to repair it.

To fix the wiretap, the Plumbers entered the Watergate Hotel and placed tape across the locks of the doors leading to the office of the DNC. After waiting for the office to empty, they noticed that someone had removed the tape. This should have alerted them that someone, possibly a guard, was aware that intruders were in the building. But rather than postponing the mission, they replaced the tape and continued their activities. Minutes later the police arrived and the Plumbers were arrested.

Two Washington Post reporters, Mr. Bob Woodard and Mr. Carl Bernstein, learned of the break-in. They interviewed people who worked closely with the president. Eventually, they learned of illegal campaign contributions that were given to President Nixon, of illegal wiretapping, and of the illegal arrests of political activists and every day citizens. And they learned that all of these actions were connected to President Richard Nixon.

When the investigation into the Watergate Scandal was complete, all of the Plumbers, many of the members of CREEP, and many other participants in the scandal went to prison. Ultimately, Richard Nixon became the only president to resign. And although he received a full pardon, his reputation and legacy as President were forever tarnished.

Richard Nixon repeated over and over that he had not done anything wrong. He believed that he and CREEP had acted in the best interest of the country and for the benefit of national security. Nixon believed the end justified the means.

He justified lying, stealing, and harassing Americans by saying it was for the good of the country. If Richard Nixon had lived by the lesson that Benjamin Franklin's father had taught young Benjamin—that evil means can only produce evil deeds—the Watergate scandal would have been prevented. In addition, he, Richard Nixon, would not have had to resign as President as of the United States of America.

Written Summation

On this list were reporters, members of his White House staff, actors, activists, Presidents of Universities, Supreme Court Justices, and regular American citizens. Nixon believed that everyone on this list was his enemy and posed a threat to the welfare of the United States.

Model Practice 1 (adapted from the original)

Model Practice 2

_____

_____

_____

_____

_____

_____

_____

_____

_____

Model Practice 3

_____

_____

_____

_____

_____

_____

_____

_____

_____

You Feed Them

adapted from a sermon by Dr. Roger DeYoung

Jesus takes the little we give and multiplies it. I saw this happen one time before in my ministry. It was a little over 20 years ago.

I was serving as the chaplain at the Hillcrest International School. And during that time, the Northern Area of Nigeria was suffering from a severe famine caused by long term drought, climate changes, and political factors that affected food distribution. In fact, the drought was so severe that Lake Chad had receded 25 miles. Lake Chad is located on the border of Nigeria and the country of Chad. I was able to travel to the shoreline of Lake Chad and see the effects of the drought for myself.

I went to places where the World Bank had sponsored a huge irrigation project. I walked in reservoirs that had inch-wide cracks in the dirt. I could see boats sitting in sand, miles away from any water. Now all the huge pivots (sprinkler system) stood idle in the middle of the desert. There was no water in the canals for irrigation. Everything was dry.

The people of the area were becoming desperate for food. They were digging in anthills to remove the weed seed that the ants had stored inside the anthills. These anthills were not like the anthills from fire ants. These were more like termite mounds, many feet tall. In fact, we had one in our backyard that we hollowed out and made into a fort for my young son. The people would take the weed seeds inside the anthills and cook them. When cooked, the seeds made a kind of porridge—something like grits.

The people of the international church knew of the suffering of the people. They would say to one another and to me, "We've got to do something." I was skeptical whether we could do anything at all. I thought what can we do? We're only a very small group of people. How can we help?

Around this time, I was preparing for a sermon on the feeding of the multitude, and I came across the biblical text "You feed them." Those three words spoke to me. Well, that Sunday when I finished the message, I said, "If you want to get involved in a hunger task force, here is your chance." I challenged the 500 people in our International Church to take those three words to heart—you feed them. What happened next was amazing.

A task force was formed. Many of the kids at the Hillcrest International School saved their money and brought it to the school. They poured the money into the swimming pool that we used to collect the donations. But the giving did not stop at the school; other people began to contribute. Word of our task force, and that something was being done for the starving, spread throughout the international community. People heard that we had responsible supervision. The kids at the international school in Japan joined in the task force. The Mennonite Central Committee in Canada and the United States joined in the task force. Christian Reform World Relief joined in the task force. Evangelical churches of West Africa joined in the task force. Groups from England and Holland began to help. In addition, over 1000 Nigerian churches gave clothes and food for the project. Before long, we had a quarter of a million dollars to buy food for famine relief.

We would take bags of money to the market place where we would buy food. To handle distribution, we came up with the strategy that the churches in the famine-stricken areas would serve as the centers. We hired guards to protect the shipments, and we delivered food to churches in areas where people were starving. Many of these churches were made out of mud with a white cross painted on the side. It was thrilling to see the church of Jesus Christ spring into action. And all of this continued on for two years until the rains came.

At first, famine relief seemed insurmountable. How could a few hundred people actually make a difference? All of us had busy lives with work or school. But when we determined to do what little we could, God honored our efforts and many, many people were fed. God took the little we gave, blessed it, and multiplied it.

Written Summation

I walked in reservoirs that had inch-wide cracks in the dirt. I could see boats sitting in sand, miles away from any water. Now, all the huge pivots stood idle in the middle of the desert. There was no water in the canals for irrigation. Everything was dry.

Model Practice 1

Model Practice 2

Model Practice 3

CHAPTER
II

Text Excerpts
from
Primary Source Documents

Lines for written summations have not been included in this section. These selections are somewhat complicated, detailed, and advanced for written summations by students at this stage. These selections are best used for oral narrations as an introduction to ideas from the time period studied.

They also serve as a great introduction to primary source material, introducing children to the idea that they are capable of evaluating history for themselves. Copywork and dictation from primary source documents are excellent selections of living literature (aka living books).

Autobiography of Abraham Lincoln

written for Jesse W. Fell
December 20, 1859

I was born February 12, 1809 in Hardin County, Kentucky. My parents were both born in Virginia of undistinguished families—second families, perhaps I should say. My mother, who died in my tenth year, was of a family of the name of Hanks, some of whom now reside in Adams and others in Macon County, Illinois. My paternal grandfather, Abraham Lincoln, emigrated from Rockingham County, Virginia to Kentucky about 1781 or 1782, where a year or two later he was killed by the Indians, not in battle, but by stealth, when he was laboring to open a farm in the forest. His ancestors, who were Quakers, went to Virginia from Berks County, Pennsylvania. An effort to identify them with the New England family of the same name ended in nothing more definite than a similarity of Christian names in both families, such as Enoch, Levi, Mordecai, Solomon, Abraham, and the like.

My father, at the death of his father, was but six years of age, and he grew up literally without education. He removed from Kentucky to what is now Spencer County, Indiana in my eighth year. We reached our new home about the time the state came into the Union. It was a wild region, with many bears and other wild animals still in the woods. There I grew up. There were some schools, so called, but no qualification was ever required of a teacher beyond "readin', writin', and cipherin'" to the rule of three. If a straggler supposed to understand Latin happened to sojourn in the neighborhood, he was looked upon as a wizard. There was absolutely nothing to excite ambition for education. Of course, when I came of age, I did not know much. Still, somehow, I could read, write, and cipher to the rule of three, but that was all. I have not been to school since. The little advance I now have upon this store of education, I have picked up from time to time under the pressure of necessity.

I was raised to farm work, which I continued till I was twenty-two. At twenty-one I came to Illinois, Macon County. Then I got to New Salem, at that time in Sangamon, now in Menard County, where I remained a year as a sort of clerk in a store.

Then came the Black Hawk war, and I was elected a captain of volunteers, a success which gave me more pleasure than any I have had since. I went the campaign, was elated, ran for the legislature the same year (1832), and was beaten—the only time I have ever been beaten by the people. The next and three succeeding biennial elections I was elected to the legislature. I was not a candidate afterward. During this legislative period I had studied law and removed to Springfield to practice it. In 1846, I was once elected to the Lower House of Congress, was not a candidate for reelection. From 1849 to 1854, both inclusive, practiced law more assiduously than ever before. Always Whig in politics and generally on the Whig electoral tickets, making active canvasses. I was losing interest in politics when the repeal of the Missouri Compromise aroused me again. What I have done since then is pretty well known.

If any personal description of me is thought desirable, it may be said I am, in height, six feet four inches, nearly; lean in flesh, weighing on an average one hundred and eighty pounds; dark complexion, with coarse black hair and gray eyes. No other marks or brands recollected.

If a straggler supposed to understand Latin happened to sojourn in the neighborhood, he was looked upon as a wizard. There was absolutely nothing to excite ambition for education. Of course, when I came of age I did not know much. Still, somehow, I could read, write, and cipher to the rule of three, but that was all.

Model Practice 1

Model Practice 2

Model Practice 3

Gettysburg Address

by Abraham Lincoln
November 19, 1863
Gettysburg, Pennsylvania, USA

Fourscore and seven years ago our fathers brought forth on this continent a new nation, conceived in liberty and dedicated to the proposition that all men are created equal.

Now we are engaged in a great civil war, testing whether that nation, or any nation so conceived and so dedicated, can long endure. We are met on a great battlefield of that war. We have come to dedicate a portion of that field as a final resting-place for those who here gave their lives that that nation might live. It is altogether fitting and proper that we should do this.

But, in a larger sense, we cannot dedicate, we cannot consecrate, we cannot hallow this ground. The brave men, living and dead, who struggled here have consecrated it far above our poor power to add or detract. The world will little note, nor long remember, what we say here; but it can never forget what they did here.

It is for us, the living, rather, to be dedicated here to the unfinished work which they who fought here have thus far so nobly advanced. It is rather for us to be here dedicated to the great task remaining before us-that from these honored dead we take increased devotion to that cause for which they gave the last full measure of devotion—that we here highly resolve that these dead shall not have died in vain—that this nation, under God, shall have a new birth of freedom—and that government of the people, by the people, for the people shall not perish from the earth.

Fourscore and seven years ago our fathers brought forth on this continent a new nation, conceived in liberty and dedicated to the proposition that all men are created equal.

Model Practice 1

Model Practice 2

_____

_____

_____

_____

_____

_____

_____

_____

_____

Model Practice 3

_____

_____

_____

_____

_____

_____

_____

_____

_____

Another Camp Meeting (excerpt)

dictated by Sojourner Truth (ca.1797-1883)
edited by Olive Gilbert

When Sojourner had been at Northampton a few months, she attended another camp meeting, at which she performed a very important part.

A party of wild young men, with no motive but that of entertaining themselves by annoying and injuring the feelings of others, had assembled at the meeting, hooting and yelling, and in various ways interrupting the services, and causing much disturbance. Those who had the charge of the meeting, having tried their persuasive powers in vain, grew impatient and tried threats.

The young men, considering themselves insulted, collected their friends, to the number of a hundred or more, dispersed themselves through the grounds, making the most frightful noises and threatening to fire the tents. It was said the authorities of the meeting sat in grave consultation, decided to have the ring-leaders arrested, and sent for the constable, to the great displeasure of some of the company, who were opposed to such an appeal to force and arms. Be that as it may, Sojourner, seeing great consternation depicted in every countenance, caught the contagion, and, ere she was aware, found herself quaking with fear.

Under the impulse of this sudden emotion, she fled to the most retired corner of a tent and secreted herself behind a trunk, saying to herself, "I am the only colored person here, and on me, probably, their wicked mischief will fall first and, perhaps, fatally." But feeling how great was her insecurity even there, as the very tent began to shake from its foundations, she began to soliloquize as follows:-

"Shall I run away and hide from the Devil? Me, a servant of the living God? Have I not faith enough to go out and quell that mob, when I know it is written—"One shall chase a thousand, and two put ten thousand to flight"? I know there are not a thousand here, and I know I am a servant of the living God. I'll go to the rescue, and the Lord shall go with and protect me.

"Oh," said she, "I felt as if I had three hearts! And that they were so large, my body could hardly hold them!"

She now came forth from her hiding-place and invited several to go with her and see what they could do to still the raging of the moral elements. They declined and considered her wild to think of it.

The meeting was in the open fields; the full moon shed its saddened light over all; and the woman who was that evening to address them was trembling on the preachers' stand. The noise and confusion were now terrific. Sojourner left the tent alone and unaided and, walking some thirty rods to the top of a small rise of ground, commenced to sing, in her most fervid manner, with all the strength of her most powerful voice, the hymn on the resurrection of Christ—

It was early in the morning—it was early in the morning,
  Just at the break of day—
When he rose—when he rose—when he rose,
  And went to heaven on a cloud.

All who have ever heard her sing this hymn will probably remember it as long as they remember her. The hymn, the tune, the style are each too closely associated with to be easily separated from herself, and when sung in one of her most animated moods, in the open air, with the utmost strength of her most powerful voice, must have been truly thrilling.

As she commenced to sing, the young men made a rush towards her, and she was immediately encircled by a dense body of the rioters, many of them armed with sticks or clubs as their weapons of defense, if not of attack. As the circle narrowed around her, she ceased singing and, after a short pause, inquired, in a gentle but firm tone, "Why do you come about me with clubs and sticks? I am not doing harm to any one."

"We ar'n't a going to hurt you, old woman; we came to hear you sing," cried many voices, simultaneously. "Sing to us, old woman," cries one. "Talk to us, old woman," says another. "Pray, old woman," says a third. "Tell us your experience," says a fourth.

"You stand and smoke so near me, I cannot sing or talk," she answered.

"Stand back," said several authoritative voices, with not the most gentle or courteous accompaniments, raising their rude weapons in the air. The crowd suddenly gave back; the circle became larger, as many voices again called for singing, talking, or praying, backed by assurances that no one should be allowed to hurt her—the speakers declaring with an oath, that they would 'knock down' any person who should offer her the least indignity.

She looked about her, and with her usual discrimination, said inwardly—"Here must be many young men in all this assemblage, bearing within them hearts susceptible of good impressions. I will speak to them." She did speak; they silently heard and civilly asked her many questions. It seemed to her to be given her at the time to answer them with truth and wisdom beyond herself. Her speech had operated on the roused passions of the mob like oil on agitated waters; they were, as a whole, entirely subdued and only clamored when she ceased to speak or sing. Those who stood in the back ground, after the circle was enlarged, cried out, "Sing aloud, old woman, we can't hear." Those who held the scepter of power among them requested that she should make a pulpit of a neighboring wagon.

She said, "If I do, they'll overthrow it."

"No, they sha'n't. He who dares hurt you, we'll knock him down instantly," cried the chiefs.

"No we won't, no we won't, nobody shall hurt you," answered the many voices of the mob. They kindly assisted her to mount the wagon from which she spoke and sung to them about an hour. Of all she said to them on the occasion, she remembers only the following:

> "Well, there are two congregations on this ground. It is written that there shall be a separation, and the sheep shall be separated from the goats. The other preachers have the sheep; I have the goats. And I have a few sheep among my goats, but they are very ragged."

This exordium produced great laughter. When she became wearied with talking, she began to cast about her to contrive some way to induce them to disperse. While she paused, they loudly clamored for "more," "more," "sing," "sing more."

She motioned them to be quiet and called out to them: "Children, I have talked and sung to you, as you asked me; and now I have a request to make of you; will you grant it?"

"Yes, yes, yes," resounded from every quarter.

"Well, it is this," she answered; "if I will sing one more hymn for you, will you then go away and leave us this night in peace?"

"Yes, yes," came faintly, feebly from a few.

"I repeat it," says Sojourner, "and I want an answer from you all, as of one accord. If I will sing you one more, will you go away and leave us this night in peace?"

"Yes, yes, yes," shouted many voices, with hearty emphasis.

"I repeat my request once more," said she, "and I want you all to answer." And she reiterated the words again.

This time a long, loud "Yes-yes-yes," came up, as from the multitudinous mouth of the entire mob.

"AMEN! it is SEALED," repeated Sojourner, in the deepest and most solemn tones of her powerful and sonorous voice. Its effect ran through the multitude, like an electric shock; and the most of them considered themselves bound by their promise, as they might have failed to do under less imposing circumstances.

Some of them began instantly to leave; others said, "Are we not to have one more hymn?"

"Yes," answered their entertainer, and she commenced to sing:

'I bless the Lord I've got my seal-to-day and to-day—
To slay Goliath in the field-to-day and to-day;
The good old way is a righteous way,
I mean to take the kingdom in the good old way.'

While singing, she heard some, enforcing obedience to their promise, while a few seemed refusing to abide by it. But before she had quite concluded, she saw them turn from her, and, in the course of a few minutes, they were running as fast as they well could in a solid body. And she says she can compare them to nothing but a swarm of bees, so dense was their phalanx, so straight their course, so hurried their march. As they passed with a rush very near the stand of the other preachers, the hearts of the people were smitten with fear, thinking that their entertainer had failed to enchain them longer with her spell and that they were coming upon them with redoubled and remorseless fury. But they found they were mistaken and that their fears were groundless; for, before they could well recover from their surprise, every rioter was gone; and not one was left on the grounds or seen there again during the meeting.

Sojourner was informed that as her audience reached the main road, some distance from the tents, a few of the rebellious spirits refused to go on and proposed returning. But their leaders said, "No! We have promised to leave-all promised, and we must go—all go, and you shall none of you return again."

"Well, there are two congregations on this ground. It is written that there shall be a separation, and the sheep shall be separated from the goats. The other preachers have the sheep; I have the goats. And I have a few sheep among my goats, but they are very ragged."

Model Practice 1

Model Practice 2

Model Practice 3

Emancipation Proclamation

January 1, 1863

Whereas, on the twenty-second day of September, in the year of our Lord one thousand eight hundred and sixty-two, a proclamation was issued by the President of the United States, containing, among other things, the following, to wit:

"That on the first day of January, in the year of our Lord one thousand eight hundred and sixty-three, all persons held as slaves within any State, or designated part of a State, the people whereof shall then be in rebellion against the United States, shall be then, thenceforward, and for ever free; and the Executive Government of the United States, including the military and naval authority thereof, will recognize and maintain the freedom of such persons, and will do no act or acts to repress such persons, or any of them, in any efforts they may make for their actual freedom.

"That the Executive will, on the first day of January aforesaid, by proclamation, designate the States and parts of States, if any, in which the people thereof respectively shall then be in rebellion against the United States; and the fact that any State, or the people thereof, shall on that day be in good faith represented in the Congress of the United States by members chosen thereto at elections wherein a majority of the qualified voters of such State shall have participated, shall in the absence of strong countervailing testimony be deemed conclusive evidence that such State and the people thereof are not then in rebellion against the United States."

Now, therefore, I, Abraham Lincoln, President of the United States, by virtue of the power in me vested as commander-in-chief of the army and navy of the United States, in time of actual armed rebellion against the authority and government of the United States, and as a fit and necessary war measure for suppressing said rebellion, do, on this first day of January, in the year of our Lord one thousand eight hundred and sixty-three, and in accordance with my purpose so to do, publicly proclaimed for the full period of one hundred days from the day first above mentioned, order and designate as the States and parts of States wherein the people thereof, respectively, are this day in rebellion against the United States, the following, to wit:

Arkansas, Texas, Louisiana (except the parishes of St. Bernard, Plaquemines, Jefferson, St. John, St. Charles, St. James, Ascension, Assumption, Terrebonne, Lafourche, St. Mary, St. Martin, and Orleans, including the city of New Orleans), Mississippi, Alabama, Florida, Georgia, South Carolina, North Carolina, and Virginia (except the forty-eight counties designated as West Virginia, and also the counties of Berkeley, Accomac, Northampton, Elizabeth City, York, Princess Anne, and Norfolk, including the cities of Norfolk and Portsmouth), and which excepted parts are for the present left precisely as if this proclamation were not issued.

And by virtue of the power and for the purpose aforesaid, I do order and declare that all persons held as slaves within said designated States and parts of States are, and henceforward shall be free; and that the Executive Government of the United States, including the military and naval authorities thereof, will recognize and maintain the freedom of said persons.

And I hereby enjoin upon the people so declared to be free to abstain from all violence, unless in necessary self-defense; and I recommend to them that, in all cases when allowed, they labor faithfully for reasonable wages.

And I further declare and make known that such persons of suitable condition will be received into the armed service of the United States to garrison forts, positions, stations, and other places, and to man vessels of all sorts in said service.

And upon this act, sincerely believed to be an act of justice, warranted by the Constitution upon military necessity, I invoke the considerate judgment of mankind and the gracious favor of Almighty God.

In witness whereof, I have hereunto set my hand, and caused the seal of the United States to be affixed.

Done at the city of Washington, this first day of January, in the year of our Lord one thousand eight hundred and sixty-three, and of the independence of the United States of America the eighty-seventh.

ABRAHAM LINCOLN.
By the President:
WILLIAM H. SEWARD,
Secretary of State.

And by virtue of the power and for the purpose aforesaid, I do order and declare that all persons held as slaves within said designated States and parts of States are, and henceforward shall be free; and that the Executive Government of the United States, including the military and naval authorities thereof, will recognize and maintain the freedom of said persons.

Model Practice 1

Model Practice 2

_____

_____

_____

_____

_____

_____

_____

_____

Model Practice 3

_____

_____

_____

_____

_____

_____

_____

_____

_____

The Trial of Susan B. Anthony

from <u>The Life and Work of Susan B. Anthony</u>
written by Ida Husted Harper 1899
Volume 1 of 2, Chapter XXV

The trial opened the afternoon of June 17, at the lovely village of Canandaigua, Associate-Justice Ward Hunt on the bench, U.S. District-Attorney Richard Crowley prosecuting, Hon. Henry R. Selden and John Van Voorhis, Esq., defending. Miss Anthony, most of the ladies who had voted with her, and also Mrs. Gage, were seated within the bar. On the right sat the jury. The courtroom was crowded, many prominent men being present, among them ex-President Fillmore. Judge Hall, of Buffalo, was an interested spectator and Miss Anthony's counsel endeavored to have him try the case with Judge Hunt in order that, if necessary, it might go to the Supreme Court, which was not possible with only one judge, but he refused.

It was conceded that Miss Anthony was a woman and that she voted on November 5, 1872. Judge Selden, for the second time in all his practice, offered himself as a witness, and testified that he advised her to vote, believing that the laws and Constitution of the United States gave her full authority. He then proposed to call Miss Anthony to testify as to the intention or belief under which she voted, but the Court held she was not competent as a witness in her own behalf. After making this decision, the Court then admitted all the testimony, as reported, which she gave on the preliminary examination before the commissioner, in spite of her counsel's protest against accepting the version which that officer took of her evidence. The prosecution simply alleged the fact of her having voted. Mr. Selden then addressed the judge and jury in a masterly argument of over three hours' duration, beginning:

The defendant is indicted under the 19th Section of the Act of Congress of May 31, 1870 (16th St. at L., 144), for "voting without having a lawful right to vote." The words of the statute, so far as they are material in this case, are as follows:

"If at any election for representative or delegate in the Congress of the United States, any person shall knowingly ... vote without having a lawful right to vote ... every such person shall be deemed guilty of a crime ... and on conviction thereof shall be punished by a fine not exceeding $500, or by imprisonment for a term not exceeding three years, or by both, in the discretion of the Court, and shall pay the costs of prosecution."

The only alleged ground of illegality of the defendant's vote is that she is a woman. If the same act had been done by her brother under the same circumstances, the act would have been not only innocent but honorable and laudable; but, having been done by a woman, it is said to be a crime. The crime therefore consists not in the act done but in the simple fact that the person doing it was a woman and not a man. I believe this is the first instance in which a woman has been arraigned in a criminal court merely on account of her sex.

Women have the same interest that men have in the establishment and maintenance of good government; they are to the same extent as men bound to obey the laws; they suffer to the same extent by bad laws and profit to the same extent by good laws; and upon principles of equal justice, as it would seem, should be allowed, equally with men, to express their preference in the choice of law-makers and rulers. But however that may be, no greater absurdity, to use no harsher term, could be presented, than that of rewarding men and punishing women for the same act, without giving to women any voice in the question which should he rewarded and which punished.

I am aware, however, that we are here to be governed by the Constitution and laws as they are, and that if the defendant has been guilty of violating the law, she must submit to the penalty, however unjust or absurd the law may be. But courts are not required to so interpret laws or constitutions as to produce either absurdity or injustice, so long as they are open to a more reasonable interpretation. This must be my excuse for what I design to say in regard to the propriety of female suffrage, because with that propriety established there is very little difficulty in finding sufficient warrant in the Constitution for its exercise. This case, in its legal aspects, presents three questions which I propose to discuss.

1. Was the defendant legally entitled to vote at the election in question?

2. If she was not entitled to vote but believed that she was, and voted in good faith in that belief, did such voting constitute a crime under the statute before referred to?

3. Did the defendant vote in good faith in that belief?

He argued the case from a legal, constitutional, and moral standpoint and concluded:

One other matter will close what I have to say. Miss Anthony believed, and was advised, that she had a right to vote. She may also have been advised, as was clearly the fact, that the question as to her right could not be brought before the courts for trial without her voting or offering to vote, and if either was criminal, the one was as much so as the other. Therefore she stands now arraigned as a criminal, for taking the only step by which it was possible to bring the great constitutional question as to her right before the tribunals of the country for adjudication. If for thus acting, in the most perfect good faith, with motives as pure and impulses as noble as any which can find place in your honor's breast in the administration of justice, she is by the laws of her country to be condemned as a criminal, she must abide the consequences. Her condemnation, however, under such circumstances, would only add another most weighty reason to those which I have already advanced, to show that women need the aid of the ballot for their protection.

The district-attorney followed with a two hours' speech. Then Judge Hunt, without leaving the bench, delivered a written opinion to the effect that the Fourteenth Amendment, under which Miss Anthony claimed the authority to vote, "was a protection, not to all our rights, but to our rights as citizens of the United States only; that is, the rights existing or belonging to that condition or capacity." At its conclusion he directed the jury to bring in a verdict of guilty.

Miss Anthony's counsel insisted that the Court had no power to make such a direction in a criminal case and demanded that the jury be permitted to bring in its own verdict. The judge made no reply except to order the clerk to take the verdict. Mr. Selden demanded that the jury be polled. Judge Hunt refused, and at once discharged the jury without allowing them any consultation or asking if they agreed upon a verdict. Not one of them had spoken a word. After being discharged, the jurymen talked freely and several declared they should have brought in a verdict of "not guilty."

The next day Judge Selden argued the motion for a new trial on seven exceptions, but this was denied by Judge Hunt. The following scene then took place in the courtroom:

Judge Hunt.—(Ordering the defendant to stand up). Has the prisoner anything to say why sentence shall not be pronounced?

Miss Anthony.—Yes, your honor, I have many things to say; for in your ordered verdict of guilty, you have trampled under foot every vital principle of our government. My natural rights, my civil rights, my political rights, my judicial rights are all alike ignored. Robbed of the fundamental privilege of citizenship, I am degraded from the status of a citizen to that of a subject; and not only myself individually, but all of my sex are, by your honor's verdict, doomed to political subjection under this so-called republican form of government.

Judge Hunt.—The Court can not listen to a rehearsal of argument which the prisoner's counsel has already consumed three hours in presenting.

Miss Anthony.—May it please your honor, I am not arguing the question, but simply stating the reasons why sentence can not, in justice, be pronounced against me. Your denial of my citizen's right to vote is the denial of my right of consent as one of the governed, the denial of my right of representation as one of the taxed, the denial of my right to a trial by a jury of my peers as an offender against law; therefore, the denial of my sacred right to life, liberty, property and—

Judge Hunt.—The Court can not allow the prisoner to go on.

Miss Anthony.—But your honor will not deny me this one and only poor privilege of protest against this high-handed outrage upon my citizen's rights. May it please the Court to remember that, since the day of my arrest last November, this is the first time that either myself or any person of my disfranchised class has been allowed a word of defense before judge or jury—

Judge Hunt.—The prisoner must sit down—the Court can not allow it.

Miss Anthony.—Of all my prosecutors, from the corner grocery politician who entered the complaint, to the United States marshal, commissioner, district-attorney, district-judge, your honor on the bench—not one is my peer, but each and all are my political sovereigns; and had your honor submitted my case to the jury, as was clearly your duty, even then I should have had just cause of protest, for not one of those men was my peer; but, native or foreign born, white or black, rich or poor, educated or ignorant, sober or drunk, each and every man of them was my political superior; hence, in no sense, my peer. Under such circumstances a commoner of England, tried before a jury of lords, would have far less cause to complain than have I, a woman, tried before a jury of men. Even my counsel, Hon. Henry R. Selden, who has argued my cause so ably, so earnestly, so unanswerably before your honor, is my political sovereign. Precisely as no disfranchised person is entitled to sit upon a jury, and no woman is entitled to the franchise, so none but a regularly admitted lawyer is allowed to practice in the courts, and no woman can gain admission to the bar—hence, jury, judge, counsel, all must be of the superior class.

Judge Hunt.—The Court must insist—the prisoner has been tried according to the established forms of law.

Miss Anthony.—Yes, your honor, but by forms of law all made by men, interpreted by men, administered by men, in favor of men and against women-and hence your honor's ordered verdict of guilty, against a United States citizen for the exercise of the "citizen's right to vote," simply because that citizen was a woman and not a man. But yesterday, the same man-made forms of law declared it a crime punishable with $1,000 fine and six months' imprisonment to give a cup of cold water, a crust of bread or a night's shelter to a panting fugitive tracking his way to Canada; and every man or woman in whose veins coursed a drop of human sympathy violated that wicked law, reckless of consequences, and was justified in so doing. As then the slaves who got their freedom had to take it over or under or through the unjust forms of law, precisely so now must women take it to get their right to a voice in this government. And I have taken mine and mean to take it at every opportunity.

Judge Hunt.—The Court orders the prisoner to sit down. It will not allow another word.

Miss Anthony.—When I was brought before your honor for trial, I hoped for a broad and liberal interpretation of the Constitution and its recent amendments, which should declare all United States citizens under its protecting aegis—which should declare equality of rights the national guarantee to all persons born or naturalized in the United States. But failing to get this justice—failing, even, to get a trial by a jury not of my peers—I ask not leniency at your hands but rather the full rigor of the law.

Judge Hunt—The Court must insist—[Here the prisoner sat down.] The prisoner will stand up. [Here Miss Anthony rose again.] The sentence of the Court is that you pay a fine of $100 and the costs of the prosecution.

Miss Anthony.—May it please your honor, I will never pay a dollar of your unjust penalty. All the stock in trade I possess is a debt of $10,000, incurred by publishing my paper—The Revolution—the sole object of which was to educate all women to do precisely as I have done, rebel against your man-made, unjust, unconstitutional forms of law, which tax, fine, imprison and hang women, while denying them the right of representation in the government; and I will work on with might and main to pay every dollar of that honest debt, but not a penny shall go to this unjust claim. And I shall earnestly and persistently continue to urge all women to the practical recognition of the old Revolutionary maxim, "Resistance to tyranny is obedience to God."

Judge Hunt.—Madam, the Court will not order you to stand committed until the fine is paid.

Thus ended the great trial, "The United States of America vs. Susan B. Anthony." From this date the question of woman suffrage was lifted from one of grievances into one of Constitutional Law.

As then the slaves who got their freedom had to take it over or under or through the unjust forms of law, precisely, so now must women take it to get their right to a voice in this government. And I have taken mine and mean to take it at every opportunity.

Model Practice 1

_____

_____

_____

_____

_____

_____

_____

_____

_____

_____

_____

_____

_____

_____

_____

Model Practice 2

_____

_____

_____

_____

_____

_____

_____

_____

_____

Model Practice 3

_____

_____

_____

_____

_____

_____

_____

_____

_____

Life and Adventures of Calamity Jane
by Herself

(Warning! This selection was written by Calamity Jane and has many errors. I have corrected a few of the more glaring ones; however, I did not correct them all. I did not want to prevent the students from hearing the "voice" of Calamity Jane.)

My maiden name was Marthy Cannary. I was born in Princeton, Missouri, May 1st, 1852. Father and mother were natives of Ohio. I had two brothers and three sisters, I being the oldest of the children. As a child I always had a fondness for adventure and out-door exercise and especial fondness for horses, which I began to ride at an early age and continued to do so until I became an expert rider, being able to ride the most vicious and stubborn of horses. In fact, the greater portion of my life in early times was spent in this manner.

In 1865 we emigrated from our homes in Missouri by the overland route to Virginia City, Montana, taking five months to make the journey. While on the way the greater portion of my time was spent in hunting along with the men and hunters of the party, in fact I was at all times with the men when there was excitement and adventures to be had. By the time we reached Virginia City I was considered a remarkable good shot and a fearless rider for a girl of my age. I remember many occurrences on the journey from Missouri to Montana. Many times in crossing the mountains the conditions of the trail were so bad that we frequently had to lower the wagons over ledges by hand with ropes for they were so rough and rugged that horses were of no use. We also had many exciting times fording streams for many of the streams in our way were noted for quicksand and boggy places, where, unless we were very careful, we would have lost horses and all. Then we had many dangers to encounter in the way of streams swelling on account of heavy rains. On occasions of that kind the men would usually select the best places to cross the streams. I, on more than one occasion, have mounted my pony and swam across the stream several times merely to amuse myself and have had many narrow escapes from having both myself and pony washed away to certain death. But as the pioneers of those days had plenty of courage, we overcame all obstacles and reached Virginia City in safety.

Mother died at Black Foot, Montana, 1866, where we buried her. I left Montana in spring of 1866, for Utah, arriving at Salt Lake City during the summer. Remained in Utah until 1867, where my father died, then went to Fort Bridger, Wyoming Territory, where we arrived May 1, 1868, then went to Piedmont, Wyoming, with U.P. Railway. Joined General Custer as a scout at Fort Russell, Wyoming, in 1870, and started for Arizona for the Indian Campaign. Up to this time I had always worn the costume of my sex. When I joined Custer I donned the uniform of a soldier. It was a bit awkward at first but I soon got to be perfectly at home in men's clothes.

Was in Arizona up to the winter of 1871 and during that time I had a great many adventures with the Indians, for as a scout I had a great many dangerous missions to perform and while I was in many close places always succeeded in getting away safely. For by this time, I was considered the most reckless and daring rider and one of the best shots in the western country.

After that campaign I returned to Fort Sanders, Wyoming, remained there until spring of 1872, when we were ordered out to the Muscle Shell or Nursey Pursey Indian outbreak. In that war Generals Custer, Miles, Terry and Crook were all engaged. This campaign lasted until fall of 1873.

It was during this campaign that I was christened Calamity Jane. It was on Goose Creek, Wyoming, where the town of Sheridan is now located. Capt. Egan was in command of the Post. We were ordered out to quell an uprising of the Indians and were out for several days, had numerous skirmishes during which six of the soldiers were killed and several severely wounded. When on returning to the Post we were ambushed about a mile and a half from our destination. When fired upon, Capt. Egan was shot. I was riding in advance and, on hearing the firing, turned in my saddle and saw the Captain reeling in his saddle as though about to fall. I turned my horse and galloped back with all haste to his side and got there in time to catch him as he was falling. I lifted him onto my horse in front of me and succeeded in getting him safely to the Fort. Capt. Egan on recovering, laughingly said: ``I name you Calamity Jane, the heroine of the plains.'' I have borne that name up to the present time. We were afterwards ordered to Fort Custer, where Custer city now stands, where we arrived in the spring of 1874; remained around Fort Custer all summer and were ordered to Fort Russell in fall of 1874, where we remained until spring of 1875; was then ordered to the Black Hills to protect miners, as that country was controlled by the Sioux Indians and the government had to send the soldiers to protect the lives of the miners and settlers in that section. Remained there until fall of 1875 and wintered at Fort Laramie. In spring of 1876, we were ordered north with General Crook to join Gen'ls Miles, Terry and Custer at Big Horn river. During this march I swam the Platte River at Fort Fetterman, as I was the bearer of important dispatches. I had a ninety-mile ride to make, being wet and cold, I contracted a severe illness and was sent back in Gen. Crook's ambulance to Fort Fetterman where I laid in the hospital for fourteen days. When able to ride I started for Fort Laramie where I met Wm. Hickock, better known as Wild Bill, and we started for Deadwood, where we arrived about June.

During the month of June I acted as a pony express rider carrying the U.S. mail between Deadwood and Custer, a distance of fifty miles, over one of the roughest trails in the Black Hills country. As many of the riders before me had been held up and robbed of their packages, mail, and money that they carried, for that was the only means of getting mail and money between these points. It was considered the most dangerous route in the Hills, but as my reputation as a rider and quick shot was well known, I was molested very little. For the toll gatherers looked on me as being a good fellow, and they knew that I never missed my mark. I made the round trip every two days which was considered pretty good riding in that country. Remained around Deadwood all that summer visiting all the camps within an area of one hundred miles. My friend, Wild Bill, remained in Deadwood during the summer with the exception of occasional visits to the camps. On the 2nd of August, while setting at a gambling table in the Bell Union saloon, in Deadwood, he was shot in the back of the head by the notorious Jack McCall, a desperado. I was in Deadwood at the time and on hearing of the killing made my way at once to the scene of the shooting and found that my friend had been killed by McCall. I at once started to look for the assassin and found him at Shurdy's butcher shop and grabbed a meat cleaver and made him throw up his hands; through the excitement on hearing of Bill's death, having left my weapons on the post of my bed. He was then taken to a log cabin and locked up, well secured as every one thought, but he got away and was afterwards caught at Fagan's ranch on Horse Creek, on the old Cheyenne road and was then taken to Yankton, Dak., where he was tried, sentenced and hung.

I remained around Deadwood locating claims, going from camp to camp until the spring of 1877, where one morning, I saddled my horse and rode towards Crook City. I had gone about twelve miles from Deadwood, at the mouth of Whitewood Creek, when I met the overland mail running from

Cheyenne to Deadwood. The horses on a run, about two hundred yards from the station, upon looking closely, I saw they were pursued by Indians. The horses ran to the barn, as was their custom. As the horses stopped I rode along side of the coach and found the driver John Slaughter, lying face downwards in the boot of the stage, he having been shot by the Indians. When the stage got to the station the Indians hid in the bushes. I immediately removed all baggage from the coach except the mail. I then took the driver's seat and with all haste drove to Deadwood, carrying the six passengers and the dead driver.

I left Deadwood in the fall of 1877, and went to Bear Butte Creek with the 7th Cavalry. During the fall and winter we built Fort Meade and the town of Sturgis. In 1878 I left the command and went to Rapid City and put in the year prospecting.

In 1879 I went to Fort Pierre and drove trains from Rapid City to Fort Pierre for Frank Witc then drove teams from Fort Pierce to Sturgis for Fred Evans. This teaming was done with oxen as they were better fitted for the work than horses, owing to the rough nature of the country.

In 1881 I went to Wyoming and returned in 1882 to Miles city and took up a ranch on the Yellow Stone, raising stock and cattle, also kept a way side inn, where the weary traveler could be accommodated with food, drink, or trouble if he looked for it. Left the ranch in 1883, went to California, going through the States and territories, reached Ogden the latter part of 1883 and San Francisco in 1884. Left San Francisco in the summer of 1884 for Texas, stopping at Fort Yuma, Arizona, the hottest spot in the United States. Stopping at all points of interest until I reached El Paso in the fall. While in El Paso, I met Mr. Clinton Burk, a native of Texas, who I married in August 1885. As I thought I had traveled through life long enough alone and thought it was about time to take a partner for the rest of my days. We remained in Texas leading a quiet home life until 1889. On October 28th, 1887, I became the mother of a girl baby, the very image of its father, at least that is what he said, but who has the temper of its mother.

Hoping that this little history of my life may interest all readers, I remain as in the older days,

Yours,

Mrs. M. BURK

BETTER KNOWN AS CALAMITY JANE

When fired upon, Capt. Egan was shot. I was riding in advance and, on hearing the firing, turned in my saddle and saw the Captain reeling in his saddle as though about to fall. I turned my horse and galloped back with all haste to his side and got there in time to catch him as he was falling.

Model Practice 1

Model Practice 2

Model Practice 3

The Atlanta Compromise
An Address at the Atlanta Exposition (excerpt)
by Booker T. Washington

Mr. President and Gentlemen of the Board of Directors and Citizens.

One-third of the population of the South is of the Negro race. No enterprise seeking the material, civil, or moral welfare of this section can disregard this element of our population and reach the highest success. I but convey to you, Mr. President and Directors, the sentiment of the masses of my race when I say that in no way have the value and manhood of the American Negro been more fittingly and generously recognized than by the managers of this magnificent Exposition at every stage of its progress. It is a recognition that will do more to cement the friendship of the two races than any occurrence since the dawn of our freedom.

Not only this, but the opportunity here afforded will awaken among us a new era of industrial progress. Ignorant and inexperienced, it is not strange that in the first years of our new life we began at the top instead of at the bottom; that a seat in Congress or the state legislature was more sought than real estate or industrial skill; that the political convention or stump speaking had more attractions than starting a dairy farm or truck garden.

A ship lost at sea for many days suddenly sighted a friendly vessel. From the mast of the unfortunate vessel was seen a signal, "Water, water; we die of thirst!" The answer from the friendly vessel at once came back, "Cast down your bucket where you are." A second time the signal, "Water, water; send us water!" ran up from the distressed vessel, and was answered, "Cast down your bucket where you are." And a third and fourth signal for water was answered, "Cast down your bucket where you are." The captain of the distressed vessel, at last heading the injunction, cast down his bucket, and it came up full of fresh, sparkling water from the mouth of the Amazon River. To those of my race who depend on bettering their condition in a foreign land or who underestimate the importance of cultivating friendly relations with the Southern white man, who is their next-door neighbor, I would say: "Cast down your bucket where you are"—cast it down in making friends in every manly way of the people of all races by whom we are surrounded.

Cast it down in agriculture, mechanics, in commerce, in domestic service, and in the professions. And in this connection it is well to bear in mind that whatever other sins the South may be called to bear, when it comes to business, pure and simple, it is in the South that the Negro is given a man's chance in the commercial world, and in nothing is this Exposition more eloquent than in emphasizing this chance. Our greatest danger is that, in the great leap from slavery to freedom, we may overlook the fact that the masses of us are to live by the productions of our hands and fail to keep in mind that we shall prosper in proportion as we learn to dignify and glorify common labor and put brains and skill into the common occupations of life; shall prosper in proportion as we learn to draw the line between the superficial and the substantial, the ornamental gewgaws of life and the useful. No race can prosper till it learns that there is as much dignity in tilling a field as in writing a poem. It is at the bottom of life we must begin, and not at the top. Nor should we permit our grievances to overshadow our opportunities.

To those of the white race who look to the incoming of those of foreign birth and strange tongue and habits of the prosperity of the South, were I permitted I would repeat what I say to my own race: "Cast down your bucket where you are." Cast it down among the eight millions of Negroes whose habits you know, whose fidelity and love you have tested in days when to have proved treacherous meant the ruin of your firesides. Cast down your bucket among these people who have, without strikes and labor wars, tilled your fields, cleared your forests, builded your railroads and cities, and brought forth treasures from the bowels of the earth, and helped make possible this magnificent representation of the progress of the South. Casting down your bucket among my people, helping and encouraging them as you are doing on these grounds, and to education of head, hand, and heart, you will find that they will buy your surplus land, make blossom the waste places in your fields, and run your factories. While doing this, you can be sure in the future, as in the past, that you and your families will be surrounded by the most patient, faithful, law-abiding, and unresentful people that the world has seen. As we have proved our loyalty to you in the past, nursing your children, watching by the sick-bed of your mothers and fathers, and often following them with tear-dimmed eyes to their graves, so in the future, in our humble way, we shall stand by you with a devotion that no foreigner can approach, ready to lay down our lives, if need be, in defense of yours, interlacing our industrial, commercial, civil, and religious life with yours in a way that shall make the interests of both races one. In all things that are purely social we can be as separate as the fingers, yet one as the hand in all things essential to mutual progress.

There is no defense or security for any of us except in the highest intelligence and development of all. If anywhere there are efforts tending to curtail the fullest growth of the Negro, let these efforts be turned into stimulating, encouraging, and making him the most useful and intelligent citizen. Effort or means so invested will pay a thousand per cent interest. These efforts will be twice blessed—blessing him that gives and him that takes.

There is no escape through law of man or God from the inevitable:—

The laws of changeless justice bind
Oppressor with oppressed;
And close as sin and suffering joined
We march to fate abreast.

Nearly sixteen millions of hands will aid you in pulling the load upward, or they will pull against you the load downward. We shall constitute one-third and more of the ignorance and crime of the South or one-third its intelligence and progress. We shall contribute one-third to the business and industrial prosperity of the South, or we shall prove a veritable body of death—stagnating, depressing, retarding every effort to advance the body politic.

We shall constitute one-third and more of the ignorance and crime of the South or one-third its intelligence and progress. We shall contribute one-third to the business and industrial prosperity of the South, or we shall prove a veritable body of death—stagnating, depressing, retarding every effort to advance the body politic.

Model Practice 1

Model Practice 2

_____

_____

_____

_____

_____

_____

_____

_____

Model Practice 3

_____

_____

_____

_____

_____

_____

_____

_____

San Juan Hill

by General John J. Pershing

Santiago, Cuba was the center of some of the heaviest fighting of the Spanish-American War. The Spanish fleet had taken refuge from the American fleet in Santiago Harbor. The Spanish army had been concentrated there to protect their fleet. The American army, under the general command of Major General Shafter, invested the city. The following extract describes picturesquely the fighting three days before the Spanish fleet put to sea.

On June 30th, the general order came to move forward, and every man felt that the final test of skill at arms would soon come. The cavalry division of six regiments, camped in its tracks at midnight on El Pozo Hill, awoke next morning to find itself in support of Grimes' Battery, which was to open fire here on the left.

The morning of July 1st was ideally beautiful. The sky was cloudless, the air soft and balmy; peace seemed to reign supreme; great palms towered here and there above the low jungle. It was a picture of a peaceful valley. There was a feeling that we had secretly invaded the Holy Land. The hush seemed to pervade all nature as though she held her bated breath in anticipation of the carnage.

Captain Capron's field guns opened fire upon the southern field at El Caney, and the hill resounded with echoes. Then followed the rattle of the musketry of the attacking invaders. The firing in our front burst forth, and the battle was on.

The artillery duel began and, in company with foreign military attachés and correspondents, we all sat watching the effect of the shots, as men witness any friendly athletic contest, eagerly trying to locate the enemy's smokeless batteries. A force of insurgents near the old Sugar Mill applauded at the explosion of each firing charge, apparently caring for little except the noise.

Now and then, a slug of iron fell among the surrounding bushes or buried itself deep in the ground near us. Finally, a projectile from an unseen Spanish gun disabled a Hotchkiss piece, wounded two cavalrymen, and smashed into the old Sugar Mill in our rear; whereupon the terrorized insurgents fled and were not seen again near the firing line until the battle was over.

When the Tenth Cavalry arrived at the crossing of San Juan River, our observation balloon had become lodged in the treetops above; and the enemy had just begun to make a target of it. A converging fire upon all the works within range opened upon us that was terrible in its effect. Our mounted officers dismounted; and the men stripped off, at the roadside, everything possible and prepared for business.

We were posted, for a time, in the bed of the stream directly under the balloon and stood in the water to our waists awaiting orders to deploy. Standing there under that galling fire of exploding shrapnel and deadly Mauser bullets, the minutes seemed like hours. General Wheeler and a part of his staff stood mounted a few minutes in the middle of the stream. Just as I raised my hand to salute, in moving up the stream to post the leading squadron of my regiment, a piece of bursting shell struck between his horse's feet and covered us both with water.

Pursuant to orders, with myself as guide, the second squadron of the Tenth forced its way through wire fence and almost impenetrable thicket to its position. The regiment was soon deployed as skirmishers in an opening across the river to the right of the road; and, our line being partly visible from the enemy's position, their fire was turned upon us; and we had to lie down in the grass a few minutes for safety. Two officers of the regiment were wounded; here and there were frequent calls for the surgeon; but no order came to move forward. Whatever may have been the intention of the commanding general as to the part to be played by the cavalry division on that day, the officers present were not long in deciding the part their command should play; and the advance began.

White regiments, black regiments, regulars and rough riders, representing the young manhood of the North and South, fought shoulder to shoulder unmindful of race or color, unmindful of whether commanded by an ex-Confederate or not, and mindful only of their common duty as Americans.

Through streams, tall grass, tropical undergrowth; under barbed-wire fences and over wire entanglements; regardless of casualties; up the hill, to the right, this gallant advance was made. As we appeared on the crest, we found the Spaniards retreating only to take up a new position farther on, spitefully firing as they retired and only yielding their ground inch by inch.

Our troopers halted and lay down for a moment to get a breath and, in the face of continued volleys, soon formed for attack on the blockhouses and intrenchments on the second hill. This attack was supported by troops including some of the Tenth who had originally moved to the left toward this second hill and had worked their way in groups—slipping through the tall grass and bushes, crawling when casualties came too often, courageously facing a sleet of bullets, and now hugging the steep southern declivity, ready to spring forward the few remaining yards into the teeth of the enemy. The fire from the Spanish position had doubled in intensity until the popping of their rifles made a continuous roar. There was a moment's lull, and our line moved forward to the charge across the valley separating the two hills. Once begun, it continued dauntless in its steady, dogged, persistent advance until, like a mighty resistless torrent, it dashed triumphant over the crest of the hill and, firing a final volley at the vanishing foe, planted the regimental colors on the enemy's breastworks and the Stars and Stripes over the blockhouse on San Juan Hill to stay.

This was a time for rejoicing. It was glorious.

—From an address given in
Chicago, November 27, 1898.

The sky was cloudless, the air soft and balmy ; peace seemed to reign supreme ; great palms towered here and there above the low jungle. It was a picture of a peaceful valley. There was a feeling that we had secretly invaded the Holy Land.

Model Practice 1

Model Practice 2

Model Practice 3

Sinking of the Titanic (excerpt)

from The Sinking of the Titanic and Great Sea Disasters
edited by Logan Marshall
chapters VIII and IX

THE CALL FOR HELP HEARD

"We have struck an iceberg. Badly damaged. Rush aid."

Seaward and landward, J. G. Phillips, the <u>Titanic</u>'s wireless man, had hurled the appeal for help. By fits and starts—for the wireless was working unevenly and blurringly—Phillips reached out to the world, crying the <u>Titanic</u>'s peril. A word or two, scattered phrases, now and then a connected sentence made up the message that sent a thrill of apprehension for a thousand miles east, west and south of the doomed liner.

The early dispatches from <u>St. John's</u>, <u>Cape Race</u>, and <u>Montreal</u> told graphic tales of the race to reach the <u>Titanic</u>, the wireless appeals for help, the interruption of the calls, then what appeared to be a successful conclusion of the race when the <u>Virginian</u> was reported as having reached the giant liner.

TITANIC SENT OUT NO MORE NEWS

It was at 12.17 A. M., while the <u>Virginian</u> was still plunging eastward, that all communication from the <u>Titanic</u> ceased. The <u>Virginian</u>'s operator, with the <u>Virginian</u>'s captain at his elbow, fed the air with blue flashes in a desperate effort to know what was happening to the crippled liner, but no message came back. The last word from the <u>Titanic</u> was that she was sinking. Then the sparking became fainter. The call was dying to nothing. The <u>Virginian</u>'s operator labored over a blur of signals. It was hopeless. So the <u>Allan</u> ship strove on, fearing that the worst had happened.

It was this ominous silence that so alarmed the other vessels hurrying to the <u>Titanic</u> and that caused so much suspense here.

IN THE DRIFTING LIFE-BOATS

SIXTEEN boats were in the procession, which entered on the terrible hours of rowing, drifting, and suspense. Women wept for lost husbands and sons; sailors sobbed for the ship which had been their pride. Men choked back tears and sought to comfort the widowed. Perhaps, they said, other boats might have put off in another direction. They strove, though none too sure themselves, to convince the women of the certainty that a rescue ship would appear.

In the distance the <u>Titanic</u> looked an enormous length, her great bulk outlined in black against the starry sky, every porthole and saloon blazing with light. It was impossible to think anything could be wrong with such a leviathan, were it not for that ominous tilt downwards in the bows, where the water was now up to the lowest row of port-holes. Presently, about 2 A. M., as near as can be determined, those in the life-boats observed her settling very rapidly with the bows and the bridge completely under water and concluded it was now only a question of minutes before she went. So it proved, She slowly tilted straight on end with the stern vertically upwards; and, as she did, the lights in the cabins and saloons, which until then had not flickered for a moment, died out, came on again for a single flash, and finally went altogether. At the same time the machinery roared down through the vessel with a rattle and a groaning that could be heard for miles, the weirdest sound surely that could be heard in the middle of the ocean, a thousand miles away from land. But this was not yet quite the end.

TITANIC STOOD UPRIGHT

To the amazement of the awed watchers in the life-boats, the doomed vessel remained in that upright position for a time estimated at five minutes; some in the boat say less, but it was certainly some minutes that at least 150 feet of the <u>Titanic</u> towered up above the level of the sea and loomed black against the sky.

SAW LAST OF BIG SHIP

Then with a quiet, slanting dive she disappeared beneath the waters, and the eyes of the helpless spectators had looked for the last time upon the gigantic vessel on which they had set out from Southampton. And there was left to the survivors only the gently heaving sea, the life-boats filled with men and women in every conceivable condition of dress and undress, above the perfect sky of brilliant stars with not a cloud. All tempered with a bitter cold that made each man and woman long to be one of the crew who toiled away with the oars and kept themselves warm thereby-a curious, deadening, bitter cold unlike anything they had felt before.

"ONE LONG MOAN"

And then with all these there fell on the ear the most appalling noise that human being has ever listened to—the cries of hundreds of fellow—beings struggling in the icy cold water, crying for help with a cry that could not be answered.

Third Officer Herbert John Pitman, in charge of one of the boats, described this cry of agony in his testimony before the Senatorial Investigating Committee, under the questioning of Senator Smith:

"I heard no cries of distress until after the ship went down," he said.

"How far away were the cries from your life-boat?"

"Several hundred yards, probably, some of them."

"Describe the screams."

"Don't, sir, please! I'd rather not talk about it."

"I'm sorry to press it, but what was it like? Were the screams spasmodic?"

"It was one long continuous moan."

The witness said the moans and cries continued an hour.

Those in the lifeboats longed to return and pick up some of the poor drowning souls, but they feared this would mean swamping the boats and a further loss of life.

Some of the men tried to sing to keep the women from hearing the cries and rowed hard to get away from the scene of the wreck, but the memory of those sounds will be one of the things the rescued will find it difficult to forget.

The waiting sufferers kept a lookout for lights, and several times it was shouted that steamers' lights were seen, but they turned out to be either a light from another boat or a star low down on the horizon. It was hard to keep up hope.

Women wept for lost husbands and sons; sailors sobbed for the ship which had been their pride. Men choked back tears and sought to comfort the widowed. Perhaps, they said, other boats might have put off in another direction. They strove, though none too sure themselves, to convince the women of the certainty that a rescue ship would appear.

Model Practice 1

_____

_____

_____

_____

_____

_____

_____

_____

_____

_____

_____

_____

_____

Model Practice 2

_____

_____

_____

_____

_____

_____

_____

_____

Model Practice 3

_____

_____

_____

_____

_____

_____

_____

_____

_____

The Sinking of the Lusitania (excerpt)

from The New York Times Current History
A Monthly Magazine
The European War Volume II
June 1915

The German Warning

On Saturday, May 1, the day that the Lusitania left New York on her last voyage, the following advertisement bearing the authentication of the German Embassy at Washington appeared in the chief newspapers of the United States, placed next the advertisement of the Cunard Line:

NOTICE!

TRAVELLERS intending to embark on the Atlantic voyage are reminded that a state of war exists between Germany and her allies and Great Britain and her allies; that the zone of war includes the waters adjacent to the British Isles; that, in accordance with formal notice given by the Imperial German Government vessels flying the flag of Great Britain, or of any of her allies, are liable to destruction in those waters and that travelers sailing in the war zone on ships of Great Britain or her allies do so at their own risk.

IMPERIAL GERMAN EMBASSY

WASHINGTON, D.C., APRIL 22, 1915

Despite this warning, relying on President Wilson's note to Germany of Feb. 10, 1915, which declared that the United States would "hold the Imperial Government of Germany to a strict accountability" for such an act within the submarine zone; relying, also, on the speed of the ship, and hardly conceiving that the threat would be carried out, over two thousand men, women, and children embarked. The total toll of the dead was 1,150, of whom 114 were known to be American citizens.

England Answers Germany (after the sinking of the Lusitania)

by The Associated Press

LONDON, Wednesday, May 12: The German Government states that responsibility for the loss of the Lusitania rests with the British Government, which through their plan of starving the civil population of Germany has forced Germany to resort to retaliatory measures. The reply to this is as follows:

As far back as last December Admiral Von Tirpitz, (the German Marine Minister,) in an interview, foreshadowed a submarine blockade of Great Britain, and a merchant ship and a hospital ship were torpedoed Jan. 30 and Feb. 1, respectively.

The German Government on Feb. 4 declared their intention of instituting a general submarine blockade of Great Britain and Ireland, with the avowed purpose of cutting off supplies for these islands. This blockade was put into effect Feb. 18.

As already stated, merchant vessels had, as a matter of fact, been sunk by a German submarine at the end of January. Before Feb. 4, no vessel carrying food supplies for Germany had been held up by his Majesty's Government except on the ground that there was reason to believe the foodstuffs were intended for use of the armed forces of the enemy or the enemy Government.

His Majesty's Government had, however, informed the State Department on Jan. 29 that they felt bound to place in a prize court the foodstuffs of the steamer Wilhelmina, which was going to a German port, in view of the Government control of foodstuffs in Germany, as being destined for the enemy Government and, therefore, liable to capture.

The decision of his Majesty's Government to carry out the measures laid down by the Order in Council was due to the action of the German Government in insisting on their submarine blockade.

This, added to other infractions of international law by Germany, led to British reprisals, which differ from the German action in that his Majesty's Government scrupulously respect the lives of noncombatants traveling in merchant vessels, and do not even enforce the recognized penalty of confiscation for a breach of the blockade, whereas the German policy is to sink enemy or neutral vessels at sight, with total disregard for the lives of noncombatants and the property of neutrals.

The Germans state that, in spite of their offer to stop their submarine war in case the starvation plan was given up, Great Britain has taken even more stringent blockade measures. The answer to this is as follows:

It was not understood from the reply of the German Government that they were prepared to abandon the principle of sinking British vessels by submarine.

They have refused to abandon the use of mines for offensive purposes on the high seas on any condition. They have committed various other infractions of international law, such as strewing the high seas and trade routes with mines, and British and neutral vessels will continue to run danger from this course, whether Germany abandons her submarine blockade or not.

It should be noted that since the employment of submarines, contrary to international law, the Germans also have been guilty of the use of asphyxiating gas. They have even proceeded to the poisoning of water in South Africa.

The Germans represent British merchant vessels generally as armed with guns and say that they repeatedly ram submarines. The answer to this is as follows:

> It is not to be wondered at that merchant vessels, knowing they are liable to be sunk without warning and without any chance being given those on board to save their lives, should take measures for self-defense.

With regard to the <u>Lusitania</u>: The vessel was not armed on her last voyage and had not been armed during the whole war.

The Germans attempt to justify the sinking of the <u>Lusitania</u> by the fact that she had arms and ammunition on board. The presence of contraband on board a neutral vessel does render her liable to capture, but certainly not to destruction, with the loss of a large portion of her crew and passengers. Every enemy vessel is a fair prize, but there is no legal provision, not to speak of the principles of humanity, which would justify what can only be described as murder because a vessel carries contraband.

The Germans maintain, that after repeated official and unofficial warnings his Majesty's Government were responsible for the loss of life, as they considered themselves able to declare that the boat ran no risk, and thus "light-heartedly assume the responsibility for the human lives on board a steamer which, owing to its armament and cargo, is liable to destruction." The reply thereto is:

> First—His Majesty's Government never declared the boat ran no risk.

> Second—The fact that the Germans issued their warning shows that the crime was premeditated. They had no more right to murder passengers after warning them than before.

> Third—In spite of their attempts to put the blame on Great Britain, it will tax the ingenuity even of the Germans to explain away the fact that it was a German torpedo, fired by a German seaman from a German submarine, that sank the vessel and caused over 1,000 deaths.

In spite of their attempts to put the blame on Great Britain, it will tax the ingenuity even of the Germans to explain away the fact that it was a German torpedo, fired by a German seaman from a German submarine, that sank the vessel and caused over 1,000 deaths.

Model Practice 1

Model Practice 2

Model Practice 3

The Women of China (excerpt)

by Yvette Borup Andrews from <u>Camps and Trails in China</u>
Chapter VIII The Women of China

The schools for native girls at Foochow and Yen-ping interested us greatly, even when we first came to China, but we could not appreciate then, as we did later, the epoch-making step toward civilization of these institutions.

How much the missionaries are able to accomplish from a religious standpoint is a question which we do not wish to discuss, but no one who has ever lived among them can deny that the opening of schools and the diffusing of western knowledge are potent factors in the development of the people. The Chinese were not slow, even in the beginning, to see the advantages of a foreign education for their boys and now, along the coast at least, some are beginning to make sacrifices for their daughters as well. The Woman's College, which was opened recently in Foochow, is one of the finest buildings of the Republic, and when one sees its bright-faced girls dressed in their quaint little pajama-like garments, it is difficult to realize that outside such schools they are still slaves in mind and body to those iron rules of Confucius which have molded the entire structure of Chinese society for over 2400 years.

The position of women in China today, and the rules which govern the household of every orthodox Chinese, are the direct heritage of Confucianism. The following translation by Professor J. Legge from the Narratives of the Confucian School, chapter 26, is illuminating:

Confucius said: "Man is the representative of heaven and is supreme over all things. Woman yields obedience to the instructions of man and helps to carry out his principles. On this account she can determine nothing of herself and is subject to the rule of the three obediences.
"(1) When young she must obey her father and her elder brother;
"(2) When married, she must obey her husband;
"(3) When her husband is dead she must obey her son.
"She may not think of marrying a second time. No instructions or orders must issue from the harem. Women's business is simply the preparation and supplying of drink and food. Beyond the threshold of her apartments, she shall not be known for evil or for good. She may not cross the boundaries of a state to attend a funeral. She may take no steps on her own motive and may come to no conclusion on her own deliberation."

The grounds for divorce as stated by Confucius are:
"(1) Disobedience to her husband's parents;
"(2) Not giving birth to a son;
"(3) Dissolute conduct;
"(4) Jealousy of her husband's attentions (to the other inmates at his harem);
"(5) Talkativeness, and
"(6) Thieving."

A Chinese bride owes implicit obedience to her mother-in-law, and as she is often reared by her husband's family, or else married to him as a mere child, and is under the complete control of his mother for a considerable period of her existence, her life in many instances is one of intolerable misery. There is, generally, little or no consideration for a girl under the best of circumstances until she becomes the mother of a male child; her condition then improves; but she approaches happiness only when she in turn occupies the enviable position of mother-in-law.

It is difficult to imagine a life of greater dreariness and vacuity than that of the average Chinese woman. Owing to her bound feet and resultant helplessness, if she is not obliged to work she rarely stirs from the narrow confinement of her courtyard, and perhaps in her entire life she may not go a mile from the house to which she was brought a bride, except for the periodical visits to her father's home.

It has been aptly said that there are no real homes in China, and it is not surprising that, ignored and despised for centuries, the Chinese woman shows no ability to improve the squalor of her surroundings. She passes her life in a dark, smoke-filled dwelling with broken furniture and a mud floor, together with pigs, chickens, and babies enjoying a limited sphere of action under the tables and chairs or in the tumble-down courtyard without. Her work is actually never done, and a Chinese bride, bright and attractive at twenty, will be old and faded at thirty.

But without doubt the crowning evil which attends woman's condition in China is foot binding, and nothing can be offered in extenuation of this abominable custom. It is said to have originated one thousand years before the Christian era and has persisted until the present day in spite of the efforts directed against it. The Empress Dowager issued edicts strongly advising its discontinuation; the "Natural Foot Society," which was formed about fifteen years ago, has endeavored to educate public opinion; and the missionaries refuse to admit girls so mutilated to their schools; but nevertheless the reform has made little progress beyond the coast cities. "Precedent" and the fear of not obtaining suitable husbands for their daughters are responsible for the continuation of the evil, and it is estimated that there are still about seventy-four millions of girls and women who are crippled in this way.

The feet are bandaged between the ages of five and seven. The toes are bent under the sole of the foot, and, after two or three years, the heel and instep are so forced together that a dollar can be placed in the cleft; gradually, also, the lower limbs shrink away until only the bones remain.

The suffering of the children is intense. We often passed through streets full of laughing boys and tiny girls where others, a few years older, were sitting on the doorsteps or curbstones holding their tortured feet and crying bitterly. In some instances, out-houses are constructed a considerable distance from the family dwelling where the girls must sleep during their first crippled years in order that their moans may not disturb the other members of the family. The child's only relief is to hang her feet over the edge of the bed in order to stop the circulation and induce numbness, or to seek oblivion from opium.

If the custom were a fad which affected only the wealthy classes it would be reprehensible enough, but it curses rich and poor alike. And almost every day we saw heavily laden coolie women steadying themselves by means of a staff, hobbling stiff-kneed along the roads or laboring in the fields.

Although the agitation against foot binding is undoubtedly making itself felt to a certain extent in the coast provinces, in Yün-nan the horrible practice continues unabated. During the year in which we traveled through a large part of the province, wherever there were Chinese, we saw bound feet. And the fact that virtually every girl over eight years old was mutilated in this way is satisfactory evidence that reform ideas have not penetrated to this remote part of the Republic.

There has been much criticism of foreign education because the girls who have had its advantages absorb western ideas so completely that they dislike to return to their homes where the ordinary conditions of a Chinese household exist. Nevertheless, if the women of China are ever to be emancipated it must come through their own education as well as that of the men.

One of the first results of foreign influence is to delay marriage, and in some instances the early betrothal with its attendant miseries. The evil which results from this custom can hardly be overestimated. It happens, not infrequently, that two children are betrothed in infancy, the respective families being in like circumstances at the time. The opportunity, perhaps, is offered to the girl to attend school; and she may even go through college; but an inexorable custom brings her back to her parents' home, forces her to submit to the engagement made in babyhood, and, perhaps, ruins her life through marriage with a man of no higher social status or intelligence than a coolie.

Among the few girls imbued with western civilization, a spirit of revolt is slowly growing; and while it is impossible for them to break down the barriers of ages, yet in many instances they waive aside what would seem an insurmountable precedent and insist upon having some voice in the choosing of their husbands.

While in Yen-ping, we were invited to attend the semi-foreign wedding of a girl who had been brought up in the Woman's School and who was qualified to be a "'Bible Woman'" or native Christian teacher. It was whispered that she had actually met her betrothed on several occasions; but on their wedding day no trace of recognition was visible; and the marriage was performed with all the punctilious Chinese observances compatible with a Christian ceremony.

Precedent required of this little bride, although she might have been radiantly happy at heart, and undoubtedly was, to appear tearful and shrinking; and as she was escorted up the aisle by her bridesmaid, one might have thought she was being led to slaughter. White is not becoming to the Chinese and besides it is a sign of mourning, so she had chosen pink for her wedding gown and had a brilliant pink veil over her carefully oiled hair.

After the ceremony the bride and bridegroom proceeded downstairs to the joyous strain of the wedding march, but with nothing joyous in their demeanor. In fact they appeared like two wooden images at the reception and endured, for over an hour, the stares and loud criticism of the guests. He assumed, during the ordeal, a look of bored indifference, while the little bride sat with her head bowed on her breast, apparently terror stricken. But once, she raised her face, and I saw a merry twinkle in her shining black eyes that made me realize that perhaps it wasn't all quite so frightful as she would have us believe. I often wonder what sort of a life she is leading in her far away Chinese courtyard.

The suffering of the children is intense. We often passed through streets full of laughing boys and tiny girls where others, a few years older, were sitting on the doorsteps or curbstones holding their tortured feet and crying bitterly

Model Practice 1

_____

_____

_____

_____

_____

_____

_____

_____

_____

_____

_____

_____

_____

_____

Model Practice 2

Model Practice 3

To Every Englishman in India

Dear Friend,

I wish that every Englishman will see this appeal and give thoughtful attention to it.

Let me introduce myself to you. In my humble opinion no Indian has co-operated with the British Government more than I have for an unbroken period of twenty-nine years of public life in the face of circumstances that might well have turned any other man into a rebel. I ask you to believe me when I tell you that my co-operation was not based on the fear of the punishments provided by your laws or any other selfish motives. It was free and voluntary co-operation based on the belief that the sum total of the activity of the British Government was for the benefit of India. I put my life in peril four times for the sake of the Empire,—at the time of the Boer war when I was in charge of the Ambulance corps whose work was mentioned in General Buller's dispatches, at the time of the Zulu revolt in Natal when I was in charge of a similar corps, at the time of the commencement of the late war when I raised an Ambulance corps and, as a result of the strenuous training, had a severe attack of pleurisy, and lastly in fulfillment of my promise to Lord Chelmsford at the War Conference in Delhi. I threw myself in such an active recruiting campaign in Kuira District involving long and trying marches that I had an attack of dysentery, which proved almost fatal. I did all this in the full belief that acts such as mine must gain for my country an equal status in the Empire. So late as last December, I pleaded hard for a trustful co-operation; I fully believed that Mr. Lloyd George would redeem his promise to the Mussalmans and that the revelations of the official atrocities in the Punjab would secure full reparation for the Punjabis. But the treachery of Mr. Lloyd George, and its appreciation by you, and the condonation of the Punjab atrocities have completely shattered my faith in the good intentions of the Government and the nation which is supporting it.

But though my faith in your good intentions is gone, I recognize your bravery; and I know that what you will not yield to justice and reason, you will gladly yield to bravery.

See what this Empire means to India:

Exploitation of India's resources for the benefit of Great Britain.

An ever-increasing military expenditure and a civil service the most expensive in the world.

Extravagant working of every department in utter disregard of India's poverty.

Disarmament and consequent emasculation of a whole nation lest an armed nation might imperil the lives of a handful of you in our midst. Traffic in intoxicating liquors and drugs for the purposes of sustaining a top-heavy administration.

Progressively representative legislation in order to suppress an ever-growing agitation seeking to give expression to a nation's agony.

Degrading treatment of Indians residing in your dominions, and you have shown total disregard of our feelings by glorifying the Punjab administration and flouting the Mosulman sentiment.

I know you would not mind if we could fight and wrest the scepter form your hands. You know that we are powerless to do that, for you have ensured our incapacity to fight in open and honorable battle. Bravery on the battlefield is thus impossible for us. Bravery of the soul still remains open to us. I know you will respond to that also. I am engaged in evoking that bravery. Non-co-operation means nothing less than training in self-sacrifice. Why should we co-operate with you when we know that by your administration of this great country we are lifting daily enslaved in an increasing degree? This response of the people to my appeal is not due to my personality. I would like you to dismiss me, and for that matter the Ali Brothers too, from your consideration. My personality will fail to evoke any response to anti-Muslim cry if I were foolish enough to rise it, as the magic name of the Ali Brothers would fail to inspire the Mussalmans with enthusiasm if they were madly to raise in anti-Hindu cry. People flock in their thousands to listen to us because we today represent the voice of a nation groaning under iron heels. The Ali Brothers were your friends as I was and still am. My religion forbids me to bear any ill will towards you. I would not raise my hand against you even if I had the power. I expect to conquer you only by my suffering. The Ali Brothers will certainly draw the sword, if they could, in defense of their religion and their country. But they and I have made common cause with the people of India in their attempt to voice their feelings and to find a remedy for their distress.

You are in search of a remedy to suppress this rising ebullition of national feeling. I venture to suggest to you that the only way to suppress it is to remove the causes. You have yet the power. You can repent of the wrongs done to Indians. You can compel Mr. Lloyd George to redeem his promises. I assure you he has kept many escape doors. You can compel the Viceroy to retire in favor of a better one; you can revise your ideas about Sir Michael O'Dwyer and General Dyer. You can compel the Government to summon a conference of the recognized lenders of the people, duly elected by them and representing all shades of opinion so as to devise means for granting Swaraj in accordance with the wishes of the people of India. But this you cannot do unless you consider every Indian to be in reality your equal and brother. I ask for no patronage; I merely point out to you, as a friend, an honorable solution of a grave problem. The other solution, namely repression, is open to YOU. I prophesy that it will fail. It has begun already. The Government has already imprisoned two brave men of Panipat for holding and expressing their opinions freely. Another is on his trial in Lahore for having expressed similar opinion. One in the Oudh District is already imprisoned. Another awaits judgment. You should know what is going on in your midst. Our propaganda is being carried on in anticipation of repression. I invite you, respectfully, to choose the better way and make common cause with the people of India whose salt you are eating. To seek to thwart their inspirations is disloyalty to the country.

I am, Your faithful friend,
M. K. GANDHI

I know you would not mind if we could fight and wrest the scepter form your hands. You know that we are powerless to do that, for you have ensured our incapacity to fight in open and honorable battle. Bravery on the battlefield is thus impossible for us. Bravery of the soul still remains open to us.

Model Practice 1

_____

_____

_____

_____

_____

_____

_____

_____

_____

_____

_____

_____

_____

_____

Model Practice 2

_____

_____

_____

_____

_____

_____

_____

_____

_____

Model Practice 3

_____

_____

_____

_____

_____

_____

_____

_____

_____

Infamy Speech
by Franklin D. Roosevelt

Mr. Vice President, Mr. Speaker, members of the Senate and the House of Representatives: yesterday, December 7th, 1941—a date which will live in infamy—the United States of America was suddenly and deliberately attacked by naval and air forces of the Empire of Japan.

The United States was at peace with that nation and, at the solicitation of Japan, was still in conversation with its Government and its Emperor looking toward the maintenance of peace in the Pacific. Indeed, one hour after Japanese air squadrons had commenced bombing in the American Island of Oahu, the Japanese Ambassador to the United States and his colleague delivered to our Secretary of State a formal reply to a recent American message. And while this reply stated that it seemed useless to continue the existing diplomatic negotiations, it contained no threat or hint of war or of armed attack.

It will be recorded that the distance of Hawaii from Japan makes it obvious that the attack was deliberately planned many days or even weeks ago. During the intervening time, the Japanese Government has deliberately sought to deceive the United States by false statements and expressions of hope for continued peace.

The attack yesterday on the Hawaiian Islands has caused severe damage to American naval and military forces. I regret to tell you that very many American lives have been lost. In addition, American ships have been reported torpedoed on the high seas between San Francisco and Honolulu.

Yesterday, the Japanese Government also launched an attack against Malaya.

Last night, Japanese forces attacked Hong Kong.

Last night, Japanese forces attacked Guam.

Last night, Japanese forces attacked the Philippine Islands.

Last night, the Japanese attacked Wake Island.

And this morning, the Japanese attacked Midway Island.

Japan has, therefore, undertaken a surprise offensive extending throughout the pacific area. The facts of yesterday and today speak for themselves. The people of the United States have already formed their opinions and well understand the implications to the very life and safety of our nation.

As Commander-in-Chief of the Army and Navy, I have directed that all measures be taken for our defense.

But always will our whole nation remember the character of the onslaught against us. No matter how long it may take us to overcome this premeditated invasion, the American people in their righteous might will win through to absolute victory.

I believe that I interpret the will of the Congress and of the people when I assert that we will not only defend ourselves to the uttermost but will make it very certain that this form of treachery shall never again endanger us.

Hostilities exist. There is no blinking at the fact that our people, our territory, and our interests are in grave danger.

With confidence in our armed forces—with the unbounded determination of our people—we will gain the inevitable triumph—so help us God.

I ask that the Congress declare that since the unprovoked and dastardly attack by Japan on Sunday, December 7th, 1941, a state of war has existed between the United States and the Japanese Empire.

Last night, Japanese forces attacked Hong Kong.

Last night, Japanese forces attacked Guam.

Last night, Japanese forces attacked the Philippine Islands.

Last night, the Japanese attacked Wake Island.

And this morning, the Japanese attacked Midway Island.

Model Practice 1

_____

_____

_____

_____

_____

_____

_____

_____

_____

_____

_____

_____

_____

Model Practice 2

Model Practice 3

The Atomic Bombings of Hiroshima and Nagasaki (excerpt)

by The Manhattan Engineer District
eyewitness account by Father John A. Siemes, professor of modern philosophy at Tokyo's Catholic University
Hiroshima - August 6th, 1945

August 6th began in a bright, clear summer morning. About seven o'clock, there was an air raid alarm which we had heard almost every day, and a few planes appeared over the city. No one paid any attention, and, at about eight o'clock, the all-clear was sounded.

I am sitting in my room at the Novitiate of the Society of Jesus in Nagatsuke; during the past half year, the philosophical and theological section of our Mission had been evacuated to this place from Tokyo. The Novitiate is situated approximately two kilometers from Hiroshima, halfway up the sides of a broad valley which stretches from the town at sea level into this mountainous hinterland, and through which courses a river. From my window, I have a wonderful view down the valley to the edge of the city.

Suddenly, the time is approximately 8:14, the whole valley is filled by a garish light, which resembles the magnesium light used in photography, and I am conscious of a wave of heat. I jump to the window to find out the cause of this remarkable phenomenon, but I see nothing more than that brilliant yellow light. As I make for the door, it doesn't occur to me that the light might have something to do with enemy planes. On the way from the window, I hear a moderately loud explosion which seems to come from a distance; and, at the same time, the windows are broken in with a loud crash. There has been an interval of perhaps ten seconds since the flash of light. I am sprayed by fragments of glass. The entire window frame has been forced into the room. I realize now that a bomb has burst, and I am under the impression that it exploded directly over our house or in the immediate vicinity.

I am bleeding from cuts about the hands and head. I attempt to get out of the door. It has been forced outwards by the air pressure and has become jammed. I force an opening in the door by means of repeated blows with my hands and feet and come to a broad hallway from which open the various rooms. Everything is in a state of confusion. All windows are broken and all the doors are forced inwards. The bookshelves in the hallway have tumbled down. I do not note a second explosion, and the fliers seem to have gone on. Most of my colleagues have been injured by fragments of glass. A few are bleeding, but none has been seriously injured. All of us have been fortunate, since it is now apparent that the wall of my room, opposite the window, has been lacerated by long fragments of glass.

We proceed to the front of the house to see where the bomb has landed. There is no evidence, however, of a bomb crater; but the southeast section of the house is very severely damaged. Not a door nor a window remains. The blast of air had penetrated the entire house from the southeast, but the house still stands. It is constructed in a Japanese style with a wooden framework, but has been greatly strengthened by the labor of our Brother Gropper as is frequently done in Japanese homes. Only along the front of the chapel which adjoins the house, three supports have given way (it has been made in the manner of Japanese temple, entirely out of wood.)

Down in the valley, perhaps one-kilometer toward the city from us, several peasant homes are on fire, and the woods on the opposite side of the valley are aflame. A few of us go over to help control the flames. While we are attempting to put things in order, a storm comes up, and it begins to rain. Over the city, clouds of smoke are rising, and I hear a few slight explosions. I come to the conclusion that an incendiary bomb with an especially strong explosive action has gone off down in the valley. A few of us saw three planes at great altitude over the city at the time of the explosion. I, myself, saw no aircraft whatsoever.

Perhaps, a half-hour after the explosion, a procession of people begins to stream up the valley from the city. The crowd thickens continuously. A few come up the road to our house. We give them first aid and bring them into the chapel, which we have in the meantime cleaned and cleared of wreckage, and put them to rest on the straw mats which constitute the floor of Japanese houses. A few display horrible wounds of the extremities and back. The small quantity of fat, which we possessed during this time of war, was soon used up in the care of the burns. Father Rektor, who, before taking holy orders, had studied medicine, ministers to the injured; but our bandages and drugs are soon gone. We must be content with cleansing the wounds.

More and more of the injured come to us. The least injured drag the more seriously wounded. There are wounded soldiers, and mothers carrying burned children in their arms. From the houses of the farmers in the valley comes word: "Our houses are full of wounded and dying. Can you help, at least by taking the worst cases?" The wounded come from the sections at the edge of the city. They saw the bright light; their houses collapsed and buried the inmates in their rooms. Those that were in the open suffered instantaneous burns, particularly on the lightly clothed or unclothed parts of the body. Numerous fires sprang up, which soon consumed the entire district. We now conclude that the epicenter of the explosion was at the edge of the city near the Jokogawa Station, three kilometers away from us. We are concerned about Father Kopp who, that same morning, went to hold Mass at the Sisters of the Poor who have a home for children at the edge of the city. He had not returned as yet.

Toward noon, our large chapel and library are filled with the seriously injured. The procession of refugees from the city continues. Finally, about one o'clock, Father Kopp returns, together with the Sisters. Their house, and the entire district where they live, has burned to the ground. Father Kopp is bleeding about the head and neck, and he has a large burn on the right palm. He was standing in front of the nunnery ready to go home. All of a sudden, he became aware of the light, felt the wave of heat; and a large blister formed on his hand. The windows were torn out by the blast. He thought that the bomb had fallen in his immediate vicinity. The nunnery, also a wooden structure made by our Brother Gropper, still remained; but soon it is noted that the house is as good as lost because the fire, which had begun at many points in the neighborhood, sweeps closer and closer; and water is not available. There is still time to rescue certain things from the house and to bury them in an open spot. Then the house is swept by flame, and they fight their way back to us along the shore of the river and through the burning streets. Soon comes news that the entire city has been destroyed by the explosion and that it is on fire.

None of us in those days heard a single outburst against the Americans on the part of the Japanese; nor was there any evidence of a vengeful spirit. The Japanese suffered this terrible blow as part of the fortunes of war—something to be borne without complaint. During this, war, I have noted relatively little hatred toward the allies on the part of the people themselves, although the press has taken occasion to stir up such feelings. After the victories at the beginning of the war, the enemy was rather looked down upon, but when allied offensive gathered momentum and especially after the advent of the majestic B-29's, the technical skill of America became an object of wonder and admiration.

We have discussed among ourselves the ethics of the use of the bomb. Some consider it in the same category as poison gas and were against its use on a civil population. Others were of the view that in total war, as carried on in Japan, there was no difference between civilians and soldiers, and that the bomb itself was an effective force tending to end the bloodshed, warning Japan to surrender and thus to avoid total destruction. It seems logical to me that he who supports total war in principle cannot complain of war against civilians. The crux of the matter is whether total war in its present form is justifiable, even when it serves a just purpose. Does it not have material and spiritual evil as its consequences which far exceed whatever good that might result? When will our moralists give us a clear answer to this question?

I jump to the window to find out the cause of this remarkable phenomenon, but I see nothing more than that brilliant yellow light. As I make for the door, it doesn't occur to me that the light might have something to do with enemy planes.

Model Practice 1

Model Practice 2

Model Practice 3

Inaugural Address of President John F. Kennedy

January 20, 1961

Vice President Johnson, Mr. Speaker, Mr. Chief Justice, President Eisenhower, Vice President Nixon, President Truman, reverend clergy, fellow citizens, we observe today not a victory of party, but a celebration of freedom—symbolizing an end, as well as a beginning—signifying renewal, as well as change. For I have sworn before you and Almighty God the same solemn oath our forebears prescribed nearly a century and three-quarters ago.

The world is very different now. For man holds in his mortal hands the power to abolish all forms of human poverty and all forms of human life. And yet the same revolutionary beliefs for which our forebears fought are still at issue around the globe—the belief that the rights of man come not from the generosity of the state, but from the hand of God.

We dare not forget today that we are the heirs of that first revolution. Let the word go forth from this time and place, to friend and foe alike, that the torch has been passed to a new generation of Americans—born in this century, tempered by war, disciplined by a hard and bitter peace, proud of our ancient heritage—and unwilling to witness or permit the slow undoing of those human rights to which this Nation has always been committed, and to which we are committed today at home and around the world.

Let every nation know, whether it wishes us well or ill, that we shall pay any price, bear any burden, meet any hardship, support any friend, oppose any foe, in order to assure the survival and the success of liberty.

This much we pledge—and more.

To those old allies whose cultural and spiritual origins we share, we pledge the loyalty of faithful friends. United, there is little we cannot do in a host of cooperative ventures. Divided, there is little we can do—for we dare not meet a powerful challenge at odds and split asunder.

To those new States whom we welcome to the ranks of the free, we pledge our word that one form of colonial control shall not have passed away merely to be replaced by a far more iron tyranny. We shall not always expect to find them supporting our view. But we shall always hope to find them strongly supporting their own freedom—and to remember that, in the past, those who foolishly sought power by riding the back of the tiger ended up inside.

To those peoples in the huts and villages across the globe struggling to break the bonds of mass misery, we pledge our best efforts to help them help themselves, for whatever period is required—not because the Communists may be doing it, not because we seek their votes, but because it is right. If a free society cannot help the many who are poor, it cannot save the few who are rich.

To our sister republics south of our border, we offer a special pledge—to convert our good words into good deeds—in a new alliance for progress—to assist free men and free governments in casting off the chains of poverty. But this peaceful revolution of hope cannot become the prey of hostile powers. Let all our neighbors know that we shall join with them to oppose aggression or subversion anywhere in the Americas. And let every other power know that this Hemisphere intends to remain the master of its own house.

To that world assembly of sovereign states, the United Nations, our last best hope in an age where the instruments of war have far outpaced the instruments of peace, we renew our pledge of support—to prevent it from becoming merely a forum for invective—to strengthen its shield of the new and the weak—and to enlarge the area in which its writ may run.

Finally, to those nations who would make themselves our adversary, we offer not a pledge but a request: that both sides begin anew the quest for peace, before the dark powers of destruction unleashed by science engulf all humanity in planned or accidental self-destruction.

We dare not tempt them with weakness. For only when our arms are sufficient beyond doubt can we be certain beyond doubt that they will never be employed.

But neither can two great and powerful groups of nations take comfort from our present course—both sides overburdened by the cost of modern weapons, both rightly alarmed by the steady spread of the deadly atom, yet both racing to alter that uncertain balance of terror that stays the hand of mankind's final war.

So let us begin anew—remembering on both sides that civility is not a sign of weakness, and sincerity is always subject to proof. Let us never negotiate out of fear. But let us never fear to negotiate.

Let both sides explore what problems unite us instead of belaboring those problems which divide us.

Let both sides, for the first time, formulate serious and precise proposals for the inspection and control of arms,—and bring the absolute power to destroy other nations under the absolute control of all nations.

Let both sides seek to invoke the wonders of science instead of its terrors. Together let us explore the stars, conquer the deserts, eradicate disease, tap the ocean depths, and encourage the arts and commerce.

Let both sides unite to heed in all corners of the earth the command of Isaiah—to "undo the heavy burdens ... and to let the oppressed go free."

And if a beachhead of cooperation may push back the jungle of suspicion, let both sides join in creating a new endeavor, not a new balance of power, but a new world of law, where the strong are just and the weak secure and the peace preserved.

All this will not be finished in the first 100 days. Nor will it be finished in the first 1,000 days, nor in the life of this Administration, nor even perhaps in our lifetime on this planet. But let us begin. In your hands, my fellow citizens, more than in mine, will rest the final success or failure of our course. Since this country was founded, each generation of Americans has been summoned to give testimony to its national loyalty. The graves of young Americans who answered the call to service surround the globe.

Now the trumpet summons us again—not as a call to bear arms, though arms we need; not as a call to battle, though embattled we are—but a call to bear the burden of a long twilight struggle, year in and year out, "rejoicing in hope, patient in tribulation"—a struggle against the common enemies of man: tyranny, poverty, disease, and war itself.

Can we forge against these enemies a grand and global alliance, North and South, East and West, that can assure a more fruitful life for all mankind? Will you join in that historic effort?

In the long history of the world, only a few generations have been granted the role of defending freedom in its hour of maximum danger. I do not shank from this responsibility—I welcome it. I do not believe that any of us would exchange places with any other people or any other generation. The energy, the faith, the devotion which we bring to this endeavor will light our country and all who serve it—and the glow from that fire can truly light the world.

And so, my fellow Americans, ask not what your country can do for you—ask what you can do for your country.

My fellow citizens of the world ask not what America will do for you, but what together we can do for the freedom of man.

Finally, whether you are citizens of America or citizens of the world, ask of us the same high standards of strength and sacrifice which we ask of you. With a good conscience our only sure reward, with history the final judge of our deeds, let us go forth to lead the land we love, asking His blessing and His help, but knowing that here on earth God's work must truly be our own.

And so, my fellow Americans: ask not what your country can do for you — ask what you can do for your country.

My fellow citizens of the world: ask not what America will do for you, but what together we can do for the freedom of man.

Model Practice 1

_____

_____

_____

_____

_____

_____

_____

_____

_____

_____

_____

_____

_____

Model Practice 2

Model Practice 3

President Nixon's Resignation Speech (excerpt)
August 8, 1974

Good evening. This is the 37th time I have spoken to you from this office in which so many decisions have been made that shape the history of this nation. Each time I have done so to discuss with you some matters that I believe affected the national interest. And all the decisions I have made in my public life, I have always tried to do what was best for the nation.

Throughout the long and difficult period of Watergate, I have felt it was my duty to persevere-to make every possible effort to complete the term of office to which you elected me.

In the past few days, however, it has become evident to me that I no longer have a strong enough political base in the Congress to justify continuing that effort. As long as there was such a base, I felt strongly that it was necessary to see the constitutional process through to its conclusion; that to do otherwise would be unfaithful to the spirit of that deliberately difficult process, and a dangerously destabilizing precedent for the future.

But with the disappearance of that base, I now believe that the constitutional purpose has been served. And there is no longer a need for the process to be prolonged.

I would have preferred to carry through to the finish whatever the personal agony it would have involved, and my family unanimously urged me to do so. But the interests of the nation must always come before any personal considerations. From the discussions I have had with Congressional and other leaders I have concluded that because of the Watergate matter I might not have the support of the Congress that I would consider necessary to back the very difficult decisions and carry out the duties of this office in the way the interests of the nation will require.

I have never been a quitter.

To leave office before my term is completed is opposed to every instinct in my body. But as President I must put the interests of America first.

America needs a full-time President and a full-time Congress, particularly at this time with problems we face at home and abroad.

To continue to fight through the months ahead for my personal vindication would almost totally absorb the time and attention of both the President and the Congress, in a period when our entire focus should be on the great issues of peace abroad and prosperity without inflation at home.

Therefore, I shall resign the Presidency effective at noon tomorrow.

Vice President Ford will be sworn in as President at that hour in this office. As I recall the high hopes for America with which we began this second term, I feel a great sadness that I will not be here in this office working on your behalf to achieve those hopes in the next two and a half years.

But in turning over direction of the Government to Vice President Ford I know, as I told the nation when I nominated him for that office 10 months ago, that the leadership of America will be in good hands.

In passing this office to the Vice President, I also do so with the profound sense of the weight of responsibility that will fall on his shoulders tomorrow, and therefore of the understanding, the patience, the cooperation he will need from all Americans.

As he assumes that responsibility he will deserve the help and the support of all of us. As we look to the future, the first essential is to begin healing the wounds of this nation. To put the bitterness and divisions of the recent past behind us and to rediscover those shared ideals that lie at the heart of our strength and unity as a great and as a free people.

By taking this action, I hope that I will have hastened the start of that process of healing which is so desperately needed in America.

I regret deeply any injuries that may have been done in the course of the events that led to this decision. I would say only that if some of my judgments were wrong—and some were wrong—they were made in what I believed at the time to be the best interests of the nation.

To those who have stood with me during these past difficult months, to my family, my friends, the many others whose joined in supporting my cause because they believed it was right, I will be eternally grateful for your support.

And to those who have not felt able to give me your support, let me say I leave with no bitterness toward those who have opposed me, because all of us in the final analysis have been concerned with the good of the country however our judgments might differ.

So let us all now join together in firming that common commitment and in helping our new President succeed for the benefit of all Americans.

I shall leave this office with regret at not completing my term but with gratitude for the privilege of serving as your President for the past five and a half years. These years have been a momentous time in the history of our nation and the world. They have been a time of achievement in which we can all be proud—achievements that represent the shared efforts of the administration, the Congress and the people. But the challenges ahead are equally great.

And they, too, will require the support and the efforts of a Congress and the people, working in cooperation with the new Administration.

We have ended America's longest war. But in the work of securing a lasting peace in the world, the goals ahead are even more far-reaching and more difficult. We must complete a structure of peace, so that it will be said of this generation—our generation of Americans—by the people of all nations, not only that we ended one war but that we prevented future wars.

I regret deeply any injuries that may have been done in the course of the events that led to this decision. I would say only that if some of my judgments were wrong — and some were wrong — they were made in what I believed at the time to be the best interests of the nation.

Model Practice 1

_____

_____

_____

_____

_____

_____

_____

_____

_____

_____

_____

_____

_____

Model Practice 2

Model Practice 3

CHAPTER III

Poetry
from
Modern History

Note: Poetry models should be written in the same manner that the author wrote them, meaning indentions and punctuation.

Each line of poetry should begin on a new line. If the student cannot fit the line of the model on one line, he should continue the sentence on the next line with an indention at the beginning.

For an example, see the cursive model to "O Captain, My Captain!" on page III-36.

The poetry selections do not lend themselves as easily to narration. Narration pages are not included for these selections.

All Things Obey God

by Anonymous from <u>The Infant's Delight</u>

"He saith to the snow, Be thou on the earth."
God's works are very great, but still
  His hands do not appear:
Though heaven and earth obey His will,
  His voice we cannot hear.

And yet we know that it is He
  Who moves and governs all,
Who stills the raging of the sea,
  And makes the showers to fall.

Alike in mercy He bestows
  The sunshine and the rain;
That which is best for us He knows,
  And we must not com-plain,

Whether He makes His winds to blow,
  And gives His tempests birth,
Or sends His frost, or bids the snow—
  "Be thou upon the earth."

Whether He makes His winds to blow,
And gives His tempests birth,
Or sends His frost, or bids the snow —
"Be thou upon the earth."

Model Practice 1

Model Practice 2

Model Practice 3

America the Beautiful

by Katharine Lee Bates

O beautiful for spacious skies,
For amber waves of grain,
For purple mountain majesties
Above the fruited plain!
America! America!
God shed His grace on thee,
And crown thy good with brotherhood
From sea to shining sea!

O beautiful for pilgrim feet,
Whose stern, impassioned stress
A thoroughfare for freedom beat
Across the wilderness!
America! America!
God mend thine every flaw,
Confirm thy soul in self-control,
Thy liberty in law!

O beautiful for heroes proved
In liberating strife,
Who more than self their country loved,
And mercy more than life!
America! America!
May God thy gold refine
Till all success be nobleness
And every gain divine!

O beautiful for patriot dream
That sees, beyond the years,
Thine alabaster cities gleam
Undimmed by human tears!
America! America!
God shed His grace on thee,
And crown thy good with brotherhood
From sea to shining sea!

O beautiful for spacious skies,
For amber waves of grain,
For purple mountain majesties
Above the fruited plain!
America! America!
God shed His grace on thee,
And crown thy good with brotherhood
From sea to shining sea!

Model Practice 1

Model Practice 2

Model Practice 3

The Battle Hymn of the Republic
by Julia Ward Howe

Mine eyes have seen the glory of the coming of the Lord:
He is trampling out the vintage where the grapes of wrath are stored;
He hath loosed the fateful lightning of His terrible swift sword:
      His truth is marching on.

I have seen Him in the watch fires of a hundred circling camps;
They have builded Him an altar in the evening dews and damps;
I can read His righteous sentence by the dim and flaring lamps;
      His day is marching on.

I have read a fiery gospel, writ in burnished rows of steel:
"As ye deal with my contemners, so with you my grace shall deal;
Let the Hero born of woman crush the serpent with his heel,
      Since God is marching on."

He has sounded forth the trumpet that shall never call retreat;
He is sifting out the hearts of men before His judgment seat:
Oh! be swift, my soul, to answer Him! be jubilant, my feet!
      Our God is marching on.

In the beauty of the lilies Christ was born across the sea,
With a glory in His bosom that transfigures you and me:
As he died to make men holy, let us die to make men free,
      While God is marching on.

Mine eyes have seen the glory of the coming of the
　　　　Lord:
He is trampling out the vintage where the grapes of
　　　　wrath are stored;
He hath loosed the fateful lightning of His terrible
　　　　swift sword:
　　　　　　His truth is marching on.

Model Practice 1

_____

_____

_____

_____

_____

_____

_____

_____

_____

_____

_____

_____

_____

_____

Model Practice 2

Model Practice 3

Bed in Summer

by Robert Louis Stevenson

In winter I get up at night
And dress by yellow candle-light.
In summer quite the other way,
I have to go to bed by day.

I have to go to bed and see
The birds still hopping on the tree,
Or hear the grown-up people's feet
Still going past me in the street.

And does it not seem hard to you,
When all the sky is clear and blue,
And I should like so much to play,
To have to go to bed by day?

In winter I get up at night
And dress by yellow candle-light.
In summer quite the other way,
I have to go to bed by day.

I have to go to bed and see
The birds still hopping on the tree,
Or hear the grown-up people's feet
Still going past me in the street.

Model Practice 1

Model Practice 2

Model Practice 3

The Charge of the Light Brigade

by Alfred Lord Tennyson

Half a league, half a league,
    Half a league onward,
All in the valley of Death
    Rode the six hundred.
"Forward, the Light Brigade!
Charge for the guns!" he said:
Into the valley of Death
    Rode the six hundred.

"Forward, the Light Brigade!"
Was there a man dismay'd?
Not tho' the soldier knew
    Some one had blunder'd:
Their's not to make reply,
Their's not to reason why,
Their's but to do and die:
Into the valley of Death
    Rode the six hundred.

Cannon to right of them,
Cannon to left of them,
Cannon in front of them
    Volley'd and thunder'd;
Storm'd at with shot and shell,
Boldly they rode and well,
Into the jaws of Death,
Into the mouth of Hell
    Rode the six hundred.

Flash'd all their sabres bare,
Flash'd as they turn'd in air
Sabring the gunners there,
Charging an army, while
    All the world wonder'd:
Plunged in the battery-smoke
Right thro' the line they broke;
Cossack and Russian
Reel'd from the sabre-stroke
Shatter'd and sunder'd.
Then they rode back, but not
    Not the six hundred.

Cannon to right of them,
Cannon to left of them,
Cannon behind them
    Volley'd and thunder'd;
Storm'd at with shot and shell,
While horse and hero fell,
They that had fought so well
Came thro' the jaws of Death,
Back from the mouth of Hell,
All that was left of them,
    Left of six hundred.

When can their glory fade?
O the wild charge they made!
    All the world wonder'd.
Honor the charge they made!
Honor the Light Brigade,
    Noble six hundred!

Half a league, half a league,
  Half a league onward,
All in the valley of Death
  Rode the six hundred.
"Forward, the Light Brigade!
Charge for the guns!" he said:
Into the valley of Death
  Rode the six hundred.

Model Practice 1

Model Practice 2

Model Practice 3

Father William

by Lewis Caroll

"You are old, Father William," the young man said,
  "And your hair has become very white;
And yet you incessantly stand on your head—
  Do you think, at your age, it is right?"

"In my youth," Father William replied to his son,
  "I feared it might injure the brain;
But now that I'm perfectly sure I have none,
  Why, I do it again and again."

"You are old," said the youth, "as I mentioned before,
  And have grown most uncommonly fat;
Yet you turned a back-somersault in at the door—
  Pray, what is the reason of that?"

"In my youth," said the sage, as he shook his gray locks,
  "I kept all my limbs very supple
By the use of this ointment—one shilling the box—
  Allow me to sell you a couple."

"You are old," said the youth, "and your jaws are too weak
  For anything tougher than suet;
Yet you finished the goose, with the bones and the beak:
  Pray, how did you manage to do it?"

"In my youth," said his father, "I took to the law,
  And argued each case with my wife;
And the muscular strength which it gave to my jaw
  Has lasted the rest of my life."

"You are old," said the youth; "one would hardly suppose
  That your eye was as steady as ever;
Yet you balanced an eel on the end of your nose—
  What made you so awfully clever?"

"I have answered three questions, and that is enough,"
  Said his father, "don't give yourself airs!
Do you think I can listen all day to such stuff?
  Be off, or I'll kick you down-stairs!"

"You are old, Father William," the young man said,
"And your hair has become very white;
And yet you incessantly stand on your head —
Do you think, at your age, it is right?"

"In my youth," Father William replied to his son,
"I feared it might injure the brain;
But now that I'm perfectly sure I have none,
Why, I do it again and again."

Model Practice 1

_____

_____

_____

_____

_____

_____

_____

_____

_____

_____

_____

_____

_____

_____

Model Practice 2

Model Practice 3

If
by Rudyard Kipling

If you can keep your head when all about you
  Are losing theirs and blaming it on you,
If you can trust yourself when all men doubt you,
  But make allowance for their doubting too;
If you can wait and not be tired by waiting,
  Or being lied about, don't deal in lies,
Or being hated don't give way to hating,
  And yet don't look too good, nor talk too wise:

If you can dream—and not make dreams your master;
  If you can think—and not make thoughts your aim,
If you can meet with Triumph and Disaster
  And treat those two imposters just the same;
If you can bear to hear the truth you've spoken
  Twisted by knaves to make a trap for fools,
Or watch the things you gave your life to, broken,
  And stoop and build 'em up with worn-out tools:

If you can make one heap of all your winnings
  And risk it on one turn of pitch-and-toss,
And lose, and start again at your beginnings
  And never breathe a word about your loss;
If you can force your heart and nerve and sinew
  To serve your turn long after they are gone,
And so hold on when there is nothing in you
  Except the Will which says to them; "Hold on!"

If you can talk with crowds and keep your virtue,
  Or walk with Kings—nor lose the common touch,
If neither foes nor loving friends can hurt you,
  If all men count with you, but none too much;
If you can fill the unforgiving minute
  With sixty seconds' worth of distance run,
Yours is the Earth and everything that's in it,
  And—which is more—you'll be a Man, my son!

If you can talk with crowds and keep your virtue,
   Or walk with Kings — nor lose the common touch,
If neither foes nor loving friends can hurt you,
   If all men count with you, but none too much;
If you can fill the unforgiving minute
   With sixty seconds' worth of distance run,
Yours is the Earth and everything that's in it,
   And — which is more — you'll be a Man, my
      son!

Model Practice 1

Model Practice 2

Model Practice 3

John Littlejohn

By Charles Mackay

John Littlejohn was stanch and strong,
Upright and downright, scorning wrong;
He gave good weight and paid his way,
He thought for himself and said his say.
Whenever a rascal strove to pass,
Instead of silver, a coin of brass,
He took his hammer and said with a frown,
"The coin is spurious—nail it down!"

John Littlejohn was firm and true,
You could not cheat him in "two and two";
When foolish arguers, might and main,
Darkened and twisted the clear and plain,
He saw through the mazes of their speech
The simple truth beyond their reach;
And crushing their logic said with a frown,
"Your coin is spurious—nail it down!"

John Littlejohn maintained the right,
Through storm and shine, in the world's despite;
When fools or quacks desired his vote,
Dosed him with arguments learned by rote,
Or by coaxing, threats, or promise tried
To gain his support to the wrong side,
"Nay, nay," said John with an angry frown,
"Your coin is spurious—nail it down!"

When told that kings had a right divine,
And that the people were herds of swine,
That nobles alone were fit to rule,
That the poor were unimproved by school,
That ceaseless toil was the proper fate
Of all but the wealthy and the great,
John shook his head and said with a frown,
"The coin is spurious—nail it down!"

When told that events might justify
A false and crooked policy,
That a decent hope of future good
Might excuse departure from rectitude,
That a lie, if white, was a small offense,
To be forgiven by men of sense,
"Nay, nay," said John with a sigh and frown,
"The coin is spurious—nail it down!"

Whenever the world our eyes would blind
With false pretenses of such a kind,
With humbug, cant, or bigotry,
Or a specious, sham philosophy,
With wrong dressed up in the guise of right,
And darkness passing itself for light,
Let us imitate John and exclaim with a frown,
"The coin is spurious—nail it down!"

Whenever the world our eyes would blind
With false pretenses of such a kind,
With humbug, cant, or bigotry,
Or a specious, sham philosophy,
With wrong dressed up in the guise of right,
And darkness passing itself for light,
Let us imitate John and exclaim with a frown,
"The coin is spurious —nail it down!"

Model Practice 1

Model Practice 2

Model Practice 3

The Lost Thought
by Emily Dickinson

I felt a clearing in my mind
   As if my brain had split;
I tried to match it, seam by seam,
   But could not make them fit.

The thought behind I strove to join
   Unto the thought before,
But sequence raveled out of reach
   Like balls upon a floor.

I felt a clearing in my mind
  As if my brain had split;
I tried to match it, seam by seam,
  But could not make them fit.

The thought behind I strove to join
  Unto the thought before,
But sequence raveled out of reach
  Like balls upon a floor.

Model Practice 1

Model Practice 2

Model Practice 3

The New Duckling

by Ella Wheeler Wilcox

"I want to be new," said the duckling.
  "O ho!" said the wise old owl,
While the guinea-hen cluttered off chuckling
  To tell all the rest of the fowl.

"I should like a more elegant figure,"
  That child of a duck went on.
"I should like to grow bigger and bigger,
  Until I could swallow a swan.

"I won't be the bond slave of habit,
  I won't have these webs on my toes.
I want to run round like a rabbit,
  A rabbit as red as a rose.

"I don't want to waddle like mother,
  Or quack like my silly old dad.
I want to be utterly other,
  And frightfully modern and mad."

"Do you know," said the turkey, "you're quacking!
  There's a fox creeping up thro' the rye;
And, if you're not utterly lacking,
  You'll make for that duck-pond. Good-bye!"

But the duckling was perky as perky.
  "Take care of your stuffing!" he called.
(This was horribly rude to a turkey!)
  "But you aren't a real turkey," he bawled.

"You're an Early Victorian Sparrow!
  A fox is more fun than a sheep!
I shall show that my mind is not narrow
  And give him my feathers—to keep."

Now the curious end of this fable,
  So far as the rest ascertained,
Though they searched from the barn to the stable,
  Was that only his feathers remained.

So he wasn't the bond slave of habit,
  And he didn't have webs on his toes;
And perhaps he runs round like a rabbit,
  A rabbit as red as a rose.

But the duckling was perky as perky.
  "Take care of your stuffing!" he called.
(This was horribly rude to a turkey!)
  "But you aren't a real turkey," he bawled.

"You're an Early Victorian Sparrow!
  A fox is more fun than a sheep!
I shall show that my mind is not narrow
  And give him my feathers—to keep."

Model Practice 1

Model Practice 2

_____

_____

_____

_____

_____

_____

_____

_____

Model Practice 3

_____

_____

_____

_____

_____

_____

_____

_____

O Captain, My Captain!

by Walt Whitman

O Captain, my Captain! our fearful trip is done;
The ship has weathered every rack, the prize we sought is won;
The port is near, the bells I hear, the people all exulting,
While follow eyes the steady keel, the vessel grim and daring;
  But, O heart, heart, heart!
  O the bleeding drops of red,
  Where on the deck my Captain lies,
   fallen cold and dead.

O Captain, my Captain! rise up and hear the bells;
Rise up—for you the flag is flung—for you the bugle trills,
For you bouquets and ribboned wreaths—for you the shores a-crowding,
For you they call, the swaying mass, their eager faces turning;
  Here, Captain, dear father!
  This arm beneath your head!
  It is some dream that on the deck,
   you've fallen cold and dead.

My Captain does not answer, his lips are pale and still;
My Captain does not feel my arm, he has no pulse nor will;
The ship is anchored safe and sound, its voyage is closed and done;
From fearful trip the victor ship comes in with object won;
  Exult, O shores, and ring,
  O bells! but I with mournful tread
  Walk the deck where my Captain lies,
   fallen cold and dead.

O Captain, my Captain! our fearful trip is done;
The ship has weathered every rack, the prize we
sought is won;
The port is near, the bells I hear, the people all
exulting,
While follow eyes the steady keel, the vessel grim and
daring;

Model Practice 1

Model Practice 2

Model Practice 3

The Pessimist
by Ben F. King

Nothing to do but work,
    Nothing to eat but food,
Nothing to wear but clothes
    To keep one from going nude.

Nothing to breathe but air,
    Quick as a flash 'tis gone;
Nowhere to fall but off,
    Nowhere to stand but on.

Nothing to comb but hair,
    Nowhere to sleep but in bed,
Nothing to weep but tears,
    Nothing to bury but dead.

Nothing to sing but songs,
    Ah, well, alas! alack!
Nowhere to go but out,
    Nowhere to come but back.

Nothing to see but sights,
    Nothing to quench but thirst,
Nothing to have but what we've got,
    Thus thro' life we are cursed.

Nothing to strike but a gait;
    Everything moves that goes.
Nothing at all but common sense
    Can ever withstand these woes.

Nothing to do but work,
  Nothing to eat but food,
Nothing to wear but clothes
  To keep one from going nude.

Nothing to breathe but air,
  Quick as a flash 'tis gone;
Nowhere to fall but off,
  Nowhere to stand but on.

Model Practice 1

Model Practice 2

_____

_____

_____

_____

_____

_____

_____

_____

_____

Model Practice 3

_____

_____

_____

_____

_____

_____

_____

_____

_____

CHAPTER
IV

Tales from
Various
Cultures

The Bonfire in the Sea

from A <u>Story Hour Reader</u>

Long, long ago, in Australia, it is said, fish could travel as easily on land as they could swim in water.

It happened, so the story goes, that the whole fish tribe had been playing tag along a sandy beach near the sea. At last they became tired of the game. Fin-fin, the leader of the fish, said, "Let us coast down the great, black rock."

Now beyond the level shore where the fish had been playing tag, there were cliffs and rocks. Some of the rocks rose straight out of the water; others sloped toward the sandy beach.

High above the rest towered the great, black rock. The fish climbed to the top. Then, one after another, they followed the leader, each gliding head foremost down the rock. It was fine sport!

Then the fish formed a circle and danced, while Fin-fin slid down the rock alone.

Again and again he climbed to the top and slid down, as swiftly as an arrow glides from the bow. Finally he turned a somersault at the foot of the rock and then called to the fish to stop dancing.

"It is time to cook dinner," said Fin-fin.

"There is a good place for a camp under the trees on the tall cliff yonder."

The fish climbed to the top of the cliff overhanging the sea. They gathered wood and heaped it high at the edge of the cliff.

When all was ready for the bonfire, Fin-fin rubbed two sticks briskly together. Soon a spark fell upon the wood, and instantly the flames leaped upward. Then the fish put some roots in front of the fire to roast.

While the roots were cooking, the fish stretched themselves under the trees. They had almost fallen asleep, when suddenly great drops of rain came splashing down.

A dark cloud, which they had not noticed, had covered the sun.

The rain fell hard and fast and soon put out the fire.

Now, you know, this was very serious, for people in those days had no matches, and it was difficult to light a fire. Then, too, an icy wind began to blow, and the fish were soon shivering in the cold.

"We shall freeze to death unless we can build a fire again," cried Fin-fin.

He tried to kindle a flame by rubbing two sticks together. He could not produce even one spark.

"It is of no use," said Fin-fin. "The wood is too wet. We shall have to wait for the sun to shine again."

A tiny fish came forward and bowed before Fin-fin, saying, "Ask my father, Flying-fish, to light the fire. He is skilled in magic, and he can do more than most fish."

So Fin-fin asked Flying-fish to light the fire once more.

Flying-fish knelt before the smoldering ashes and fanned briskly with his fins.

A tiny thread of smoke curled upward, and a feeble red glow could be seen in the ashes.

When the tribe of fish saw this, they crowded close around Flying-fish, keeping their backs toward the cold wind. He told them to go to the other side, because he wanted to fan the fire.

By and by the spark grew into a flame, and the bonfire burned brightly.

"Bring more wood," cried Flying-fish.

The fish gathered wood and piled it upon the fire. The red flames roared, sputtered, and crackled.

"We shall soon be warm now," said Fin-fin.

Then the fish crowded around the fire, closer and closer. Suddenly a blast of wind swept across the cliff from the direction of the land and blew the fire toward the fish.

They sprang back, forgetting that they were on the edge of the cliff. And down, down, down went the whole fish tribe to the bottom of the sea.

The water felt warm, for the strong wind had driven the fire down below, too.

There, indeed, was the bonfire at the bottom of the sea, burning as brightly as ever.

More wonderful still, the fire never went out, as fires do on land. The water at the bottom of the sea has been warm ever since that day.

That is why, on frosty days, the fish disappear from the surface of the water. They dive to the bottom of the sea, where they can keep warm and comfortable, around the magic bonfire.

AT LEAST, SO SOME PEOPLE SAY.

Written Summation

"We shall freeze to death unless we can build a fire again," cried Fin-fin.

He tried to kindle a flame by rubbing two sticks together. He could not produce even one spark.

"It is of no use," said Fin-fin. "The wood is too wet. We shall have to wait for the sun to shine again."

Model Practice 1

_____

_____

_____

_____

_____

_____

_____

_____

_____

_____

_____

_____

_____

Model Practice 2

Model Practice 3

The Capture of Father Time

by L. Frank Baum

Jim was the son of a cowboy and lived on the broad plains of Arizona. His father had trained him to lasso a bronco or a young bull with perfect accuracy, and had Jim possessed the strength to back up his skill, he would have been as good a cowboy as any in all Arizona.

When he was twelve years old, he made his first visit to the east where Uncle Charles, his father's brother, lived. Of course Jim took his lasso with him, for he was proud of his skill in casting it, and wanted to show his cousins what a cowboy could do.

At first the city boys and girls were much interested in watching Jim lasso posts and fence pickets, but they soon tired of it, and even Jim decided it was not the right sort of sport for cities.

But one day the butcher asked Jim to ride one of his horses into the country, to a pasture that had been engaged, and Jim eagerly consented. He had been longing for a horseback ride, and to make it seem like old times, he took his lasso with him.

He rode through the streets demurely enough; but on reaching the open country roads his spirits broke forth into wild jubilation; and, urging the butcher's horse to full gallop, he dashed away in true cowboy fashion.

Then he wanted still more liberty, and letting down the bars that led into a big field he began riding over the meadow and throwing his lasso at imaginary cattle, while he yelled and whooped to his heart's content.

Suddenly, on making a long cast with his lasso, the loop caught upon something and rested about three feet from the ground, while the rope drew taut and nearly pulled Jim from his horse.

This was unexpected. More than that, it was wonderful; for the field seemed bare of even a stump. Jim's eyes grew big with amazement, but he knew he had caught something when a voice cried out:

"Here, let go! Let go, I say! Can't you see what you've done?"

No, Jim couldn't see, nor did he intend to let go until he found out what was holding the loop of the lasso. So he resorted to an old trick his father had taught him and, putting the butcher's horse to a run, began riding in a circle around the spot where his lasso had caught.

As he thus drew nearer and nearer his quarry, he saw the rope coil up, yet it looked to be coiling over nothing but air. One end of the lasso was made fast to a ring in the saddle, and when the rope was almost wound up and the horse began to pull away and snort with fear, Jim dismounted. Holding the reins of the bridle in one hand, he followed the rope, and an instant later saw an old man caught fast in the coils of the lasso.

His head was bald and uncovered, but long white whiskers grew down to his waist. About his body was thrown a loose robe of fine white linen. In one hand he bore a great scythe, and beneath the other arm he carried an hourglass.

While Jim gazed wonderingly upon him, this venerable old man spoke in an angry voice:

"Now, then—get that rope off as fast as you can! You've brought everything on earth to a standstill by your foolishness! Well—what are you staring at? Don't you know who I am?"

"No," said Jim, stupidly.

"Well, I'm Time—Father Time! Now, make haste and set me free—if you want the world to run properly."

"How did I happen to catch you?" asked Jim, without making a move to release his captive.

"I don't know. I've never been caught before," growled Father Time. "But I suppose it was because you were foolishly throwing your lasso at nothing."

"I didn't see you," said Jim.

"Of course you didn't. I'm invisible to the eyes of human beings unless they get within three feet of me, and I take care to keep more than that distance away from them. That's why I was crossing this field, where I supposed no one would be. And I should have been perfectly safe had it not been for your beastly lasso. Now, then," he added, crossly, "are you going to get that rope off?"

"Why should I?" asked Jim.

"Because everything in the world stopped moving the moment you caught me. I don't suppose you want to make an end of all business and pleasure, and war and love, and misery and ambition and everything else, do you? Not a watch has ticked since you tied me up here like a mummy!"

Jim laughed. It really was funny to see the old man wound round and round with coils of rope from his knees up to his chin.

"It'll do you good to rest," said the boy. "From all I've heard you lead a rather busy life."

"Indeed I do," replied Father Time with a sigh. "I'm due in Kamchatka this very minute. And to think one small boy is upsetting all my regular habits!"

"Too bad!" said Jim with a grin. "But since the world has stopped anyhow, it won't matter if it takes a little longer recess. As soon as I let you go Time will fly again. Where are your wings?"

"I haven't any," answered the old man. "That is a story cooked up by someone who never saw me. As a matter of fact, I move rather slowly."

"I see, you take your time," remarked the boy. "What do you use that scythe for?"

"To mow down the people," said the ancient one. "Every time I swing my scythe, someone dies."

"Then I ought to win a life-saving medal by keeping you tied up," said Jim. "Some folks will live this much longer."

"But they won't know it," said Father Time with a sad smile; "so it will do them no good. You may as well untie me at once."

"No," said Jim with a determined air. "I may never capture you again; so I'll hold you for awhile and see how the world wags without you."

Then he swung the old man, bound as he was, upon the back of the butcher's horse, and, getting into the saddle himself, started back toward town, one hand holding his prisoner and the other guiding the reins.

When he reached the road his eye fell on a strange tableau. A horse and buggy stood in the middle of the road, the horse in the act of trotting, with his head held high and two legs in the air, but perfectly motionless. In the buggy a man and a woman were seated; but had they been turned into stone they could not have been more still and stiff.

"There's no Time for them!" sighed the old man. "Won't you let me go now?"

"Not yet," replied the boy.

He rode on until he reached the city, where all the people stood in exactly the same positions they were in when Jim lassoed Father Time. Stopping in front of a big dry goods store, the boy hitched his horse and went in. The clerks were measuring out goods and showing patterns to the rows of customers in front of them, but everyone seemed suddenly to have become a statue.

There was something very unpleasant in this scene, and a cold shiver began to run up and down Jim's back; so he hurried out again.

On the edge of the sidewalk sat a poor, crippled beggar, holding out his hat, and beside him stood a prosperous-looking gentleman who was about to drop a penny into the beggar's hat. Jim knew this gentleman to be very rich but rather stingy, so he ventured to run his hand into the man's pocket and take out his purse in which was a $20 gold piece. This glittering coin he put in the gentleman's fingers instead of the penny and then restored the purse to the rich man's pocket.

"That donation will surprise him when he comes to life," thought the boy.

He mounted the horse again and rode up the street. As he passed the shop of his friend, the butcher, he noticed several pieces of meat hanging outside.

"I'm afraid that meat'll spoil," he remarked.

"It takes Time to spoil meat," answered the old man.

This struck Jim as being queer, but true.

"It seems Time meddles with everything," said he.

"Yes; you've made a prisoner of the most important personage in the world," groaned the old man; "and you haven't enough sense to let him go again."

Jim did not reply, and soon they came to his uncle's house, where he again dismounted. The street was filled with teams and people, but all were motionless. His two little cousins were just coming out the gate on their way to school, with their books and slates underneath their arms; so Jim had to jump over the fence to avoid knocking them down.

In the front room sat his aunt, reading her Bible. She was just turning a page when Time stopped. In the dining room was his uncle, finishing his luncheon. His mouth was open and his fork poised just before it, while his eyes were fixed upon the newspaper folded beside him. Jim helped himself to his uncle's pie, and while he ate it, he walked out to his prisoner.

"There's one thing I don't understand," said he.

"What's that?" asked Father Time.

"Why is it that I'm able to move around while everyone else is—is—froze up?"

"That is because I'm your prisoner," answered the other. "You can do anything you wish with Time now. But unless you are careful you'll do something you will be sorry for."

Jim threw the crust of his pie at a bird that was suspended in the air, where it had been flying when Time stopped.

"Anyway," he laughed, "I'm living longer than anyone else. No one will ever be able to catch up with me again."

"Each life has its allotted span," said the old man. "When you have lived your proper time my scythe will mow you down."

"I forgot your scythe," said Jim, thoughtfully.

Then a spirit of mischief came into the boy's head, for he happened to think that the present opportunity to have fun would never occur again. He tied Father Time to his uncle's hitching post, that he might not escape, and then crossed the road to the corner grocery.

The grocer had scolded Jim that very morning for stepping into a basket of turnips by accident. So the boy went to the back end of the grocery and turned on the faucet of the molasses barrel.

"That'll make a nice mess when Time starts the molasses running all over the floor," said Jim, with a laugh.

A little further down the street was a barbershop, and sitting in the barber's chair Jim saw the man that all the boys declared was the "meanest man in town." He certainly did not like the boys and the boys knew it. The barber was in the act of shampooing this person when Time was captured. Jim ran to the drug store, and, getting a bottle of mucilage, he returned and poured it over the ruffled hair of the unpopular citizen.

"That'll probably surprise him when he wakes up," thought Jim.

Near by was the schoolhouse. Jim entered it and found that only a few of the pupils were assembled. But the teacher sat at his desk, stern and frowning as usual.

Taking a piece of chalk, Jim marked upon the blackboard in big letters the following words:

"Every scholar is requested to yell the minute he enters the room. He will also please throw his books at the teacher's head. Signed, Prof. Sharpe."

"That ought to raise a nice rumpus," murmured the mischief-maker, as he walked away.

On the corner stood Policeman Mulligan, talking with old Miss Scrapple, the worst gossip in town, who always delighted in saying something disagreeable about her neighbors. Jim thought this opportunity was too good to lose. So he took off the policeman's cap and brass-buttoned coat and put them on Miss Scrapple, while the lady's feathered and ribboned hat he placed jauntily upon the policeman's head.

The effect was so comical that the boy laughed aloud, and as a good many people were standing near the corner, Jim decided that Miss Scrapple and Officer Mulligan would create a sensation when Time started upon his travels.

Then the young cowboy remembered his prisoner, and, walking back to the hitching post, he came within three feet of it and saw Father Time still standing patiently within the toils of the lasso. He looked angry and annoyed, however, and growled out:

"Well, when do you intend to release me?"

"I've been thinking about that ugly scythe of yours," said Jim.

"What about it?" asked Father Time.

"Perhaps if I let you go, you'll swing it at me the first thing, to be revenged," replied the boy.

Father Time gave him a severe look, but said:

"I've known boys for thousands of years, and of course I know they're mischievous and reckless. But I like boys, because they grow up to be men and people my world. Now, if a man had caught me by accident, as you did, I could have scared him into letting me go instantly; but boys are harder to scare. I don't know as I blame you. I was a boy myself, long ago, when the world was new. But surely you've had enough fun with me by this time, and now I hope you'll show the respect that is due to old age. Let me go, and in return I will promise to forget all about my capture. The incident won't do much harm, anyway, for no one will ever know that Time has halted the last three hours or so."

"All right," said Jim, cheerfully, "since you've promised not to mow me down, I'll let you go." But he had a notion some people in the town would suspect Time had stopped when they returned to life.

He carefully unwound the rope from the old man, who, when he was free, at once shouldered his scythe, rearranged his white robe and nodded farewell.

The next moment he had disappeared, and with a rustle and rumble and roar of activity the world came to life again and jogged along as it always had before.

Jim wound up his lasso, mounted the butcher's horse, and rode slowly down the street.

Loud screams came from the corner, where a great crowd of people quickly assembled. From his seat on the horse Jim saw Miss Scrapple, attired in the policeman's uniform, angrily shaking her fists in Mulligan's face, while the officer was furiously stamping upon the lady's hat, which he had torn from his own head amidst the jeers of the crowd.

As he rode past the schoolhouse he heard a tremendous chorus of yells and knew Prof. Sharpe was having a hard time to quell the riot caused by the sign on the blackboard.

Through the window of the barber shop, he saw the "mean man" frantically belaboring the barber with a hair brush, while his hair stood up stiff as bayonets in all directions. And the grocer ran out of his door and yelled "Fire!" while his shoes left a track of molasses wherever he stepped.

Jim's heart was filled with joy. He was fairly reveling in the excitement he had caused when someone caught his leg and pulled him from the horse.

"What're ye doin' hear, ye rascal?" cried the butcher, angrily. "Didn't ye promise to put that beast inter Plympton's pasture? An' now I find ye ridin' the poor nag around like a gentleman o' leisure!"

"That's a fact," said Jim with surprise; "I clean forgot about the horse!"

* * * * *

This story should teach us the supreme importance of Time and the folly of trying to stop it. For should you succeed, as Jim did, in bringing Time to a standstill, the world would soon become a dreary place and life decidedly unpleasant.

Written Summation

"Then I ought to win a life-saving medal by keeping you tied up," said Jim. "Some folks will live this much longer."

"But they won't know it," said Father Time with a sad smile; "so it will do them no good. You may as well untie me at once."

Model Practice 1

Model Practice 2

Model Practice 3

The Half-Chick

by Andrew Lang

Once upon a time there was a handsome black Spanish hen who had a large brood of chickens. They were all fine, plump little birds, except the youngest, who was quite unlike his brothers and sisters. Indeed, he was such a strange, queer-looking creature, that when he first chipped his shell his mother could scarcely believe her eyes; he was so different from the twelve other fluffy, downy, soft little chicks who nestled under her wings. This one looked just as if he had been cut in two. He had only one leg and one wing and one eye, and he had half a head and half a beak. His mother shook her head sadly as she looked at him and said:

"My youngest born is only a half-chick. He can never grow up a tall handsome cock like his brothers. They will go out into the world and rule over poultry yards of their own, but this poor little fellow will always have to stay at home with his mother." And she called him Medio Pollito, which is Spanish for half-chick.

Now though Medio Pollito was such an odd, helpless-looking little thing, his mother soon found that he was not at all willing to remain under her wing and protection. Indeed, in character he was as unlike his brothers and sisters as he was in appearance. They were good, obedient chickens, and when the old hen chicked after them, they chirped and ran back to her side. But Medio Pollito had a roving spirit in spite of his one leg, and when his mother called to him to return to the coop, he pretended that he could not hear because he had only one ear.

When she took the whole family out for a walk in the fields, Medio Pollito would hop away by himself and hide among the Indian corn. Many an anxious minute his brothers and sisters had looking for him, while his mother ran to and fro cackling in fear and dismay.

As he grew older he became more self-willed and disobedient, and his manner to his mother was often very rude, and his temper to the other chickens very disagreeable.

One day he had been out for a longer expedition than usual in the fields. On his return he strutted up to his mother with the peculiar little hop and kick which was his way of walking, and cocking his one eye at her in a very bold way he said:

"Mother, I am tired of this life in a dull farmyard, with nothing but a dreary maize field to look at. I'm off to Madrid to see the King."

"To Madrid, Medio Pollito!" exclaimed his mother. "Why, you silly chick, it would be a long journey for a grown-up cock, and a poor little thing like you would be tired out before you had gone half the distance. No, no, stay at home with your mother, and some day, when you are bigger, we will go on a little journey together."

But Medio Pollito had made up his mind, and he would not listen to his mother's advice, nor to the prayers and entreaties of his brothers and sisters.

"What is the use of our all crowding each other up in this poky little place?" he said. "When I have a fine courtyard of my own at the King's palace, I shall perhaps ask some of you to come and pay me a short visit," and, scarcely waiting to say good-bye to his family, away he stumped down the high road that led to Madrid.

"Be sure that you are kind and civil to everyone you meet," called his mother, running after him; but he was in such a hurry to be off, that he did not wait to answer her or even to look back.

A little later in the day, as he was taking a short cut through a field, he passed a stream. Now the stream was all choked up, and overgrown with weeds and water-plants, so that its waters could not flow freely.

"Oh! Medio Pollito," it cried, as the half-chick hopped along its banks, "do come and help me by clearing away these weeds."

"Help you, indeed!" exclaimed Medio Pollito, tossing his head, and shaking the few feathers in his tail. "Do you think I have nothing to do but to waste my time on such trifles? Help yourself, and don't trouble busy travelers. I am off to Madrid to see the King," and hoppity-kick, hoppity-kick, away stumped Medio Pollito.

A little later he came to a fire that had been left by some gypsies in a wood. It was burning very low, and would soon be out.

"Oh! Medio Pollito," cried the fire in a weak, wavering voice as the half-chick approached, "in a few minutes I shall go quite out, unless you put some sticks and dry leaves upon me. Do help me, or I shall die!"

"Help you, indeed!" answered Medio Pollito. "I have other things to do. Gather sticks for yourself and don't trouble me. I am off to Madrid to see the King," and hoppity-kick, hoppity-kick, away stumped Medio Pollito.

The next morning, as he was getting near Madrid, he passed a large chestnut tree, in whose branches the wind was caught and entangled. "Oh! Medio Pollito," called the wind, "do hop up here, and help me to get free of these branches. I cannot come away, and it is so uncomfortable."

"It is your own fault for going there," answered Medio Pollito. "I can't waste all my morning stopping here to help you. Just shake yourself off, and don't hinder me, for I am off to Madrid to see the King." And hoppity-kick, hoppity-kick, away stumped Medio Pollito in great glee, for the towers and roofs of Madrid were now in sight. When he entered the town, he saw before him a great splendid house with soldiers standing before the gates. This he knew must be the King's palace, and he determined to hop up to the front gate and wait there until the King came out. But as he was hopping past one of the back windows the King's cook saw him:

"Here is the very thing I want," he exclaimed, "for the King has just sent a message to say that he must have chicken broth for his dinner." And opening the window, he stretched out his arm, caught Medio Pollito, and popped him into the broth-pot that was standing near the fire. Oh! How wet and clammy the water felt as it went over Medio Pollito's head, making his feathers cling to his side.

"Water, water!" he cried in his despair, "do have pity upon me and do not wet me like this."

"Ah! Medio Pollito," replied the water, "you would not help me when I was a little stream away on the fields, and now you must be punished."

Then the fire began to burn and scald Medio Pollito, and he danced and hopped from one side of the pot to the other, trying to get away from the heat and crying out in pain.

"Fire, fire! Do not scorch me like this; you can't think how it hurts."

"Ah! Medio Pollito," answered the fire, "you would not help me when I was dying away in the wood. You are being punished."

At last, just when the pain was so great that Medio Pollito thought he must die, the cook lifted up the lid of the pot to see if the broth was ready for the King's dinner.

"Look here!" he cried in horror, "this chicken is quite useless. It is burnt to a cinder. I can't send it up to the royal table;" and opening the window he threw Medio Pollito out into the street. But the wind caught him up and whirled him through the air so quickly that Medio Pollito could scarcely breathe, and his heart beat against his side till he thought it would break.

"Oh, wind!" at last he gasped out, "if you hurry me along like this you will kill me. Do let me rest a moment, or—" but he was so breathless that he could not finish his sentence.

"Ah! Medio Pollito," replied the wind, "when I was caught in the branches of the chestnut tree you would not help me; now you are punished." And he swirled Medio Pollito over the roofs of the houses till they reached the highest church in the town, and there he left him fastened to the top of the steeple.

And there stands Medio Pollito to this day. And if you go to Madrid and walk through the streets till you come to the highest church, you will see Medio Pollito perched on his one leg on the steeple, with his one wing drooping at his side, and gazing sadly out of his one eye over the town.

Spanish Tradition.

Written Summation

"Help you, indeed!" exclaimed Medio Pollito, tossing his head, and shaking the few feathers in his tail. "Do you think I have nothing to do but to waste my time on such trifles? Help yourself, and don't trouble busy travelers. I am off to Madrid to see the King," and hoppity-kick, hoppity-kick, away stumped Medio Pollito.

Model Practice 1 (adapted from the original)

Model Practice 2

Model Practice 3

The Lion and the Gnat

by Sara Cone Bryant

Far away in Central Africa, that vast land where dense forests and wild beasts abound, the shades of night were once more descending, warning all creatures that it was time to seek repose.

All day long the sun had been like a great burning eye, but now, after painting the western sky with crimson and scarlet and gold, he had disappeared into his fleecy bed; the various creatures of the forest had sought their holes and resting-places; the last sound had rumbled its rumble, the last bee had mumbled his mumble, and the last bear had grumbled his grumble; even the grasshoppers that had been chirruping, chirruping, through all the long hours without a pause, at length had ceased their shrill music, tucked up their long legs, and given themselves to slumber.

There on a nodding grass-blade, a tiny Gnat had made a swinging couch, and he too had folded his wings, closed his tiny eyes, and was fast asleep. Darker, darker, darker became the night until the darkness could almost be felt. Over all was a solemn stillness as though some powerful finger had been raised; some potent voice had whispered, "Hush!"

Just when all was perfectly still, there came suddenly from the far away depths of the forest, like the roll of thunder, a mighty ROAR-R-R-R!

In a moment all the beasts and birds were wide-awake, and the poor little Gnat was nearly frightened out of his little senses, and his little heart went pit-a-pat. He rubbed his little eyes with his feelers and then peered all around trying to penetrate the deep gloom as he whispered in terror: "What—was—that?"

What do you think it was? Yes, a LION! A great, big lion who, while most other denizens of the forest slept, was out hunting for prey. He came rushing and crashing through the thick undergrowth of the forest, swirling his long tail and opening wide his great jaws, and as he rushed he RO-AR-R-R-ED!

Presently he reached the spot where the little Gnat hung panting at the tip of the waving grass-blade. Now the little Gnat was not afraid of lions, so when he saw it was only a lion, he cried out-

"Hi, stop, stop! What are you making that horrible noise about?"

The Lion stopped short, then backed slowly, and regarded the Gnat with scorn.

"Why, you tiny, little, mean, insignificant creature you; how dare you speak to me?" he raged.

"How dare I speak to you?" repeated the Gnat quietly. "By the virtue of right, which is always greater than might. Why don't you keep to your own part of the forest? What right have you to be here, disturbing folks at this time of night?"

By a mighty effort the Lion restrained his anger-he knew that to obtain mastery over others one must be master over oneself.

"What right?" he repeated in dignified tones. "Because I'm King of the Forest. That's why. I can do no wrong, for all the other creatures of the forest are afraid of me. I DO what I please, I SAY what I please, I EAT whom I please, I GO where I please-simply because I'm King of the Forest."

"But who told you you were King?" demanded the Gnat. "Just answer me that!"

"Who told ME?" roared the Lion. "Why, everyone acknowledges it; didn't I tell you that everyone is afraid of me?"

"Indeed!" cried the Gnat disdainfully. "Pray don't say all, for I'm not afraid of you. And further, I deny your right to be King."

This was too much for the Lion. He now worked himself into a perfect fury.

"You-you-YOU deny my right as King?"

"I do, and, what is more, you shall never be King until you have fought and conquered me."

The Lion laughed a great lion laugh, and a lion laugh cannot be laughed at like a cat laugh, as everyone ought to know.

"Fight! Did you say fight?" he asked. "Who ever heard of a lion fighting a gnat? Here, out of my way, you atom of nothing! I'll blow you to the other end of the world."

But though the Lion puffed his cheeks until they were like great bellows, and then blew with all his might, he could not disturb the little Gnat's hold on the swaying grass-blade.

"You'll blow all your whiskers away if you are not careful," he said with a laugh, "but you won't move me. And if you dare leave this spot without fighting me, I'll tell all the beasts of the forest that you are afraid of me, and they'll make me King."

"Ho, ho!" roared the Lion. "Very well, since you will fight, let it be so."

"You agree to the conditions, then? The one who conquers shall be King?"

"Oh, certainly," laughed the Lion, for he expected an easy victory. "Are you ready?"

"Quite ready."

"Then—GO!" roared the Lion.

And with that he sprang forward with open jaws, thinking he could easily swallow a million gnats. But just as the great jaws were about to close upon the blade of grass whereto the Gnat clung, what should happen but that the Gnat suddenly spread his wings and nimbly flew—where do you think?—right into one of the Lion's nostrils! And there he began to sting, sting, sting. The Lion wondered, and thundered, and blundered—but the Gnat went on stinging. He foamed, and he moaned, and he groaned—still the Gnat went on stinging. He rubbed his head on the ground in agony; he swirled his tail in furious passion; he roared, he spluttered, he sniffed, he snuffed—and still the Gnat went on stinging.

"O my poor nose, my nose, my nose!" the Lion began to moan. "Come down, come DOWN, come DOWN! My nose, my NOSE, my NOSE!! You're King of the Forest, you're King, you're King—only come down. My nose, my NOSE, my NOSE!"

So at last the Gnat flew out from the Lion's nostril and went back to his waving grass-blade, while the Lion slunk away into the depths of the forest with his tail between his legs—beaten, and by a tiny Gnat!

"What a fine fellow am I, to be sure!" exclaimed the Gnat, as he proudly plumed his wings. "I've beaten a lion—a lion! Dear me, I ought to have been King long ago, I'm so clever, so big, so strong—oh!"

The Gnat's frightened cry was caused by finding himself entangled in some silky sort of threads. While gloating over his victory, the wind had risen, and his grass-blade had swayed violently to and fro unnoticed by him. A stronger gust than usual had bent the blade downward close to the ground, and then something caught it and held it fast and with it the victorious Gnat. Oh, the desperate struggles he made to get free! Alas! he became more entangled than ever. You can guess what it was—a spider's web, hung out from the overhanging branch of a tree. Then—flipperty-flopperty, flipperty-flopperty, flop, flip, flop—down his stairs came cunning Father Spider and quickly gobbled up the little Gnat for his supper, and that was the end of him.

A strong Lion—and what overcame him? A Gnat!

A clever Gnat—and what overcame him? A Spider's web! He who had beaten the strong lion had been overcome by the subtle snare of a spider's thread.

Written Summation

"Why, you tiny, little, mean, insignificant creature you; how dare you speak to me?" he raged.

"How dare I speak to you?" repeated the Gnat quietly. "By the virtue of right, which is always greater than might. Why don't you keep to your own part of the forest? What right have you to be here, disturbing folks at this time of night?"

Model Practice 1

Model Practice 2

_____

_____

_____

_____

_____

_____

_____

_____

_____

_____

Model Practice 3

_____

_____

_____

_____

_____

_____

_____

_____

_____

_____

Persevere and Prosper
adapted by A. R. Montalba

"He that seeketh shall find, and to him that knocketh, it shall be opened," says an old Arab proverb.

"I will try that," said a youth one day. To carry out his intention, he journeyed to Baghdad, where he presented himself before the Vizier.

"Lord," said he, "for many years I have lived a quiet and solitary life, the monotony of which wearies me. I have never permitted myself earnestly to will anything. But as my teacher daily repeated to me, 'He that seeketh shall find, and to him that knocketh shall be opened,' so have I now come to the resolution with might and heart to will, and the resolution of my will is nothing less than to have the Caliph's daughter for my wife."

The Vizier thought the poor man was mad and told him to call again some other time.

Perseveringly, he daily returned and never felt disconcerted at the same often-repeated answer. One day, the Caliph called on the Vizier, as the youth was repeating his statement.

Full of astonishment the Caliph listened to the strange demand, and being in no humor for having the poor youth's head taken off, but on the contrary, being rather inclined for pleasantry, his Mightiness condescendingly said: "For the great, the wise, or the brave, to request a Princess for wife, is a moderate demand; but what are your claims? To be the possessor of my daughter you must distinguish yourself by one of these attributes, or else by some great undertaking. Ages ago a carbuncle of inestimable value was lost in the Tigris; he who finds it shall have the hand of my daughter."

The youth, satisfied with the promise of the Caliph, went to the shores of the Tigris. With a small vessel, he went every morning to the river, scooping out the water and throwing it on the land; and after having for hours thus employed himself, he knelt down and prayed. The fish became at last uneasy at his perseverance; and being fearful that, in the course of time, he might exhaust the waters, they assembled in great council.

"What is the purpose of this man?" demanded the monarch of the fish.

"The possession of the carbuncle that lies buried in the bottom of the Tigris," was the reply.

"I advise you, then," said the aged monarch, "to give it up to him; for, if he has the steady will and has positively resolved to find it, he will work until he has drained the last drop of water from the Tigris rather than deviate a hair's breadth from his purpose."

The fish, out of fear, threw the carbuncle into the vessel of the youth; and the latter, as a reward, received the daughter of the Caliph for his wife.

"He who earnestly wills, can do much!"

Written Summation

"He that seeketh shall find, and to him that knocketh, it shall be opened," says an old Arab proverb.

"I'll try that," said a youth one day. To carry out his intention he journeyed to Baghdad, where he presented himself before the Vizier.

Model Practice 1 (adapted from the original)

Model Practice 2

Model Practice 3

The Star Wife

from <u>Childhood's Favorites and Fairy Stories</u>
edited by Hamilton Wright Mabie, Edward Everett Hale, and William Byron Forbush

In the days when the buffalo raced and thundered over the earth and the stars danced and sang in the sky, a brave young hunter lived on the bank of Battle River. He was fond of the red flowers and the blue sky; and when the rest of the Indians went out to hunt in waistcloths of skin, he put on his fringed leggings all heavy with blue beads and painted red rings and stripes on his face till he was as gay as the earth and the sky himself. High-feather was his name, and he always wore a red swan's feather on his head.

One day, when High-feather was out with his bow and arrows, he came on a little beaten trail that he had never seen before, and he followed it—but he found that it went round and round and brought him back to where he had started. It came from nowhere, and it went to nowhere.

"What sort of animal has made this?" he said. And he lay down in the middle of the ring to think, looking up into the blue sky.

While he lay thinking, he saw a little speck up above him in the sky, and thought it was an eagle. But the speck grew bigger and sank down and down, till he saw it was a great basket coming down out of the sky. He jumped up and ran back to a little hollow and lay down to hide in a patch of tall red flowers. Then he peeped out and saw the basket come down to the earth and rest on the grass in the middle of the ring. Twelve beautiful maidens were leaning over the edge of the basket. They were not Indian maidens, for their faces were pink and white, and their long hair was bright red-brown like a fox's fur, and their clothes were sky-blue and floating light as cobwebs.

The maidens jumped out of the basket and began to dance round and round the ring-trail, one behind the other, drumming with their fingers on little drums of eagle-skin, and singing such beautiful songs as High-feather had never heard.

Then High-feather jumped up and ran towards the ring, crying out, "Let me dance and sing with you!"

The maidens were frightened and ran to the basket and jumped in, and the basket flew up into the sky and grew smaller till at last he could not see it at all.

The young man went home to his wigwam, and his mother roasted buffalo meat for his dinner; but he could not eat, and he could not think of anything but the twelve beautiful maidens. His mother begged him to tell her what the matter was, and at last he told her and said he would never be happy till he brought one of the maidens home to be his wife.

"Those must be the Star-people," said his mother, who was a great magician—the prairie was full of magic in those days, before the white man came and the buffalo went. "You had better take an Indian girl for your wife. Don't think any more of the Star-maidens, or you will have much trouble."

"I care little how much trouble I have, so long as I get a Star-maiden for my wife," he said; "and I am going to get one, if I have to wait till the world ends."

"If you must, you must," said his mother.

So next morning she sewed a bit of gopher's fur on to his feather; and he ate a good breakfast of buffalo meat and tramped away over the prairie to the dancing ring. As soon as he came into the ring, he turned into a gopher; but there were no gophers' holes there for him to hide in, so he had to lie in the grass and wait.

Presently he saw a speck up in the sky, and the speck grew larger and larger till it became a basket, and the basket came down and down till it rested on the earth in the middle of the ring.

The eldest maiden put her head over the edge and looked all around, north and east and south and west.

"There is no man here," she said. So they all jumped out to have their dance. But before they came to the beaten ring, the youngest maiden spied the gopher and called out to her sisters to look at it.

"Away! Away!" cried the eldest maiden. "No gopher would dare to come on our dancing ground. It is a conjuror in disguise!"

So she took her youngest sister by the arm and pulled her away to the basket. They all jumped in, and the basket went sailing up into the sky before High-feather could get out of his gopher skin or say a word.

The young man went home very miserable. But when his mother heard what had happened she said: "It is a hard thing you want to do; but if you must, you must. Tonight I will make some fresh magic, and you can try again tomorrow."

Next morning High-feather asked for his breakfast; but his mother said, "You must not have any buffalo meat, or it will spoil the magic. You must not eat anything but the wild strawberries you find on the prairie as you go."

Then she sewed a little bit of a mouse's whisker on to his red feather; and he tramped away across the prairie, picking wild strawberries and eating them as he went, till he came to the dancing ring. As soon as he was inside the ring, he turned into a little mouse and made friends with the family of mice that lived in a hole under the grass. The mother mouse promised to help him all she could.

They had not waited long when the basket came, dropping down out of the sky. The eldest sister put her head over the edge and looked all around, north and west and south and east and down on the ground.

"There is no man here," she said, "and I do not see any gopher. But you must be very careful."

So they all got out of the basket, and began to dance round the ring, drumming and singing as they went. But when they came near the mouse's nest the eldest sister held up her hand, and they stopped dancing and held their breath. Then she tapped on the ground and listened.

"It does not sound so hollow as it did," she said. "The mice have a visitor."

And she tapped again and called out, "Come and show yourselves, you little traitors, or we will dig you up!"

But the mother mouse had made another door to her nest, just outside the ring, working very fast with all her toes. And while the maidens were looking for her inside the ring, she came out at the other door with all her children and scampered away across the prairie.

The maidens turned round and ran after them; all but the youngest sister, who did not want any one to be killed; and High-feather came out of the hole and turned himself into what he was and caught her by the arm.

"Come home and marry me," he said, "and dance with the Indian maidens. And I will hunt for you, and my mother will cook for you, and you will be much happier than up in the sky."

Her sisters came, rushing round her, and begged her to go back home to the sky with them; but she looked into the young man's eyes and said she would go with him wherever he went. So the other maidens went weeping and wailing up into the sky, and High-feather took his Star-wife home to his tent on the bank of the Battle River.

High-feather's mother was glad to see them both; but she whispered in his ear: "You must never let her out of your sight if you want to keep her; you must take her with you everywhere you go."

And he did so. He took her with him every time he went hunting, and he made her a bow and arrows, but she would never use them. She would pick wild strawberries and gooseberries and raspberries as they went along, but she would never kill anything; and she would never eat anything that any one else had killed. She only ate berries and crushed corn.

One day, while the young man's wife was embroidering feather stars on a dancing-cloth, and his mother was gossiping in a tent at the end of the village, a little yellow bird flew in and perched on High-feather's shoulder and whispered in his ear:

"There is a great flock of wild red swans just over on Loon Lake. If you come quickly and quietly you can catch them before they fly away; but do not tell your wife, for red swans cannot bear the sight of a woman, and they can tell if one comes within a mile of them."

High-feather had never seen or heard of a red swan before. All the red feathers he wore he had had to paint. He looked at his wife, and as she was sewing busily and looking down at her star embroidering, he thought he could slip away and get back before she knew he had gone. But as soon as he was out of sight the little yellow bird flew in and perched on her shoulder and sang her such a beautiful song about her sisters in the sky that she forgot everything else. So she slipped out and ran like the wind and got to the dancing ring just as her sisters came down in their basket. Then they all gathered round her and begged her to go home with them.

But she only said, "High-feather is a brave man, and he is very good to me. I will never leave him."

When they saw they could not make her leave her husband, the eldest sister said: "If you must stay, you must. But just come up for an hour, to let your father see you, because he has been mourning for you ever since you went away."

The Star-wife did not wish to go, but she wanted to see her father once more. So she got into the basket, and it sailed away up into the sky. Her father was very glad to see her, and she was very glad to see him. They talked and they talked till the blue sky was getting gray. Then she remembered that she ought to have gone home long before.

"Now I must go back to my husband," she said.

"That you shall never do!" said her father.

And he shut her up in a white cloud and said she should stay there till she promised never to go back to the prairie. She begged to be let out, but it was no use.

Then she began to weep; and she wept so much that the cloud began to weep too, and it was weeping itself quite away. So her father saw she would go down to the earth in rain if he kept her in the cloud any longer, and he let her out.

"What must I do for you," he said, "to make you stay with us here and be happy?"

"I will not stay here," she said, "unless my husband comes and lives here too."

"I will send for him at once," said her father. So he sent the basket down empty, and it rested in the middle of the dancing ring.

Now when High-feather reached Loon Lake, he found it covered with red swans. He shot two with one arrow; then all the rest flew away. He picked up the two swans and hurried back to his tent, and there lay the dancing-cloth with the feather stars on it half finished, but no wife could he see. He called her, but she did not answer. He rushed out, with the two red swans still slung round his neck and hanging down his back, and ran to the dancing ring, but nobody was there.

"I will wait till she comes back," he said to himself, "if I have to wait till the world ends." So he threw himself down on the grass and lay looking up at the stars till he went to sleep.

Early in the morning he heard a rustling on the grass, and when he opened his eyes he saw the great basket close beside him. He jumped up, with the two red swans still slung round his neck, and climbed into the basket. There was nobody there; and when he began to climb out again he found that the basket was half way up to the sky. It went up and up, and at last it came into the Star-country, where his wife was waiting for him. Her father gave them a beautiful blue tent to live in, and High-feather was happy enough for a while. But he soon grew tired of the cloudberries that the Star-people ate, and he longed to tramp over the solid green prairie, so he asked his wife's father to let him take her back to the earth.

"No," said the Star-man, "because then I should never see her again. If you stay with us you will soon forget the dull old earth."

The young man said nothing. Secretly, he put on the wings of one of the red swans, and he put the other red swan's wings on his wife. Then they leapt over the edge of the Star-country and flew down through the air to the prairie and came to the tent where High-feather's mother was mourning for them. And there was a great feast in the village because they had come back safe and sound. The Star-wife finished embroidering her dancing-cloth that day; and whenever the Indians danced, she danced with them. She never went back to the Star-maidens' dancing ring; but she still lived on berries and corn, because she would never kill anything—except one thing, and that was the little yellow bird. It flew into the tent one day when High-feather had his back turned and began to whisper into the Star-wife's ear; but it never came to trouble her again.

Written Summation

"There is no man here," she said. So they all jumped out to have their dance. But before they came to the beaten ring, the youngest maiden spied the gopher and called out to her sisters to look at it.

"Away! Away!" cried the eldest maiden. "No gopher would dare to come on our dancing ground. It is a conjuror in disguise!"

Model Practice 1

Model Practice 2

Model Practice 3

The Story of Caliph Stork

from <u>Childhood's Favorites and Fairy Stories</u>
edited by Hamilton Wright Mabie, Edward Everett Hale, and William Byron Forbush

Caliph Charid, of Bagdad, was reclining on his divan one pleasant afternoon, smoking his long pipe and sipping coffee from a handsome dish, which a slave was holding for him when his Grand Vizier, Mansor, entered and told him of a peddler in the court below whose wares might interest him. The Caliph, being in an affable state of mind, summoned the peddler, who, delighted with the opportunity, displayed all the treasures of his pack. There were pearls, rings, silks, and many other rich things. The Caliph selected something for himself, a handsome present for the Vizier, and another for the Vizier's wife.

Just as the peddler was putting the things back into his box, the Caliph noticed a small drawer and asked what it contained.

"Only something of no value, which I picked up in a street of Mecca," the peddler replied. He thereupon opened the drawer and showed the Caliph a small box containing a black powder and a scroll written in characters which neither the Caliph nor his Grand Vizier could make out. The Caliph immediately decided that he wanted this strange scroll, and the peddler was persuaded to part with it for a trifle. Then the Vizier was asked to find someone to decipher its meaning.

Near the mosque lived a man called Selim, who was so learned that he knew every language in the world. When the Vizier brought him to interpret the scroll, the Caliph said to him:

"They tell me that you are a scholar and can read all languages. If you can decipher what is written here, I shall know that it is true and will give you a robe of honor; but if you fail, I shall have you punished with many strokes because you are falsely named."

Selim prostrated himself at the feet of the Caliph and then took the scroll. He had not looked at it long when he exclaimed:

"My lord and master, I hope to die if this is not Latin."

"Well, if so, let us hear what it says," the Caliph impatiently answered. Selim at once began.

"Let him who finds this box praise Allah. If he sniffs the powder it contains, at the same time pronouncing the word 'Matabor,' he will be transformed into any creature that he desires and will understand the language of all animals. When he wishes to return to his own form, let him bow to the east three times, repeating the word 'Matabor.' But remember if, while he is bird or beast, he should laugh, the magic word would be forgotten, and the enchantment would be on him forever."

The Caliph was delighted with the knowledge of Selim. He made him a splendid present and told him to keep the secret. When he had dismissed the learned man, he turned to the Grand Vizier and expressed a wish to try the powder.

"Come tomorrow morning early," said he, "and we will go together to the country and learn what the animals are talking about."

The Vizier came as he was ordered, and they left the palace without attendants. Beyond the town was a large pond where some handsome storks were often seen, and to this place they presently came. A grave and stately stork was hunting for frogs, while another flew about and kept him company.

"Most gracious lord," said the Vizier, "what think you of these dignified long legs, and how would you like to know their chatter?"

The Caliph replied that the stork had always interested him, and he would very much like a more intimate acquaintance. Taking the box from his girdle, he helped himself to a pinch of powder and offered it to the Vizier, who followed his example.

Together they cried, "Matabor," and instantly their beards disappeared and feathers covered their bodies; their necks stretched out long and slender, and their legs shriveled into red and shapeless sticks. The Caliph lifted up his foot to stroke his beard in astonishment, but found a long bill in its place.

"By the beard of the Prophet, since I have not one of my own to swear by, but we are a pretty pair of birds, Mansor!"

"If I may say so, your Highness, you are equally handsome as a stork as when you were a Caliph," replied the Vizier. "I see our two relations are conversing over there; shall we join them?"

When they came near to where the storks were smoothing their feathers and touching bills in the most friendly manner, this was the conversation they overheard, "Will you have some of my frog's legs for breakfast, Dame Yellowlegs?" "No, thank you; I am obliged to practice a dance for my father's guests and cannot eat." Thereupon Dame Yellowlegs stepped out and began to pose most gracefully. The Caliph and the Vizier watched her, until she stood on one foot and spread her wings; then they both, at the same time, burst into such peals of laughter that the two storks flew away.

Suddenly, however, the Vizier ceased his mirth and commenced bowing to the east. The Caliph recovered himself and did the same, but neither could think of the magic word.

"Mansor, just recall that unholy word, and I will become Caliph once more, and you my Grand Vizier. I have had enough of being a bird for one day."

"Most gracious lord, that dancing stork has undone us, for, since laughing at her antics, I cannot remember the word that will restore us to human shape."

So at last, in despair, the two unhappy birds wandered through the meadows. They appeased their hunger with fruits, for they could not bring themselves to eat frogs and lizards. As they dared not return to Bagdad and tell the people their chagrin, they flew over the city and had the satisfaction of seeing signs of mourning and confusion.

In a few days, however, while sitting on the roof of a house, they saw a most splendid procession coming up the street. The people welcomed the new ruler, shouting, "Hail! Hail Mirza, ruler of Bagdad!" As the procession came nearer, the Caliph saw, at the head of it, a man dressed in scarlet and gold, riding a handsome horse. He at once recognized the new ruler as the son of his worst enemy.

"Behold," said he, "the explanation of our enchantment! This is the son of Kaschnur, the magician, who is my great enemy who seeks revenge. Let us not lose hope, but fly to the sacred grave of the Prophet and pray to be released from the spell."

They at once spread their wings and soared away toward Medina, but not being accustomed to such long flights, they soon became fatigued and descended to a ruin which stood in a valley below. The two enchanted birds decided to remain there for the night; then wandered through the deserted rooms and corridors, which gave of evidence of former splendor. Suddenly the Vizier stopped and remarked that if it were not ridiculous for a stork to be afraid of ghosts, he would feel decidedly nervous. The Caliph listened and heard a low moaning and sobbing which seemed to come from a room down the passage. He started to rush toward it, but the Vizier held him fast by a wing. He had retained the brave heart that he had possessed when a Caliph, however, and, freeing himself from the Vizier's bill, he hurried to the room whence came the pitiful sounds. The moon shone through a barred window and showed him a screech owl sitting on the floor of the ruined chamber, lamenting in a hoarse voice. The Vizier had cautiously stolen up beside the Caliph; and at sight of the two storks, the screech owl uttered a cry of pleasure. To their astonishment it addressed them in Arabic in the following words:

"I have abandoned myself to despair, but I believe my deliverance is near, for it was prophesied in my youth that a stork would bring me good fortune."

The Caliph, thus appealed to, arched his neck most gracefully and replied:

"Alas! Screech Owl, I fear we are unable to aid you, as you will understand when you have heard our miserable story."

He then related how the magician, Kaschnur, had changed them into storks and made his own son ruler of Bagdad. The screech owl became very much excited and exclaimed:

"How strange that misfortune should have come to us through the same man. I am Tusa, the daughter of the King of the Indies. The magician, Kaschnur, came one day to my father to ask my hand in marriage for his son Mirza. My father ordered him thrown downstairs, and in revenge he managed to have me given a powder which changed me into this hideous shape. He then conveyed me to this lonely castle and swore I should remain here until someone asked me to be his wife, and so freed me from the enchantment."

At the conclusion of her story, the screech owl wept anew and would not be consoled. Suddenly, however, she wiped her eyes on her wing and said:

"I have an idea that may lead to our deliverance. Once every month the magician, Kaschnur, and his companions meet in a large hall at this castle, where they feast and relate their evil deeds. We will listen outside the door, and perhaps you may hear the forgotten word. Then, when you have resumed human form, one of you can ask to marry me, that I too may be freed from this wretched enchantment; and the prophecy that a stork would bring me happiness would be fulfilled."

The Caliph and the Vizier withdrew and consulted over the situation. "It is unfortunate," said the Caliph, "but if we are to meet again, I think you will have to ask the screech owl to marry you."

"Not so, your Highness, I already have a wife, and would rather remain a stork forever than take another; besides, I am an old man, while you are young and unmarried and much better suited to a beautiful Princess."

"That is it," said the Caliph. "How do I know that she will not prove to be some old fright?" As the Vizier was firm, the Caliph at last said he would take the chances and do as the screech owl required.

That very night it so happened that the magicians met at the ruined castle. The screech owl led the two storks through difficult passages till they came to a hole in the wall, through which they could plainly see all that transpired in the lighted hall. Handsomely carved pillars adorned the room, and a table was spread with many dishes. About the table sat eight men, among whom was their enemy, the magician. He entertained the company with many stories, and at last came to his latest—that of turning the Caliph and Vizier into storks—which in relating he pronounced the magic word. The storks did not wait to hear more, but ran to the door of the castle. The screech owl followed as fast as she could, and when the Caliph saw her he exclaimed:

"To prove my gratitude, O our deliverer! I beg you to take me for your husband."

Then the two storks faced the rising sun and bowed their long necks three times. "Matabor!" they solemnly cried, together. In an instant they were no longer storks, but stood before each other in their natural forms. In their joy they fell on each other's necks and forgot all about the screech owl, until they heard a sweet voice beside them, and turning beheld a beautiful Princess. When the Caliph recovered from his astonishment he said that he was now, indeed, enchanted and hoped to remain so always.

They then started at once for the gate of Bagdad; and when they arrived, the people were overjoyed, for they had believed their ruler dead. The magician was taken to the ruined castle and hanged, and his son was given the choice of the black powder or death. Choosing the powder, he was changed into a stork and was kept in the palace gardens.

Caliph Charid and the Princess were married; and when their children grew old enough, the Caliph often amused them with imitations of the Grand Vizier when he was a stork—while Mansor sat smiling and pulling his long beard.

Written Summation

Suddenly, however, the Vizier ceased his mirth and commenced bowing to the east. The Caliph recovered himself and did the same, but neither could think of the magic word.

"Mansor, just recall that unholy word, and I will become Caliph once more, and you my Grand Vizier. I have had enough of being a bird for one day."

Model Practice 1

Model Practice 2

Model Practice 3

The Young Head of the Family

from Childhood's Favorites and Fairy Stories
edited by Hamilton Wright Mabie, Edward Everett Hale, and William Byron Forbush

There was once a family consisting of a father, his three sons, and his two daughters-in-law. The two daughters-in-law, wives of the two older sons, had but recently been brought into the house and were both from one village a few miles away. Having no mother-in-law living, they were obliged to appeal to their father-in-law whenever they wished to visit their former homes, and as they were lonesome and homesick they perpetually bothered the old man by asking leave of absence.

Vexed by these constant petitions, he set himself to invent a method of putting an end to them. And at last gave them leave in this wise: "You are always begging me to allow you to go and visit your mothers and thinking that I am very hard-hearted because I do not let you go. Now you may go, but only upon condition that when you come back you will each bring me something I want. The one shall bring me some fire wrapped in paper, and the other some wind in a paper. Unless you promise to bring me these, you are never to ask me to let you go home; and if you go, and fail to get these for me, you are never to come back."

The old man did not suppose that these conditions would be accepted, but the girls were young and thoughtless, and in their anxiety to get away, did not consider the impossibility of obtaining the articles required. So they made ready with speed, and in great glee started off on foot to visit their mothers. After they had walked a long distance, chatting about what they should do and whom they should see in their native village, the high heel of one of them slipped from under her foot, and she fell down. Owing to this mishap both stopped to adjust the misplaced footgear, and while doing this the conditions under which alone they could return to their husbands came to mind, and they began to cry.

While they sat there crying by the roadside a young girl came riding along from the fields on a water buffalo. She stopped and asked them what was the matter, and whether she could help them. They told her she could do them no good; but she persisted in offering her sympathy and inviting their confidence, till they told their story, and then she at once said that if they would go home with her she would show them a way out or their trouble. Their case seemed so hopeless to themselves, and the child was so sure of her own power to help them, that they finally accompanied her to her father's house, where she showed them how to comply with their father-in-law's demand.

For the first a paper lantern only would be needed. When lighted it would be a fire, and its paper surface would compass the blaze, so that it would truly be "some fire wrapped in paper." For the second a paper fan would suffice. When flapped, wind would issue from it, and the "wind wrapped in paper" could thus be carried to the old man.

The two young women thanked the wise child and went on their way rejoicing. After a pleasant visit to their old homes, they took a lantern and a fan and returned to their father-in-law's house. As soon as he saw them he began to vent his anger at their light regard for his commands, but they assured him that they had perfectly obeyed him and showed him that what they had brought fulfilled the conditions prescribed. Astonished, he inquired how it was that they had suddenly become so much more astute, and they told him the story of their journey, and of the little girl who had so opportunely come to their relief. He inquired whether the little girl was already betrothed, and, finding that she was not, engaged a go-between to see if he could get her for a wife for his youngest son.

Having succeeded in securing the girl as a daughter-in-law, he brought her home and told all the rest of the family that as there was no mother in the house—and as this girl had shown herself to be possessed of extraordinary wisdom—she should be the head of the household.

The wedding festivities being over, the sons of the old man made ready to return to their usual occupations on the farm; but, according to their father's order, they came to the young bride for instructions. She told them that they were never to go to or from the fields empty-handed. When they went they must carry fertilizers of some sort for the land, and when they returned they must bring bundles of sticks for fuel. They obeyed, and soon had the land in fine condition, and so much fuel gathered that none need be bought. When there were no more sticks, roots, or weeds to bring, she told them to bring stones instead. And they soon accumulated an immense pile of stones, which were heaped in a yard, near their house.

One day an expert in the discovery of precious stones came along, and saw in this pile a block of jade of great value. In order to get possession of this stone at a small cost, he undertook to buy the whole heap, pretending that he wished to use it in building. The little head of the family asked an exorbitant price for them, and, as he could not induce her to take less, he promised to pay her the sum she asked, and to come two days later to bring the money and to remove the stones. That night the girl thought about the reason for the buyer's being willing to pay so large a sum for the stones, and concluded that the heap must contain a gem. The next morning she sent her father-in-law to invite the buyer to supper, and she instructed the men of her family in regard to his entertainment. The best of wine was to be provided, and the father-in-law was to induce him to talk of precious stones and to cajole him into telling in what way they were to be distinguished from other stones.

The head of the family, listening behind a curtain, heard how the valuable stone in her heap could be discovered. She hastened to find and remove it from the pile; and, when her guest had recovered from the effect of the banquet, he saw that the value had departed from his purchase. He went to negotiate again with the seller, and she conducted the conference with such skill that she obtained the price originally agreed upon for the heap of stones and a large sum besides for the one in her possession.

The family, having become wealthy, built an ancestral hall of fine design and elaborate workmanship and put the words "No Sorrow" as an inscription over the entrance. Soon after, a mandarin passed that way, and, noticing this remarkable inscription, had his sedan-chair set down, that he might inquire who were the people that professed to have no sorrow. He sent for the head of the family, was much surprised on seeing so young a woman thus appear, and remarked: "Yours is a singular family. I have never before seen one without sorrow, nor one with so young a head. I will fine you for your impudence. Go and weave me a piece of cloth as long as this road."

"Very well," responded the little woman, "so soon as your Excellency shall have found the two ends of the road and informed me as to the number of feet in its length, I will at once begin the weaving."

Finding himself at fault, the mandarin added, "And I also fine you as much oil as there is water in the sea."

"Certainly," responded the woman, "as soon as you shall have measured the sea and sent me correct information as to the number of gallons, I will at once begin to press out the oil from my beans."

"Indeed," said the mandarin, "since you are so sharp, perhaps you can penetrate my thoughts. If you can, I will fine you no more. I hold this pet quail in my hand; now tell me whether I mean to squeeze it to death, or to let it fly in the air."

"Well," said the woman, "I am an obscure commoner, and you are a famed magistrate. If you are no more knowing than I, you have no right to fine me at all. Now I stand with one foot on one side my threshold, and the other foot on the other side; tell me whether I mean to go in or come out. If you cannot guess my riddle, you should not require me to guess yours."

Being unable to guess her intention the mandarin took his departure, and the family lived long in opulence and good repute under its chosen head.

Written Summation

There was once a family consisting of a father, his three sons, and his two daughters-in-law. The two daughters-in-law, wives of the two older sons, had but recently been brought into the house and were both from one village a few miles away; the youngest son, as of yet, had not married.

Model Practice 1 (adapted from the original)

Model Practice 2

_____

_____

_____

_____

_____

_____

_____

_____

_____

_____

Model Practice 3

_____

_____

_____

_____

_____

_____

_____

_____

_____

_____

APPENDIX

Models Only

For Teacher Use

Note: Paragraph-sized models from Chapters I and IV are treated as independent models and are indented.

Oral Narration Questions

(Your student may not need these questions, if he can retell the story easily.)

Questions for Chapter I, historical narratives, or Chapter IV, cultural tales.

1. Who was the main character?
2. What was the character like?
3. Where was the character?
4. What time was it in the story? Time of day? Time of year?
5. Who else was in the story?
6. Does the main character have an enemy? What is the enemy's name?
   (The enemy may also be self or nature.)
7. Does the main character want something? If not, does the main character have a problem?
8. What does the main character do? What does he say? If there are others, what do they do or say?
9. Why does the character do what he does?
10. What happens to the character as he tries to solve his problem?
11. Does the main character solve his problem? How does he solve his problem?
12. What happens at the end of the story?
13. Is there a moral to the story? If so, what was it?

Questions for Chapter II, primary source documents.
(This may be difficult for grammar stage students, help them to answer the questions. Over time, it will become easier.)
1. Who is speaking?
2. To whom is he speaking?
3. What is the main idea from the speaker?
4. Does he give facts to support his message?
5. Why is he telling this information?

Questions for Chapter III, poetry.
1. Is the poem about a character, an event, or an idea?
2. Does this poem express a feeling of happiness, sadness, anger, excitement, joy, hope, determination, or fear?
3. How does the poem make you feel?
4. Do you think the author of the poem had a message?
5. What do you think the message of the poem is?

Written Summations

(Have your student sum up the story in no more than six sentences—two for each question. Less is best)

1. What happened at the beginning of the story?
2. What happened at the middle of the story?
3. What happened at the end of the story?

Principle of Praise

Encourage, build up, praise, and celebrate your student's successes.

Let no corrupt communication
proceed out of your mouth, but
that which is good to the use of edifying,
that it may minister grace
unto the hearers.

Using the Grammar Guide

The Grammar Guide only provides an overview with definitions and a few examples of the grammar concepts. For 3rd – 5th graders, this will more than likely be enough, since the students are working with the grammar in context. But for some, this may not be enough. To supplement, you may use a separate yearlong grammar curriculum, or you, as the teacher, may purchase a guide to provide you with further explanations to pass on to your student. If you use the guide in this book, please note that the guide is not all inclusive. More advanced grammar terms, such as relative pronouns and indefinite adjectives, are not included.

1. Have your student read the model.
2. Have your student copy the selection before he marks up the model.
3. Return to the model and circle the part of speech being learned in the proper color. See page 4.
4. **For older students, have them label the parts of speech according to the definitions and abbreviations below.**
5. For adjectives, adverbs, and prepositional phrases, have your student draw an arrow to the word being modified.

Label		**Definition**

nouns   **DO, IO, PN**   **direct object, indirect object, or predicate nominative**

Subject is the noun that is or does something. (Who ran? What stinks?)	I ran. **The dog** stinks.
Direct objects answers what. (I ate what?)	I ate **the cookie**.
Indirect objects tell for whom the action of the verb was done.	I gave **her** the cookie.
Predicate Nominative (Noun Linking Verb Noun.)	John is my **dad**.

verbs   **AV, SB, LV**   **action verb, state of being, or linking verb**

Action verbs with a direct object are transitive verbs.	(He kicked the ball.)
Action verbs without a direct object are intransitive.	(He kicked.)
State of being verbs are the "to be" verbs.	(am, are, is, was, were, be, being, been)
Helping verbs help the main verb express time and mood.	(do run, can clean, am eating, might hit)
Linking verbs link the subject to the predicate.	(The wind grew chilly. The wind was chilly.)
	(If I can replace grew with was, it is a LV.)

pronouns   **SP, OP, PP, DP**   **Subject, Object, Possessive, Demonstrative**

Subject Pronouns	I, you, he, she, it, we, they	We love to read. It was outside.
Object Pronouns	me, you, him, her, it, us, them	She took it. I handed them the candy.
Possessive Pronouns	mine, yours, his, hers, theirs, ours, its, whose	That is **mine**! Ours is blue.
Demonstrative Pronouns	this, that, these, those	**That** is mine! We love that.

adjectives   **AA, PA, DA**   **Attributive, Predicate, or Demonstrative Adjectives**

Attributive Adjectives modify the noun and are right next to it.	(The **big** car.)
Predicate Adjectives follow linking verbs.	(The car is **big**.)
Demonstrative Adjectives (This, that, these, those)	**That** flower grew.

adverbs   **where, how, when, extent**

Adverbs that tell where, how, and when modify an adverb.	(up, down, quickly, softly, yesterday, now)
Adverbs that tell extent modify an adverb or adjective.	(almost, also, only, very, enough, rather, too)

prepositions   **OP**   **object of the preposition**

GRAMMAR GUIDE
Month 1
Memorize the definitions for each part of speech. Review Weekly.
Teach the following with copywork. Circle the nouns in the copywork.

Nouns   **circle blue**   a word that names a person, place, thing, or idea

Common nouns	**man, city, car, happiness**
Proper nouns	**David, Lake Charles, Mustang**
Subject	**Children** should appreciate their pastor.
Direct object	My parents bought **a birthday present**. (noun phrase)
Indirect object	My parents gave **the pastor** the present. (noun phrase)
Predicate Nominative	The queen is a **pilot**. (A noun that renames a noun, queen = **pilot**.)

Capitalization   Beginning of a sentence, I, proper nouns.

Month 2
Teach everything in month one and the following. Color-code the nouns and verbs in the copywork.

Verbs   **circle red**   a word that expresses action, state of being, or links two words together

Action verbs	**jump, run, think, have, skip, throw, say, dance, smell**
State of being	any form of to be = **am, are, is, was, were, be, being, been**
Linking verbs	**any "to be" verb** and any verb that can logically be replaced by a "to be" verb
	She **seems** nice. She is nice. The flower **smells** stinky. The flower is stinky.
Helping verbs	am, are, is, was, were, be, being, been, do, does, did, has, have, had, may, might, must
	shall, will, can, should, would, could

Month 3
Teach everything previous and the following.

Pronouns   **circle green**   a word that replaces the noun

Jack ran.	**He** ran.
Ike hit Al and Mary.	Ike hit **them**
The car is very nice.	**That** is very nice.

Types of sentences and punctuation

Declarative or statement	I have a blue dress. The ground is wet from the rain.
Interrogative or question	Will we have dessert today? What time is it?
Imperative or demand	Come here. Sit down. Mop the floor at 2:00.
Exclamation	I sold my painting for ten million dollars!

Month 4
Teach everything previous and the following.

Adjectives   **circle yellow**   a word that describes a noun or a pronoun
(When studying adverbs, you may have your student draw an arrow to the word being modified.)

I want candy.	I want **five** candies.	
the car	the **red** car	
I like shoes.	I like **those** shoes.	
The tall girl	The girl is **tall**.	Predicate adjectives (tall, stinky, angry)
The stinky dog	The dog smells **stinky**.	
The angry man	The man appeared **angry**.	

4

Month 5

Adverbs <u>circle orange</u> a word that describes a verb, another adverb, or an adjective

		Modifies the verb
Don't run.	Don't run **inside**.	tells where
The man ran.	The man ran **swiftly**.	tells how
It will rain.	It will rain **soon**.	tells when
		Modifies adjectives or other adverbs
The dog is hairy.	The dog is **very** hairy.	tells extent (modifies hairy)

Possessives words that show ownership

Mine, yours, his, hers, ours, theirs, whose	possessive pronouns (used alone)
My car, **your** house, **his** shirt, **her** computer	possessive pronouns (used with a noun)
Jane's car, Mike's shoes, Jesus' parables,	singular possessive nouns
Mom and Dad's sons, my sisters' names, children's books	plural possessive nouns

Month 6

Preposition <u>circle purple</u> a word that shows relationship between one noun and another word in the sentence
(Prepositional phrases are to be underlined)

He is <u>**on** the box</u>.   He is <u>**under** the box</u>.   He went <u>**around** the box</u>.   He is <u>**in** the box</u>.

Commas 3 items or more in a series
The elephant**,** the mouse**,** and the gnat are best friends.
I like red**,** green**,** and orange vegetables.

Month 7

Conjunction <u>circle brown</u> a word that links words, phrases, or clauses (and, but, or, nor, so, for, yet)

Jamie **and** I left.
        (words)
The blue sky, the warm sun, **and** the rainbow of flowers brightened my spirits.
        (phrases)
He is tall, **for** both of his parents are tall.
        (independent clauses, must have a comma when combining main clauses)

Quotation Marks Use quotation marks to set off direct quotations.

"No, I don't like peas," answered the little boy.	beginning of a sentence
The little boy answered, "I don't like peas."	end of a sentence
"No," answered the little boy, "I don't like peas."	middle of a sentence

Month 8

Interjection <u>circle black</u> a word that expresses emotion, sometimes but not always, sudden or intense.

Yes! I want ice cream too! **Well**, we're late because the car broke down.

Semi-colons replace commas and conjunction when combining two independent clauses

My family is going to the farm**, and** we are going to have a grand time riding horses.

My family is going to the farm**;** we are going to have a grand time riding horses.

Models from Chapter I

(The first model is the same copywork model that follows that historical narrative. The second model, which is italicized, is provided for dictation. See page ix for information on studied dictation.)

Note: Paragraph sized models are treated as independent models and are indented.

from **The Uplift of a Slave Boy's Ideal**
by Orison Swett Marden

While being broken in to field labor under the lashes of the overseer, chained and imprisoned for the crime of attempting to escape from slavery, the spirit of the youth never quailed. He believed in himself and in the right to freedom for all men.

The boy's wits, sharpened instead of blunted by repression, saw opportunities where more favored children could see none. He gave himself his first writing lesson in his master's shipyard by copying the letters written on various pieces of timber.

from **The Rescue of Jerry**
by Lawton B. Evans

In a moment, Jerry had risen from his seat, slipped through the bystanders, run down the steps, and was in the street below. The crowd cheered him and made way for him. There was no vehicle for him to escape in, but Jerry was a swift runner and disappeared up the street.

"Never!" answered the fugitive and made one last despairing effort before they closed in on him. Jerry fought like a tiger against overwhelming odds. He was surrounded, by the police and their followers, and struck from before and behind. He was thrown down and bruised, his clothes being sadly torn.

from **The Lady with the Lamp**
by F. J. Cross

Her father was a good and wealthy man who took great interest in the poor, and her mother was ever seeking to do them some kindness. Thus Florence saw no little of cottage folk. She took them dainties when they were ailing and delighted to nurse them when ill.

The fact that even her dolls were properly bandaged when their limbs became broken or the sawdust began to run out of their bodies will show that even then she was a thoughtful, kindly little person. Even as a child, one of her greatest wishes was to learn how to nurse the sick.

from **A True Story about a Girl**
by Sara Cone Bryant

Another story that they acted was <u>Cinderella</u>. They made a wonderful big pumpkin out of the wheelbarrow, trimmed with yellow paper. Cinderella rolled away in it when the fairy godmother waved her wand.

One other beautiful story they used to play was the story of <u>Pilgrim's Progress</u>. The little girls used to put shells in their hats for a sign they were on a pilgrimage, as the old pilgrims used to do. Then they made journeys over the hill behind the house, through the woods, and down the lanes. When the pilgrimage was over they had apples and nuts to eat in the happy land of home.

from **Dog Was "A Leetle Bit Ahead"**
by Colonel Alexander K. McClure

The dog, however, was glad enough to go, and so the party started out. Wolves were in plenty, and soon a pack was discovered. But when the wolfhound saw the ferocious animals, he lost heart and, putting his tail between his legs, endeavored to slink away.

These fellows remind me of the fellow who owned a dog which, so he said, just hungered and thirsted to combat and eat up wolves. It was a difficult matter, so the owner declared, to keep that dog from devoting the entire twenty-four hours of each day to the destruction of his enemies. He just hankered to get at them.

from **Elizabeth Van Lew (excerpt)**
by Kate Dickinson Sweetser

One day a cautious guard noticed a strange dish carried by Crazy Bet into the prison. It was an old French platter with a double bottom in which water was supposed to be placed to keep the food on the platter hot. The dish roused the guard's suspicions, and to a nearby soldier he muttered something about it.

Important messages were carried back and forth in her baskets of fruit and flowers in a way that would have been dangerous had not Crazy Bet established such a reputation for harmless kindness. She had even won over Lieutenant Todd, Mrs. Lincoln's brother, who was in charge of the Libby, by the personal offerings she brought him of delectable buttermilk and gingerbread. Clever Bet!

from **Peter Petersen**
A Story of the Minnesota Indian War
by Edward Eggleston

The town was crowded with frightened people. Many were living in woodsheds and barns. In their hurry, these country people had not brought food enough with them. Before long they began to suffer hunger. Peter Petersen's father thought of the potato field he had at home. If he could only go back to his house long enough to dig his potatoes, his family would have enough to eat.

Peter opened the door into the kitchen and went through. In a moment two arms were about him. He knew what home meant then. Peter's sister, Matilda, had recognized her lost brother Peter in the little soldier boy. The next day he was put into a wagon and sent out to Rushford, where his mother was living. The little captive's wanderings were over now over.

from **The Soldier's Reprieve**
from <u>The New York Observer</u>

I thought, Father, that I might meet death on the battlefield, for my country, and that when I fell it would be fighting gloriously. But to be shot down like a dog for nearly betraying it! To die for neglect of duty! O, Father! I wonder the very thought does not kill me!

Blossom went to him; he put his hand tenderly on her shoulder and turned up the pale face toward his. How tall he seemed! And President of the United States, too! A dim thought of this kind passed for a minute through Blossom's mind, but she told her simple, straightforward story and handed Mr. Lincoln Bennie's letter to read.

from **Robert E. Lee**
by Lawton B. Evans

The officer hesitated and respectfully answered, "If I fire this gun, the enemy will return the fire at once in great force. Some of us will be killed, but that does not matter so long as you are not here. If you will retire out of danger, I shall fire it as long as you order, but I beg you not to have it fired while you are standing here."

General Lee ever felt kindly toward Union soldiers. He never called them the enemy but always spoke of them as those people. Once, he remarked about the Northern troops, "Now, I wish all those people would go back to their homes and leave us to do the same."

from **Stonewall Jackson**
by Lawton B. Evans

Thomas grew up rosy-cheeked and blue-eyed with waving brown hair, very determined to have his way and full of confidence in himself. Fortunately, his was a good way, and from the start he was a very dependable boy.

He was fond of arithmetic and easily learned all the hard rules and could work any of the problems given him. His other studies were not so easy, but he never stopped anything he had once started until he had mastered it, or it had mastered him. One of the maxims of his life was, "You may be whatever you resolve to be."

from **The Surrender of General Lee**
by Lawton B. Evans

Lee was the first to arrive, and when Grant entered he arose and bowed profoundly. Grant and his officers returned the greeting. Grant then sat at a marble top table, in the center of the room, while Lee sat at a small oval table, near a window.

General Grant began the conversation by saying, "I met you once before, General Lee, while we were serving in Mexico. I have always remembered your appearance, and I think I should have recognized you anywhere."

from **The War Is Over**
by Mara L. Pratt

The assassin, as he leaped from the box upon the stage, had caught his foot in the American flag, which draped the front of the President's box. He fell forward and broke his leg in the fall. A party was at once sent in pursuit of him. On April 21, 1865, he was found in a barn near Fredericksburg.

But nobody was happier than Lincoln himself. Washington was all one blaze of light; fireworks were shooting, bonfires were blazing, and bands were playing.

from **Thomas A. Edison the Great Inventor**
by Lawton B. Evans

Edison sat down and for four hours and a half wrote the message as it came over the wire. Not once did he ask the operator to go more slowly, but kept up with him easily. Faster and faster ticked the instrument, while Edison's fingers flew over the pages. The other operators gathered around in amazement to see this exhibition of speed, but Edison paid them no attention.

He next persuaded some men in New York to furnish him the money to experiment in making a lamp for the electric light. They agreed to pay all his expenses, and, if it were a success, a share of the profits would be theirs. Edison moved to Menlo Park, New Jersey and opened himself a little shop and laboratory.

from **Clara Barton and the Red Cross**
by Lawton B. Evans

After the siege of Strasbourg, there were twenty thousand people without homes and employment, and starvation threatened them all. Clara Barton secured materials for thirty thousand garments and gave them out to the poor women of the city to be made up. She paid the women good wages for the work. Everywhere she went, the soldiers and people lent a helping hand.

After the war, the city of Paris was in the hands of lawless men of the lowest character. The Army of the Republic besieged the city, and the most dreadful scenes of conflict occurred. There was fighting on the streets, and many innocent persons were killed. In the midst of these horrors, Clara Barton entered the city on foot and offered the sick and wounded care and comfort.

from **Hobson and the Merrimac**
by Lawton B. Evans

When the Spaniards discovered the approach of the collier, they opened fire upon her from the shore, batteries on both sides. It seemed that the shells must certainly pierce her through and through. Escape for the men aboard appeared impossible.

When the Merrimac *was sunk in the channel, Hobson and his men took to a raft, and there they clung till morning. It was impossible to escape the searching fire of the enemy, afloat as they were in the open harbor. But, when day came and the Spaniards saw their helpless plight, they sent the men a rescue boat and took them prisoners.*

from **Conquering the Yellow Fever**
by Lawton B. Evans

There was an enemy that for hundreds of years no one learned to conquer. Its presence spread terror wherever it appeared. It lurked in Southern cities, but, often, it stalked broadcast over the whole country, scattering death wherever it came. That enemy was the yellow fever.

Yellow fever had always been present in Cuba. Ships from that island brought it into Southern cities, and the contagion, once started, went on its ravages for months at a time. When Cuba was occupied by the United States, the problem of the yellow fever became the concern of our Government.

from **The Wright Brothers and Their Secret Experiments (excerpt)**
by William J. Claxton

The first airplane made by the two brothers was a very simple one. There were two main planes made of long spreads of canvas arranged one above another, and on the lower plane, the pilot lay. A little plane, which could be moved by the pilot, was known as the elevator. When the elevator was tilted up, the airplane ascended; when lowered, the machine descended.

But it was in the balancing control of their machine that the Wrights showed such great ingenuity. Running from the edges of the lower plane were some wires which met at a point where the pilot could control them. The edges of the plane were flexible; that is, they could be bent slightly either up or down, and this movement of the flexible plane is known as wing warping.

from **Saved by a Child's Wit (excerpt)**
by Ruth Royce from <u>The Children of France</u>

"Have no fears, Mother; I will listen for every sound in the street and will go no further than the door. They shall neither see nor hear me.

"The mother reluctantly gave Jeanne her consent, and Jeanne crept upstairs, stepped quietly to the door and unbolted it, intending to open the door a few inches and peer out.

"Halt!" he commanded, the lances of his men thrust out so close to the little girl that it seemed as if they already had pierced her. "Listening, are you?"
"Yes, monsieur," she answered truthfully.
"Why?"
"That I might know if you had gone, so I might once more go out to the street."

from **The Sinking of the Lusitania**
by Lawton B. Evans

Then a long white line, making a train of bubbles across the water, started from the black object. It came straight for the ship. No one spoke until it was about sixty yards away. Then someone cried out, "It is a torpedo!"

The vessel began to settle, and the lifeboats on the starboard side were launched. The first boat dropped clear of the ship and floated away with no one in it. One man jumped from the deck, swam toward the boat, and got in alone.

from **General J'offre**
by Donald A. Mackenzie

The lad fretted under the restriction and at length began to steal out of the house before any-one was up. So he was put to sleep in a room in a second story of the old-fashioned country house, and his mother locked him in every night. The river was strictly forbidden. "He can't be trusted," declared his mother; "he seems to enjoy risking his life."

His mother's tears hurt him more than his injury. So he resolved to be obedient to her wishes in future. To please her he began to study seriously, and when he was going about on crutches he got into the habit of reading a good deal.

from **The Exploits of Sergeant York**
by Lawton B. Evans

"Who are you? Are you English troops?" shouted the German Major.

"No. We are a force of Americans," was the reply, which seemed to bring no great surprise to the Major.

"How many men have you in your command?" asked the Major.

"I have plenty to hold you prisoners," answered Sgt. York. "Drop your guns and equipment and move on!" The Germans obeyed promptly.

from **Caught in the Dust**
by R. J. M. Marks

The words streamed into my head, and the dust into my mouth. I didn't need to turn around to see if it was coming. It was here. The sky grew darker and darker; it was gritty with dirt. We were finally close enough to see the shape of the house, but it seemed so far away.

Jimmy was hanging back more and more; I tightened my grip. My legs were burning and my arm hurt from half-pulling, half-dragging Jim down the road. I needed air; but the harder I breathed, the more dust I swallowed. It was everywhere, swirling around us. .

from **The Navajo Code Talkers**
by R. J. M. Marks

From the age of four years old, Johnston had lived with the Navajo Indians. His father, Rev. William Johnston, had moved his family from Kansas City, Kansas to the Navajo Reservation, hoping to bring Christianity to the Navajo people. Young Philip had played with the Navajo children, had learned the Navajo ways, and had become fluent in the Navajo language.

Based on his experience with military codes, the Colonel James E. Jones responded that no code could be completely secure. Mr. Johnston proceeded to explain his idea of using an Indian language to build a code using Indian words such as iron rain for a barrage and fast shooter to designate a machine gun. Interest slowly crept into the Colonel's eyes as understanding set in.

from **Rosa Parks**
by R. J. M. Marks

"Why aren't you standing up?" the angry driver demanded.

"I should not have to," answered Mrs. Rosa Parks, calmly, politely, and wearily.

"Are you going to stand up?"

"No, I am not."

"Stand up or I'm going to have you arrested!"

Don't ride the bus to work, town, school, or any place Monday, December 5. Another Negro woman has been arrested and put in jail because she refused to give up her bus seat. Don't ride the buses to work, town, school, or anywhere on Monday. If you work, take a cab, share a ride, or walk. Come to a mass meeting, Monday at 7:00 P.M, at the Holt Street Baptist Church for further instruction.

from **The Cuban Missile Crisis**
by R. J. M. Marks

"Mr. President," added Robert McNamara, "if we conduct an air strike, we must attack before the missiles are fully operational. If the Soviets deploy these missiles, we can expect chaos in a radius of 600 to 1000 miles from Cuba."

"How effective can the air strikes be?" he asked and turned to General Taylor.

"Mr. President, they'll never be 100 percent effective. We hope to take out a vast majority in the first strike, but there would be a continuous air attack whenever we discover a missile site."

from **The Watergate Scandal**
by R. J. M. Marks

On this list were reporters, members of his White House staff, actors, activists, Presidents of Universities, Supreme Court Justices, and regular American citizens. Nixon believed that everyone on this list was his enemy and posed a threat to the welfare of the United States.

The Plumbers disguised themselves in business suits, carried briefcases, and held a fake banquet in a small room near the elevator leading to the DNC office. There they ate dinner, watched films, and waited for the DNC office to empty.

from **You Feed Them**
adapted from A Sermon by Dr. Roger DeYoung

I walked in reservoirs that had inch-wide cracks in the dirt. I could see boats sitting in sand, miles away from any water. Now all the huge pivots stood idle in the middle of the desert. There was no water in the canals for irrigation. Everything was dry.

At first, famine relief seemed insurmountable. How could a few hundred people actually make a difference? All of us had busy lives with work or school. But when we determined to do what little we could, God honored our efforts and many, many people were fed. God took the little we gave, blessed it, and multiplied it.

Models from Chapter II

from Autobiography of Abraham Lincoln

Written for Jesse W. Fell, December 20, 1859

If a straggler supposed to understand Latin happened to sojourn in the neighborhood, he was looked upon as a wizard. There was absolutely nothing to excite ambition for education. Of course, when I came of age I did not know much. Still, somehow, I could read, write, and cipher to the rule of three, but that was all.

In 1846, I was once elected to the Lower House of Congress, but was not a candidate for reelection. From 1849 to 1854, both inclusive, I practiced law more assiduously than ever before. I was always Whig in politics and generally on the Whig electoral tickets, making active canvasses. I was losing interest in politics when the repeal of the Missouri Compromise aroused me again.

from Gettysburg Address

by Abraham Lincoln
November 19, 1863
Gettysburg, Pennsylvania, USA

Fourscore and seven years ago our fathers brought forth on this continent a new nation, conceived in liberty, and dedicated to the proposition that all men are created equal.

But, in a larger sense, we cannot dedicate, we cannot consecrate, we cannot hallow this ground. The brave men, living and dead, who struggled here have consecrated it far above our poor power to add or detract. The world will little note, nor long remember, what we say here; but it can never forget what they did here.

from Another Camp Meeting(excerpt)

dictated by Sojourner Truth (ca. 1797-1883)
edited by Olive Gilbert

"Well, there are two congregations on this ground. It is written that there shall be a separation, and the sheep shall be separated from the goats. The other preachers have the sheep; I have the goats. And I have a few sheep among my goats, but they are very ragged."

The meeting was in the open fields, the full moon shed its saddened light over all, and the woman who was that evening to address them was trembling on the preachers' stand. The noise and confusion were now terrific. Sojourner left the tent alone and unaided and, walking some thirty rods to the top of a small rise of ground, commenced to sing, in her most fervid manner.

from **Emancipation Proclamation**
by Abraham Lincoln

And by virtue of the power and for the purpose aforesaid, I do order and declare that all persons held as slaves within said designated States and parts of States are, and henceforward shall be free; and that the Executive Government of the United States, including the military and naval authorities thereof, will recognize and maintain the freedom of said persons.

And I further declare and make known that such persons of suitable condition will be received into the armed service of the United States to garrison forts, positions, stations, and other places, and to man vessels of all sorts in said service.

from **The Trial of Susan B. Anthony**
from <u>The Life and Work of Susan B. Anthony</u>
by Ida Husted Harper 1899
Volume 1 of 2, Chapter XXV

As then the slaves who got their freedom had to take it over or under or through the unjust forms of law, precisely, so now must women take it to get their right to a voice in this government. And I have taken mine and mean to take it at every opportunity.

My natural rights, my civil rights, my political rights, my judicial rights are all alike ignored. Robbed of the fundamental privilege of citizenship, I am degraded from the status of a citizen to that of a subject. And not only myself individually, but all of my sex are, by your honor's verdict, doomed to political subjection under this so-called republican form of government.

from **Life and Adventures of Calamity Jane**
by Herself

When fired upon, Capt. Egan was shot. I was riding in advance and, on hearing the firing, turned in my saddle and saw the Captain reeling in his saddle as though about to fall. I turned my horse and galloped back with all haste to his side and got there in time to catch him as he was falling.

Capt. Egan on recovering, laughingly said, ``I name you Calamity Jane, the heroine of the plains.'' I have borne that name up to the present time.

from **The Atlanta Compromise**
An Address at the Atlanta Exposition (excerpt)
by Booker T. Washington

We shall constitute one-third and more of the ignorance and crime of the South, or one-third its intelligence and progress. We shall contribute one-third to the business and industrial prosperity of the South, or we shall prove a veritable body of death—stagnating, depressing, retarding every effort to advance the body politic.

No race can prosper till it learns that there is as much dignity in tilling a field as in writing a poem. It is at the bottom of life we must begin, and not at the top. Nor should we permit our grievances to overshadow our opportunities.

from **San Juan Hill**
by General John J. Pershing

The sky was cloudless, the air soft and balmy; peace seemed to reign supreme; great palms towered here and there above the low jungle. It was a picture of a peaceful valley. There was a feeling that we had secretly invaded the Holy Land.

Captain Capron's field guns opened fire upon the southern field at El Caney, and the hill resounded with echoes. Then followed the rattle of the musketry of the attacking invaders. The firing in our front burst forth, and the battle was on.

from **Sinking of the <u>Titanic</u> (excerpt)**
from <u>Sinking of the Titanic and Great Sea Disasters</u>
edited by Logan Marshall
Chapters VIII and IX

Women wept for lost husbands and sons; sailors sobbed for the ship which had been their pride. Men choked back tears and sought to comfort the widowed. Perhaps, they said, other boats might have put off in another direction. They strove, though none too sure themselves, to convince the women of the certainty that a rescue ship would appear.

To the amazement of the awed watchers in the lifeboats, the doomed vessel remained in that upright position for a time estimated at five minutes. Some in the boat say less, but it was certainly some minutes that at least 150 feet of the <u>Titanic</u> towered up above the level of the sea and loomed black against the sky.

from **The Sinking of the <u>Lusitania</u>** (excerpt)
from <u>The New York Times Current History</u>
   A Monthly Magazine
   The European War Volume II
   June 1915

In spite of their attempts to put the blame on Great Britain, it will tax the ingenuity even of the Germans to explain away the fact that it was a German torpedo, fired by a German seaman from a German submarine, that sank the vessel and caused over 1,000 deaths.

The fact that the Germans issued their warning shows that the crime was premeditated. They had no more right to murder passengers after warning them than before.

from **The Women of China** (excerpt)
   _by_ Yvette Borup Andrews from <u>Camps and Trails in China</u>
   Chapter VIII The Women of China

The suffering of the children is intense. We often passed through streets full of laughing boys and tiny girls where others, a few years older, were sitting on the doorsteps or curbstones holding their tortured feet and crying bitterly.

She passes her life in a dark, smoke-filled dwelling with broken furniture and a mud floor, together with pigs, chickens, and babies enjoying a limited sphere of action under the tables and chairs or in the tumbledown courtyard without. Her work is actually never done, and a Chinese bride, bright and attractive at twenty, will be old and faded at thirty.

from **To Every Englishman in India**
   _by_ M. K. Gandhi

I know you would not mind if we could fight and wrest the scepter form your hands. You know that we are powerless to do that, for you have ensured our incapacity to fight in open and honorable battle. Bravery on the battlefield is thus impossible for us. Bravery of the soul still remains open to us.

You are in search of a remedy to suppress this rising ebullition of national feeling. I venture to suggest to you that the only way to suppress it is to remove the causes. You have yet the power. You can repent of the wrongs done to Indians.

from **Infamy Speech**
by Franklin D. Roosevelt

Last night, Japanese forces attacked Hong Kong.
Last night, Japanese forces attacked Guam.
Last night, Japanese forces attacked the Philippine Islands.
Last night, the Japanese attacked Wake Island.
And this morning, the Japanese attacked Midway Island.

It will be recorded that the distance of Hawaii from Japan makes it obvious that the attack was deliberately planned many days or even weeks ago. During the intervening time, the Japanese Government has deliberately sought to deceive the United States by false statements and expressions of hope for continued peace.

from **The Atomic Bombings of Hiroshima and Nagasaki (excerpt)**
by The Manhattan Engineer District
eyewitness account by Father John A. Siemes, professor of modern philosophy at Tokyo's Catholic University
Hiroshima - August 6th, 1945

I jump to the window to find out the cause of this remarkable phenomenon, but I see nothing more than that brilliant yellow light. As I make for the door, it doesn't occur to me that the light might have something to do with enemy planes.

I am bleeding from cuts about the hands and head. I attempt to get out of the door. It has been forced outwards by the air pressure and has become jammed. I force an opening in the door by means of repeated blows with my hands and feet and come to a broad hallway from which open the various rooms. Everything is in a state of confusion. All windows are broken and all the doors are forced inwards. The bookshelves in the hallway have tumbled down.

from **Inaugural Address of President John F. Kennedy**

And so, my fellow Americans: ask not what your country can do for you—ask what you can do for your country.

My fellow citizens of the world: ask not what America will do for you, but what together we can do for the freedom of man.

Let both sides seek to invoke the wonders of science instead of its terrors. Together let us explore the stars, conquer the deserts, eradicate disease, tap the ocean depths, and encourage the arts and commerce.

from **President Nixon's Resignation Speech (excerpt)**

I regret deeply any injuries that may have been done in the course of the events that led to this decision. I would say only that if some of my judgments were wrong—and some were wrong—they were made in what I believed at the time to be the best interests of the nation.

And to those who have not felt able to give me your support, let me say I leave with no bitterness toward those who have opposed me, because all of us in the final analysis have been concerned with the good of the country however our judgments might differ.

Models from Chapter III

from **All Things Obey God**
by Anonymous from <u>The Infant's Delight</u>

Whether He makes His winds to blow,
  And gives His tempests birth,
Or sends His frost, or bids the snow—
  "Be thou upon the earth."

And yet we know that it is He
  Who moves and governs all,
Who stills the raging of the sea,
  And makes the showers to fall.

from **America the Beautiful**
by Katharine Lee Bates

O beautiful for spacious skies,
For amber waves of grain,
For purple mountain majesties
Above the fruited plain!
America! America!
God shed His grace on thee,
And crown thy good with brotherhood
From sea to shining sea!

O beautiful for pilgrim feet,
Whose stern, impassioned stress
A thoroughfare for freedom beat
Across the wilderness!
America! America!
God mend thine every flaw,
Confirm thy soul in self-control,
Thy liberty in law!

from **The Battle Hymn of the Republic**

by Julia Ward Howe

Mine eyes have seen the glory of the coming of the Lord:
He is trampling out the vintage where the grapes of wrath are stored;
He hath loosed the fateful lightning of His terrible swift sword:
     His truth is marching on.

In the beauty of the lilies Christ was born across the sea,
With a glory in His bosom that transfigures you and me:
As he died to make men holy, let us die to make men free,
     While God is marching on.

from **Bed in Summer**

by Robert Louis Stevenson

In winter I get up at night
And dress by yellow candle-light.
In summer quite the other way,
I have to go to bed by day.

I have to go to bed and see
The birds still hopping on the tree,
Or hear the grown-up people's feet
Still going past me in the street.

And does it not seem hard to you,
When all the sky is clear and blue,
And I should like so much to play,
To have to go to bed by day?

from **The Charge of the Light Brigade**

by Alfred Lord Tennyson

Half a league, half a league,
   Half a league onward,
All in the valley of Death
   Rode the six hundred.
"Forward, the Light Brigade!
Charge for the guns!" he said:
Into the valley of Death
   Rode the six hundred.

Cannon to right of them,
Cannon to left of them,
Cannon in front of them
   Volley'd and thunder'd;
Storm'd at with shot and shell,
Boldly they rode and well,
Into the jaws of Death,
Into the mouth of Hell
   Rode the six hundred.

from **Father William**
by Lewis Caroll

"You are old, Father William," the young man said,
  "And your hair has become very white;
And yet you incessantly stand on your head—
  Do you think, at your age, it is right?"

"In my youth," Father William replied to his son,
  "I feared it might injure the brain;
But now that I'm perfectly sure I have none,
  Why, I do it again and again."

"You are old," said the youth, "as I mentioned before,
  And have grown most uncommonly fat;
Yet you turned a back-somersault in at the door—
  Pray, what is the reason of that?"

"In my youth," said the sage, as he shook his gray locks,
  "I kept all my limbs very supple
By the use of this ointment—one shilling the box—
  Allow me to sell you a couple."

from **IF**
by Rudyard Kipling

If you can talk with crowds and keep your virtue,
  Or walk with Kings—nor lose the common touch,
If neither foes nor loving friends can hurt you,
  If all men count with you, but none too much;
If you can fill the unforgiving minute
  With sixty seconds' worth of distance run,
Yours is the Earth and everything that's in it,
  And—which is more—you'll be a Man, my son!

If you can keep your head when all about you
  Are losing theirs and blaming it on you,
If you can trust yourself when all men doubt you,
  But make allowance for their doubting too;
If you can wait and not be tired by waiting,
  Or being lied about, don't deal in lies,
Or being hated don't give way to hating,
  And yet don't look too good, nor talk too wise:

from **John Littlejohn**
by Charles Mackay
Whenever the world our eyes would blind
With false pretenses of such a kind,
With humbug, cant, or bigotry,
Or a specious, sham philosophy,
With wrong dressed up in the guise of right,
And darkness passing itself for light,
Let us imitate John and exclaim with a frown,
"The coin is spurious—nail it down!"

John Littlejohn was stanch and strong,
Upright and downright, scorning wrong;
He gave good weight and paid his way,
He thought for himself and said his say.
Whenever a rascal strove to pass,
Instead of silver, a coin of brass,
He took his hammer and said with a frown,
"The coin is spurious—nail it down!"

from **The Lost Thought**
by Emily Dickinson
I felt a clearing in my mind
  As if my brain had split;
I tried to match it, seam by seam,
  But could not make them fit.

The thought behind I strove to join
  Unto the thought before,
But sequence raveled out of reach
  Like balls upon a floor.
    (complete poem)

from **The New Duckling**

by Ella Wheeler Wilcox

But the duckling was perky as perky.
  "Take care of your stuffing!" he called.
(This was horribly rude to a turkey!)
  "But you aren't a real turkey," he bawled.

"You're an Early Victorian Sparrow!
  A fox is more fun than a sheep!
I shall show that my mind is not narrow
  And give him my feathers—to keep."

"I don't want to waddle like mother,
  Or quack like my silly old dad.
I want to be utterly other,
  And frightfully modern and mad."

"Do you know," said the turkey, "you're quacking!
  There's a fox creeping up thro' the rye;
And, if you're not utterly lacking,
  You'll make for that duck-pond. Good-bye!"

from **O Captain, My Captain!**

by Walt Whitman

O Captain, my Captain! our fearful trip is done;
The ship has weathered every rack, the prize we sought is won;
The port is near, the bells I hear, the people all exulting,
While follow eyes the steady keel, the vessel grim and daring;

My Captain does not answer, his lips are pale and still;
My Captain does not feel my arm, he has no pulse nor will;
The ship is anchored safe and sound, its voyage is closed and done;
From fearful trip the victor ship comes in with object won;

from **The Pessimist**

by Ben F. King

Nothing to do but work,
      Nothing to eat but food,
Nothing to wear but clothes
      To keep one from going nude.

Nothing to breathe but air,
      Quick as a flash 'tis gone;
Nowhere to fall but off,
      Nowhere to stand but on.

Nothing to comb but hair,
      Nowhere to sleep but in bed,
Nothing to weep but tears,
      Nothing to bury but dead.

Nothing to sing but songs,
      Ah, well, alas! alack!
Nowhere to go but out,
      Nowhere to come but back.

Models from Chapter IV

from **The Bonfire in the Sea**
from A <u>Story Hour Reader</u>

"We shall freeze to death unless we can build a fire again," cried Fin-fin.

He tried to kindle a flame by rubbing two sticks together. He could not produce even one spark.

"It is of no use," said Fin-fin. "The wood is too wet. We shall have to wait for the sun to shine again."

A tiny fish came forward and bowed before Fin-fin, saying, "Ask my father, Flying-fish, to light the fire. He is skilled in magic, and he can do more than most fish."

So Fin-fin asked Flying-fish to light the fire once more.

Flying-fish knelt before the smoldering ashes and fanned briskly with his fins.

from **The Capture of Father Time**
by L. Frank Baum

"Then I ought to win a life-saving medal by keeping you tied up," said Jim. "Some folks will live this much longer."

"But they won't know it," said Father Time with a sad smile; "so it will do them no good. You may as well untie me at once."

"Well, when do you intend to release me?"

"I've been thinking about that ugly scythe of yours," said Jim.

"What about it?" asked Father Time.

"Perhaps if I let you go, you'll swing it at me the first thing, to be revenged," replied the boy.

from **The Half-Chick**
by Andrew Lang

"Help you, indeed!" exclaimed Medio Pollito, tossing his head, and shaking the few feathers in his tail. "Do you think I have nothing to do but to waste my time on such trifles? Help yourself, and don't trouble busy travelers. I am off to Madrid to see the King," and hoppity-kick, hoppity-kick, away stumped Medio Pollito.

"Oh! Medio Pollito," cried the fire in a weak, wavering voice as the half-chick approached, "in a few minutes I shall go quite out, unless you put some sticks and dry leaves upon me. Do help me, or I shall die!"

27

from **The Lion and the Gnat**
by Sara Cone Bryant

"Why, you tiny, little, mean, insignificant creature you; how dare you speak to me?" he raged.

"How dare I speak to you?" repeated the Gnat quietly. "By the virtue of right, which is always greater than might. Why don't you keep to your own part of the forest? What right have you to be here, disturbing folks at this time of night?"

"Who told me?" roared the Lion. "Why, everyone acknowledges it; didn't I tell you that everyone is afraid of me?"

"Indeed!" cried the Gnat disdainfully. "Pray don't say all, for I'm not afraid of you. And further, I deny your right to be King."

from **Persevere and Prosper**
adapted by A. R. Montalba

"He that seeketh, shall find, and to him that knocketh shall be opened," says an old Arab proverb.

"I'll try that," said a youth one day. To carry out his intention he journeyed to Baghdad, where he presented himself before the Vizier.

"What is the purpose of this man?" demanded the monarch of the fish.

"The possession of the carbuncle that lies buried in the bottom of the Tigris," was the reply.

"I advise you, then," said the aged monarch, "to give it up to him, for if he has the steady will and has positively resolved to find it, he will work until he has drained the last drop of water from the Tigris," and with that the old monarch left the council.

from **The Star Wife**
from <u>Childhood's Favorites and Fairy Stories</u>
edited by Hamilton Wright Mabie, Edward Everett Hale, and William Byron Forbush pg.462

"There is no man here," she said. So they all jumped out to have their dance. But before they came to the beaten ring, the youngest maiden spied the gopher and called out to her sisters to look at it.

"Away! Away!" cried the eldest maiden. "No gopher would dare to come on our dancing ground. It is a conjuror in disguise!"

"What must I do for you," he said, "to make you stay with us here and be happy?"

"I will not stay here," she said, "unless my husband comes and lives here too."

"I will send for him at once," said her father. So he sent the basket down empty, and it rested in the middle of the dancing ring.

from **The Story of Caliph Stork**
by <u>Childhood's Favorites and Fairy Stories</u>
edited by Hamilton Wright Mabie, Edward Everett Hale, and William Byron Forbush pg.468

Suddenly, however, the Vizier ceased his mirth and commenced bowing to the east. The Caliph recovered himself and did the same, but neither could think of the magic word.

"Mansor, just recall that unholy word, and I will become Caliph once more, and you my Grand Vizier. I have had enough of being a bird for one day."

The Caliph and the Vizier withdrew and consulted over the situation. "It is unfortunate," said the Caliph, "but if we are to meet again, I think you will have to ask the screech owl to marry you."

"Not so, your Highness, I already have a wife, and would rather remain a stork forever than take another.

from **The Young Head of the Family**
from <u>Childhood's Favorites and Fairy Stories</u>
edited by Hamilton Wright Mabie, Edward Everett Hale, and William Byron Forbush pg.481

There was once a family consisting of a father, his three sons, and his two daughters-in-law. The two daughters-in-law, wives of the two older sons, had but recently been brought into the house and were both from one village a few miles away.

The next morning she sent her father-in-law to invite the buyer to supper, and she instructed the men of her family in regard to his entertainment. The best of wine was to be provided, and the father-in-law was to induce him to talk of precious stones and to cajole him into telling in what way they were to be distinguished from other less valuable stones.

Made in the USA
Lexington, KY
26 August 2019